JUN 12 2007

P9-BID-556

Insulating, Sealing & Ventilating Your House

William P. Spence

NAPA CITY-COUNTY LIBRARY
580 COOMBS STREET
NAPA, CA 94559

Library of Congress Cataloging-in-Publication Data

Spence, William Perkins, 1925-
  Insulating, sealing & ventilating your house / William P. Spence.
    p. cm.
  Includes index.
  ISBN 1-4027-2409-8
  1. Dwellings—Insulation. 2. Buildings—Air tightness. 3. Sealing (Technology) 4. Dwellings—Heating and ventilation. I. Title: Insulating, sealing, and ventilating your house. II. Title.

TH1715.S6554 2006
693.8'3—dc22

                                    2005020345

10 9 8 7 6 5 4 3 2 1

Published by Sterling Publishing Co., Inc.
387 Park Avenue South, New York, NY 10016
© 2006 by William P. Spence
Distributed in Canada by Sterling Publishing
℅ Canadian Manda Group, 165 Dufferin Street
Toronto, Ontario, Canada M6K 3H6
Distributed in the United Kingdom by GMC Distribution Services
Castle Place, 166 High Street, Lewes, East Sussex, England BN7 1XU
Distributed in Australia by Capricorn Link (Australia) Pty. Ltd.
P.O. Box 704, Windsor, NSW 2756, Australia

Printed in China
All rights reserved

Sterling ISBN 13: 978-1-4027-2409-1
       ISBN 10: 1-4027-2409-8

For information about custom editions, special sales, premium and
corporate purchases, please contact Sterling Special Sales
Department at 800-805-5489 or specialsales@sterlingpub.com.

CONTENTS

1 PRELIMINARY ENERGY CONSIDERATIONS 4

2 CONTROLLING AIR LEAKS AND WATER VAPOR 14

3 INSULATION MATERIALS 45

4 INSTALLING INSULATION AND VAPOR BARRIERS 57

5 ADDING INSULATION TO AN EXISTING HOUSE 108

6 INSULATING BASEMENTS, CRAWL SPACES, AND ATTIC ROOMS 140

7 HOME VENTILATION 156

METRIC EQUIVALENTS CHART 188

INDEX 189

BOOKS BY WILLIAM SPENCE 192

PRELIMINARY ENERGY CONSIDERATIONS

A house is a complex structure which has many things influencing energy consumption and the comfort of the occupants. The choice, condition, and installation of the heating and air-conditioning systems; installations of plumbing and electrical systems; the insulation chosen; and the tightness of the structure all influence energy consumption.

The goal of a properly sealed and insulated house is to control the transfer of heat into and out of the living area. Thermal insulation that has been correctly installed and is of the proper thickness is used to reduce the transfer of heat so the heating and cooling costs are reasonable and the occupants can live in a controlled, conditioned living area.

This book will address three major considerations that are of importance in producing an energy-efficient and comfortable house: insulation, ventilation, and sealing air leaks.

■ Principles of Heat Flow

Heat moves from a hot source to a cold source (**1–1**). The flow will occur by convection, conduction, or radiation.

Convection refers to the movement of heat through the motion of air or liquid. The heat is transferred by actions such as a hot air furnace blowing heat into the living area. Hot water moving through the plumbing system also moves heat by convection.

Conduction refers to the transmittance of heat through a solid material, such as metal or concrete. When heat strikes the material, the heat is conducted through it by passing from one molecule to another. If

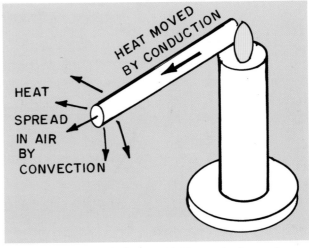

1–1. Heat moves through a material by conduction and through air by convection.

you hold one end of a metal rod and heat the other end with a torch, pretty soon the heat will get to your hand.

Thermal radiation occurs when heat energy is projected by a source through space and is absorbed by the surface it strikes. A typical example is the heat radiated from the sun that warms items inside the house which the rays from the sun strike, such as furniture in the room.

HOW HEAT IS TRANSFERRED

Heat is transferred from a hot source to a cold source. Notice in **1–2** that heat from the outside moves to the cool air-conditioned interior living areas and from the hot attic through the ceiling. In the winter, the heat from the warm interior will move through the walls and ceiling to the cold outside.

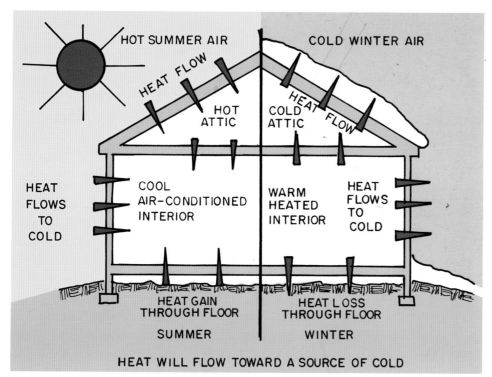

1–2. Heat flows toward cold. Heat is transferred through most construction materials and through leaks in the assembly.

Insulation is used to break the flow of heat by providing a heat barrier to the transfer of heat to a material which, when heated, would conduct heat into the house, where it is transferred by **convection** to the air in the living area. For example, attic insulation keeps the drywall ceiling from getting very hot and conducting heat into the room. If the attic is not insulated, the ceiling will get very hot. The inside air hits the hot ceiling, is warmed, and moves the heat into the house by convection.

Radiation depends upon the difference in temperature between the surfaces of objects in the room. Radiated heat moves as infrared energy through the air and warms any object that it strikes directly. It moves from a warmer surface to a colder surface and does not heat the air.

A major consideration in the effect of radiant heat is the windows. On a cold day, heat is lost to the outside because window glass absorbs heat and radiates it to the outside. On hot days, the process is reversed (**1–3**). If you sit near a window on a cold day, your body radiates heat to the cold glass, making you feel cold (**1–4**) even if the air temperature in the room is at a comfortable level. The glass is absorbing heat from your body and radiating it to the outdoors.

■ Home Energy Rating System

As you seek professional help to analyze the energy needs of your house, you will find that local contractors, state agencies, or possibly the utility company will run the Home Energy Rating System programs. These programs follow national standards governing the activity of those who rate energy. The rater should be from an accredited HERS organization.

The 1992 Energy Policy Act included the Home Rating Systems. As the associations involved in various parts of the construction industry related to energy and energy efficiency met to establish a uniform rating method, considerable differences of opinion arose. In 1999, the Board of Directors of the National Association of State Energy Officials adopted the National Home Energy Rating Guidelines. Some parts of the industry do not agree with this decision, so check

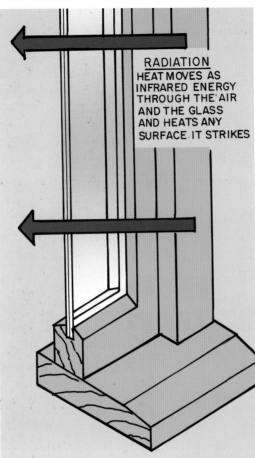

1–3. Windows are a major source of heat loss and gain due to radiation.

RADIATION
HEAT MOVES AS INFRARED ENERGY THROUGH THE AIR AND THE GLASS AND HEATS ANY SURFACE IT STRIKES

with your state energy officials agency for clarification of the current situation.

The energy analyst report from the accredited organization includes an evaluation of your energy needs and recommendations to upgrade the house and the related systems. This service will typically cost several hundred dollars. The local HERS contractor may also be available to manage the upgrading process for an additional fee.

■ Energy Star

The United States Department of Energy and the United States Environmental Protection Agency created the Energy Star label to help consumers identify home products that save energy. The Energy Star label indicates the product is more efficient than required under current federal standards (1–5). By choosing Energy Star qualifying products, homeowners can use energy more efficiently, save money on utility bills, help make their homes more comfortable, and reduce

1–4. If you sit near a cold window, your body will lose heat to the cold glass, making you feel a chill.

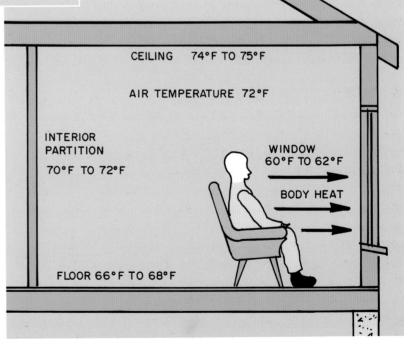

CEILING   74°F TO 75°F

AIR TEMPERATURE 72°F

INTERIOR PARTITION
70°F TO 72°F

WINDOW
60°F TO 62°F

BODY HEAT

FLOOR 66°F TO 68°F

ENERGY STAR HOME SEALING

EPA recommends sealing the "envelope" that surrounds your living space: • the ceiling • outer walls • windows • floors ENERGY STAR is a program of the U.S. Environmental Protection Agency and the U.S. Department of Energy.	To save on your heating and cooling bill and increase the comfort of your home: • Add insulation • Seal air leaks • Choose ENERGY STAR qualified windows when replacing windows www.energystar.gov

1–5. This Energy Star label indicates that the window upon which it is attached can be used in all three climate regions.

air pollution. For residential construction, the system includes heating and cooling systems, lighting, appliances, and building products used in the building envelope such as windows.

■ How Much Insulation Do You Need?

If remodeling an existing house, you first need to find out what kinds of insulation have been used and how much is in place. Then using established recommendations for R-values in various areas of the country, determine how much needs to be added. Also observe areas with no insulation. These problems are discussed in detail in Chapters 4 and 5.

■ Air Leaks

Air leaks are another factor to consider when plans are being developed to improve energy efficiency in a house. These occur in poorly constructed new houses and in older houses built when construction standards were less strict than now. Old houses also have materials that deteriorate, resulting in air leaks. Also, there are new materials and improved energy-efficient products that were not available years ago.

Occupant comfort and energy costs are directly affected by air leaks. Air infiltration involves leakage of air through places such as poorly fitting window sashes and cracks around the window frame (1–6). Even a very small crack will allow outside air to enter the house. On very windy days the amount of air infiltration is increased and quite noticeable by occupants of older houses because it is harder to get the house warm.

Considerable energy is also lost to air leakage from inside the house to the outside. Leaks occur not only around windows but in poorly fitted structural members and around plumbing and heating ducts (1–7) and other things that penetrate the walls, ceilings, and floors.

Adding insulation will, in most cases, not completely seal a leak. Cellulose and fiberglass insulation are open, fibrous materials and are especially poor leakage sealers. Rigid insulation does provide a better seal, but since even a slight crack allows air leakage, you would have to caulk around the edges to completely seal an area. Foam insulation does form an effective seal over air infiltration sources. Reflective insulation provides a good seal and a vapor barrier. The installation of house wrap provides a helpful way to seal leaks between the sheathing panels and around door and window openings (1–8).

Chapter 2 gives considerable detail to finding and controlling air leaks.

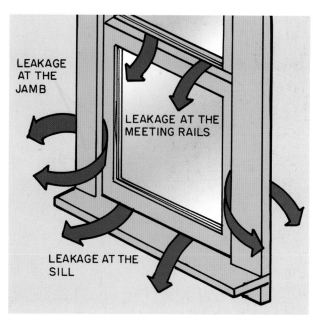

1–6. Air can infiltrate poorly made or deteriorated windows. It does not take long for leakage to allow a large amount of air to flow in or out around a window.

1-7. Things that pierce the ceiling, such as this heat register, can allow considerable air to leak into the attic unless it is caulked, sealing it to the drywall.

■ The Importance of Controlling Water Vapor

Water vapor consists of minute molecules suspended in air so when you seal air leaks you also help seal passages where moisture can enter the house, wall, ceiling, and floors. This is important because it protects the structure and reduces the chance of mold developing in these hidden areas. It also helps you control the humidity of the indoor air.

Sealing air leaks into the house also reduces the chances of radon and other harmful substances from entering the house.

■ Ventilation

Another preliminary consideration as the house is sealed and insulated is the regulation of the quality of the interior air. After the house is sealed and insulated,

1-8. Covering the sheathing with house wrap and wrapping it around the rough openings for doors and windows helps reduce air leakage through the framing.

fresh exterior air cannot get into the house through leaks as has happened for years, so plans for moving fresh air into the house and stale or polluted air out are an important thing to be considered.

Every house has one or more devices that move air within the house, exhaust interior air to the outdoors, or bring in outdoor air to the interior. All of these influence the comfort of the occupants and the cost of energy to heat and cool the house.

The heating and cooling system is designed to move conditioned air to the rooms within the house. It does not exhaust air or bring in fresh air. When ducts are not insulated and are not airtight, heat or cooling is lost to the crawl space, basement or attic, where they are typically located. This increases the cost of operation. Leaky air-return ducts can bring undesirable things into the airflow and spread them throughout the house.

Various exhaust fans and air exchange units also influence the comfort and cost of maintaining a satisfactory interior environment. Chapter 7 discusses various ventilation systems.

If the house is heated by combustion type furnaces such as gas- or oil-fired furnaces, the burned fuel gases must be vented. These furnaces produce deadly carbon monoxide, so the vent pipes must be airtight. Inexpensive carbon monoxide warning units are available and can be placed near vents and in some of the rooms (**1–9**). Gas logs in fireplaces produce nice heat and are pleasant to have on during a cold winter evening. They are supposed to be made to burn the gas so efficiently that carbon monoxide is not produced; however, it is recommended a carbon monoxide monitor be installed in the room with the fireplace.

Ventilation practices are discussed in detail in Chapter 7.

■ Insulation

Yet another preliminary consideration is the selection of the type and amount of insulation to be used in the various parts of the house.

Insulation serves to block the passage of heat. It is used to seal the rooms that are to be heated and cooled from the variations in temperature of the outdoors. This

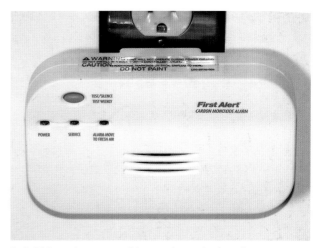

1–9. This carbon monoxide warning unit plugs into a standard 120v electric outlet and monitors the level of carbon monoxide in the air. It has a battery, so it will operate if the electricity goes off.

allows the heating and cooling units to more economically maintain the desired indoor temperature and provide a comfortable living space. The selection of the kind of insulation and how it is installed is very important for the material to be effective (**1–10**). Insulation materials are discussed in Chapter 3, and insulation installation techniques are covered in Chapters 4 and 5.

1–10. Insulation blankets are one form of insulation widely used in residential construction.

■ The Stack Effect

As you plan to improve the energy efficiency of the house, another preliminary consideration is to plan to control the stack effect. The stack effect is a convective force that moves heat flow within a house due to differences in temperature in the air in and outside the house. Warm air rises when it is surrounded by colder air. Air leakage in walls, ceilings, and floors provides passageways for air to flow into and out of a house. This flow (stack effect) influences air temperatures in various rooms, occupant comfort, indoor air quality, and heating and air-conditioning costs. The stack effect has greater influence on interior air temperatures in very cold or very hot climates than in mild year-round climates.

The stack effect in the summer is shown in **1–11**. When the outside air is hotter than the inside air, the cool, heavy inside air settles to the lower levels and leaks out of unsealed spots in windows, doors, and other openings in the floor and lower wall. Meanwhile, the hotter outside air leaks in through leakage spots at the top of the house. This is why second-floor rooms tend to be hotter than first-floor rooms and require more air-conditioning to get the air temperature down to a comfortable level.

In the winter, the stack effect reverses from the summer heat flow. The warm interior airflows out of the house through leaks at the top of the house, while the cold outside air moves into the house through leaks in the lower levels (**1–12**). This illustrates that considerable heat loss and gain can occur by convection if the house has many leaks in the walls, floors, ceilings, windows, and doors.

One major leak often overlooked is the fireplace. If the damper is open, the loss up the chimney in winter is about like leaving a window open. Always close the damper; however, this still allows considerable loss. Tight-fitting glass doors will help reduce heat loss considerably, even with the damper closed.

1–11. In the summer, the cool, heavy air inside the house sinks to the lower levels and leaks out through air leaks that exist in the wall and floor. The air lost is replaced by the hot, lighter outside air, which enters the house through leaks in the top of the structure.

HOT, LIGHT SUMMER AIR FLOWS IN THROUGH OPENINGS AT THE UPPER LEVELS

HOT, LIGHT SUMMER AIR

COOL, HEAVIER INTERIOR AIR FLOWS OUT THROUGH OPENINGS AT THE LOWER LEVELS

COOL, HEAVY INTERIOR AIR

SUMMER STACK EFFECT

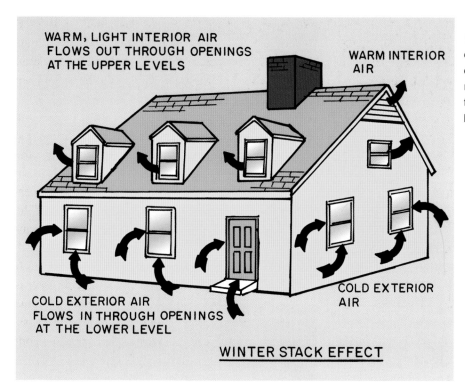

WARM, LIGHT INTERIOR AIR
FLOWS OUT THROUGH OPENINGS
AT THE UPPER LEVELS

WARM INTERIOR
AIR

COLD EXTERIOR AIR
FLOWS IN THROUGH OPENINGS
AT THE LOWER LEVEL

COLD EXTERIOR
AIR

WINTER STACK EFFECT

1–12. In the winter, the warm interior air can flow out of leaks in the walls and ceiling at the top of the house. It is replaced by an inflow of cold exterior air that can enter through leaks on the lower levels of the house.

■ Additional Insulation Factors

If you are trying to decide whether to add additional insulation, one factor is how much it will save on energy bills. Another consideration is the greater comfort in the living area. Comfort must not be overlooked when making this decision. It is possible the cost would be large enough that it will take several years of lower energy bills before the expense is paid back; however, comfort is worth some cost. Increased insulation may also be a positive factor when the house is sold. Buyers do not want to have to get into upgrading insulation.

The process to get an estimate of the savings can be very technical, involving calculating square feet of exposed wall area, ceiling area, floor area, and foundations. Then the area of windows and doors can be calculated. For each of these, there will be energy loss. After improvements, the reduced energy loss and the difference is savings can be calculated. This is converted to dollars by using tables giving the price of energy and how much less is required due to the improvements. The actual energy loss varies in the northern to southern climates. The more severe the weather, the larger the loss, and the more energy it will take to replace it.

This is a simplified explanation. Many local utility companies can run energy studies on the house or recommend someone trained to do the job. This will cost several hundred dollars.

An excellent publication giving a detailed step by step procedure including forms and charts is *Savings by Insulation,* Building Research Council, 1 East St. Mary's Road, Champaign, IL 61820. Local building codes specify the minimum amount of insulation required. Recommendations for exterior walls, ceilings, and floors for various parts of the United States are shown in Chapter 4.

■ Where to Start?

As you think about adding some insulation, generally the ceiling would be the most beneficial place if the existing insulation is substandard. This is the most likely place for the largest heat loss. Also plan to seal any leaks in the ceiling. This could be as important as the additional insulation.

Generally, the walls should receive the next consideration. Again, plug those leaks. Next, plug leaks in the floor and add more insulation if needed.

If the house is old and the existing insulation is near the recommended thickness, then start on the windows. The cheapest step is to install storm windows and caulk all windows to seal leaks (1–13). Consider weatherstripping old windows. Weatherstripping is available at building supply dealers. If the windows are really bad, replace them. There are a number of excellent replacement windows available. This expense could be more effective than adding additional insulation.

Another insulation job that will save some energy cost is to insulate the water heater. A wraparound insulating blanket is available at building supply dealers (1–14 to 1–16). Also insulate all hot water pipes. Polyethylene foam insulation sections that fit over the pies and are tied in place are available in 48-inch lengths (1–17 and 1–18). Heat ducts in uninsulated areas such as an attic or crawl space also should be insulated (1–19).

1–14. Water-heat insulation has a fiberglass pad bonded to a heavy vinyl sheet. Do not use on gas water heaters.

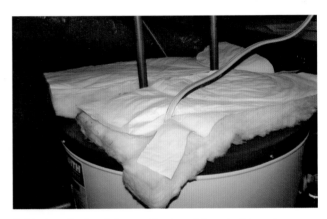

1–15. Lay the insulation on the top of the electric water heater. Cut it to fit around the pipes and electric wire. If the relief valve is on top, cut a hole in the insulation so it does not cover the valve. Tape the edges of the cut together.

1–13. Storm windows are an easy way to reduce air infiltration around old windows. They also form a dead air space, which has some insulation value.

1–16. Finally, tape the top insulation to the water heater. If the heater is old, tape insulation panels around the sides.

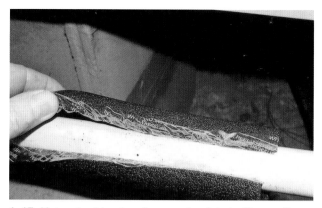

1–17. Hot and cold water pipes are insulated with pre-slit tubes of close-cell polyethylene foam. Slip the tube over the pipe. Remove the paper covering the edges of the slit to expose the adhesive coating on the edges. Press the edges together to seal the insulation around the pipe.

1–18. After the slit is bonded together, the pipe is completely surrounded by the insulation.

1–19. This is a flexible heat duct. It is manufactured surrounded with insulation. If the heat ducts are not insulated, wrap them with insulation panels and tape all joints.

CONTROLLING AIR LEAKS AND WATER VAPOR

Concern about increasing the energy efficiency of a house usually leads to the installation of additional insulation. While this is a good move, it will not produce the maximum results desired if the house has substantial air leaks. Airtight homes are more comfortable and will have lower heating and cooling costs. Airtight construction also reduces the movement of moist humid air into wall cavities and floor and ceiling insulation, which reduces the chances for mold and mildew and even rot of the wood framing.

If a house is very airtight, it is necessary to supply combustion air through a ventilation system to appliances that use combustible fuel to heat the house and provide hot water. The burners need oxygen to burn properly. If starved for oxygen, combustion will not be complete, and life-threatening carbon monoxide can be created and possibly released to the air in the house.

Observe the local building requirements for air inlets to appliances requiring combustion air. Ventilation systems are discussed in Chapter 7. A whole house ventilation system is needed to change the air in the house on a regular basis.

Before making any major changes in the heating and air-conditioning system or adding considerable additional insulation, make a study of the house and look for possible sources of air leaks. Sealing these may be the least expensive way to improve the conditions. A larger furnace or air-conditioner may not be needed.

Following are suggestions of things you can do to find and eliminate air leaks. Be observant for other places leaks might occur.

■ Air Leakage Analysis

If you are concerned about air leaks increasing heat loss and gain in the living areas, an insulation contractor can conduct a blower-door test. The blower-door is installed in an exterior door and blows air into or out of the house with a large fan (**2–1**). Blowing into the house places the interior of the house under a measured elevated pressure. The controls run records of how much air the fan must put into the house to sustain the air pressure difference between that developed indoors and the outdoors. If the house has few air leaks, the fan will have to move in less air to maintain the pressure inside the house.

When a test is made, close all exterior doors and windows. Leave interior doors and doors to a second floor or basement open. Some people prefer to close off the basement if it has not been developed into heated and cooled living space. Turn off all combustion appliances and other units such as dryers and air-conditioners. Seal exhaust fans, fireplace dampers, and other items designed to remove air from inside the house.

The person making the test will bring the house to several different pressure levels, noticing changes in air leakage as the pressures increase.

If the fan is reversed and blows inside air to the outside, a digital manometer measures the difference between the inside and outside air pressures. This will make air leak into the house through any openings. You can sometimes find some of these by feeling the flow of air into the house such as around an electric outlet (**2–2**) or a recessed light in the ceiling.

When the house interior is under pressure, leaks can be found by releasing smoke from a bottle referred to as a **smoke pencil** or **smoke generator.** This is a plastic bottle containing mineral wool and titanium tetrachloride. When these combine, smoke is generated. Release the smoke in areas where leaks commonly are found, such as holes around wiring and plumbing, ceiling lights, ducts, and recessed fans (**2–3**). If the smoke is pulled into the area and disappears, there is a leak. Caulk these leaks and test again. If they are sealed, the smoke will hang in the air along the area that was leaking.

2–2. Airflow from various items penetrating the wall, ceiling, or floor can sometimes be felt while the blower-door is removing air from inside the house. Smaller leaks are detected by blowing smoke over possible leak areas.

2–1. The blower door is sealed in an exterior door opening and all windows, exterior doors, and other openings are closed. The large fan at the bottom of the door can pull air from the house and exhausts it outdoors. The controls on the wall include a digital manometer which measures the difference between the inside and outside air pressures. It may be set to pull outside air into the houses, elevating the interior air pressure. This blower door is being used to check a new house before the finish wall covering is applied. It is also used to check older houses. *(Courtesy the Energy Conservatory)*

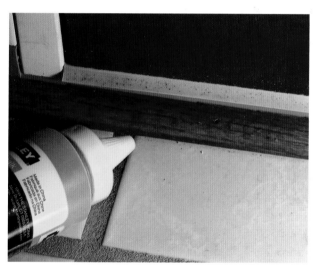

2–3. When the blower-door moves air into the house and the interior air is under pressure, leaks can be found by releasing puffs of smoke from a smoke generator placed near where leaks are possible. If the smoke flows into the spot and disappears, you have found an air leak. If no leak exists, the smoke will hang in the air.

In some areas, the local electric utility company will make an energy audit of your home for a fee. Others have the equipment to make a study using a heat-sensitive infrared video scanner, which shows where a house is losing heat to the outside.

Even if these services are not available, you can greatly reduce air leaks by physically checking the many sources of leaks discussed in this chapter. Stay alert for other sources unique to the design and construction of the house.

◼ International Energy Conservation Code (IECC)

Many states have adopted the International Energy Conservation Code (IECC), which is directed toward new residential construction. If you plan to expand your home, the new addition will be expected to meet the requirements of this code. It is possible that some requirements may apply to a remodeling project, so check with your local building inspection department before proceeding. You may be required to get a building permit for some energy-related renovations.

◼ Radon

Radon is an invisible cancer-causing underground radioactive gaseous element produced by the disintegration of radium. It can occur in various geographic areas in the United States. It can be found in basements and crawl spaces and will work its way into the upstairs living area through air leaks in the floor and exterior walls. A check with the local building-inspection department will verify if radon is found in your area. You can also check with the environmental protection agency in your area.

The U.S. Environmental Protection Agency can advise on the best way to reduce levels of radon gas and how to keep it from penetrating into the below-grade area of the building. Small radon test kits are available at the local building supply dealer (**2–4**) and will indicate whether radon is present in your basement and the amount. Expose the test packet as directed and mail it to the indicated laboratory. Results will be sent to you by mail.

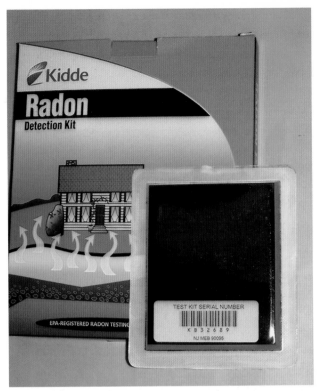

2–4. Radon test kits can tell if radon is seeping into the basement or crawl space.

Radon is measured in picoCuries. A picoCurie is one trillionth of a curie. A curie is a unit of radioactivity. A reading of 4 picoCuries per liter indicates radon is at a harmful level.

It is important to completely seal the foundation and the floor. Concrete cracks must be sealed and crawl-space floors sealed airtight with plastic sheeting. It may be such a hazard that the area will require mechanical ventilation.

◼ Water Vapor

In older houses, the exterior wall is often rather porous. New construction typically will seal all possible air leaks.

The following information is typical of what has been accepted for many years. Following it is information about some recent developments regarding the use of vapor barriers to control moisture in various climates.

Exterior walls that are not airtight will in cold weather allow the heat in the living area to move through the wall by convection and conduction to the outside. The cold exterior air infiltrates the wall through various leaks. The warm inside air is at a higher pressure than the cold outside air and forces its way into the wall. If the house has leaks in the ceiling, warm air tends to flow up out of them, which creates a partial vacuum within the house. This is referred to as the **stack effect.** This action sucks cold air into the wall through any leaks that are present. In warm, humid climates, water vapor moves from the hot, humid outside air to the cool, air-conditioned interior air, which is drier because the air-conditioning unit removes moisture from the air.

Water vapor also moves through solid materials. It is made up of individual molecules that are suspended in the air. The flow through solid materials is called **diffusion.** Control of moisture in a wall occurs when air leaks are controlled and moisture is prevented from diffusing through solid materials.

The inside air is usually heavy with water vapor generated by activities such as cooking, bathing, and growing plants. Vapor is water in a gaseous state suspended in the air. Warm air holds more water vapor than cold air. The amount of water vapor in the air and its temperature establish its dew point. The **dew point** is the temperature at which the water vapor in the air begins to condense into water. This can cause moisture to form on surfaces inside a wall, in the attic, and below the floor. Over the years, these wood members deteriorate and have to be replaced.

When the exterior wall has no insulation or a vapor barrier, warm interior air containing water vapor can penetrate the wall and strike the cold interior surface of the exterior wall. If it is cold enough, it might freeze. Some of this frozen water vapor may return to a gas when the temperature in the wall cavity rises above the dew point. Some will condense into liquid water, which is absorbed by the sheathing and framing. While vapor may vent through leaks in the wall, over many years the wood members will begin to deteriorate and develop mold (**2–5**). The leakage does increase the cost of heating and cooling the house.

If the uninsulated wall has a vapor barrier installed on the warm side of the room under the finish wall

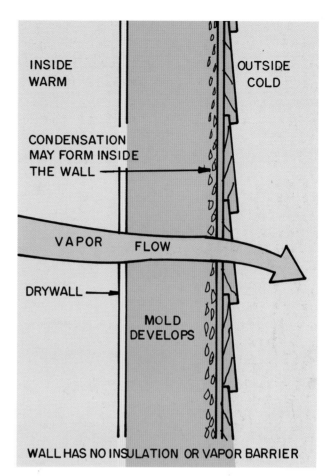

2–5. If the exterior wall has no insulation or a vapor barrier, condensation may collect on the sheathing. Air leaks in this construction may vent some of the moisture to the outside air.

material, condensation may form on interior wall surfaces in rooms with unusually high humidity, such as a bathroom (**2–6**). This can be helped by providing mechanical ventilation for rooms with high humidity. See Chapter 7 for information on ventilation.

A wall that has been insulated but has no vapor barrier is shown in **2–7**. The insulation greatly reduces the convection currents that could carry water vapor to the outside. When the temperature in the wall cavity gets below the dew point, the water vapor will condense, wetting the framing and the insulation. Wet insulation loses much of its insulating value. Mold could also begin to form in the wall cavity. This is a major health problem.

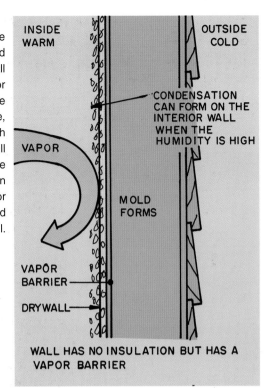

2–6. If the uninsulated exterior wall has a vapor barrier on the warm side, rooms with high humidity will produce condensation on the vapor barrier behind the drywall.

INSIDE WARM

OUTSIDE COLD

CONDENSATION CAN FORM ON THE INTERIOR WALL WHEN THE HUMIDITY IS HIGH

VAPOR

MOLD FORMS

VAPOR BARRIER

DRYWALL

WALL HAS NO INSULATION BUT HAS A VAPOR BARRIER

If the wall contains insulation and a vapor barrier on the inside wall below the finish wall material, any water vapor in the air will be deflected back into the house (2–8). It will be removed from the interior air with a mechanical dehumidifier or ventilators. Since no water vapor hits the cold exterior surface, no condensation will occur inside the wall. The vapor barrier will allow heat to move into the wall, and the heat's flow is controlled by the insulation.

Blocking air leaks will make it easier to control condensation within the wall and regulate the humidity in the air so it is at a comfortable level.

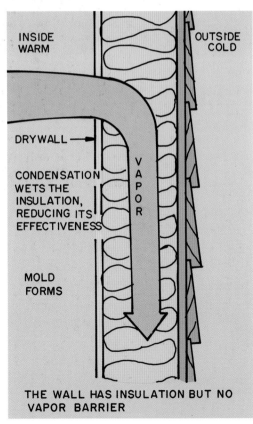

2–7. This insulated exterior wall does not have a vapor barrier on the warm side. Moisture will penetrate the wall cavity wetting the insulation and reducing its insulation value. Mold can also develop.

INSIDE WARM

OUTSIDE COLD

DRYWALL

CONDENSATION WETS THE INSULATION, REDUCING ITS EFFECTIVENESS

VAPOR

MOLD FORMS

THE WALL HAS INSULATION BUT NO VAPOR BARRIER

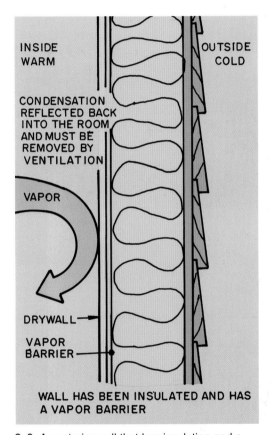

INSIDE WARM

OUTSIDE COLD

CONDENSATION REFLECTED BACK INTO THE ROOM AND MUST BE REMOVED BY VENTILATION

VAPOR

DRYWALL

VAPOR BARRIER

WALL HAS BEEN INSULATED AND HAS A VAPOR BARRIER

2–8. An exterior wall that has insulation and a vapor barrier on the warm side will deflect vapor back into the house. If the humidity is high, the vapor must be removed by a ventilation system or a dehumidifier.

RECENT DEVELOPMENTS IN THE USE OF VAPOR BARRIERS

Recent tests have led those developing building codes to reconsider where to place vapor barriers. Should the vapor barrier be installed on the interior or exterior side of the insulation? When the vapor barrier is not located on the warmer side of the wall, condensation from the interior will be trapped inside the wall. Therefore, in cold climates the vapor barrier is located on the interior side of the insulation. In hot, humid climates the moisture problems occur from the hot, moist exterior air penetrating the wall; therefore, the vapor barrier should be placed on the exterior side of the insulation. In some areas where the heating and cooling seasons cover about the same number of months, vapor barriers are sometimes completely omitted. Check with the local building inspector to see what is recommended in your area.

OTHER PLACES THAT HAVE MOISTURE PROBLEMS

Another place to check for moisture problems is the attic. If the ceiling has unsealed penetrations such as plumbing, lighting, and heating ducts, the moisture-laden air in the living area will flow into the attic. If it does not have considerable ventilation, the water vapor will condense on the sheathing in cold weather and actually freeze. As temperatures warm, this will melt and drop on the insulation (**2–9**). This reduces the insulating value of the insulation and eventually rafters will be damaged and mold will form. Seal the leaks in the ceiling and provide adequate attic ventilation.

MOLD AND MILDEW

Mold and mildew frequently occur within the walls, ceiling, floors, basements, and crawl spaces. In addition, they develop on surfaces inside the house such as

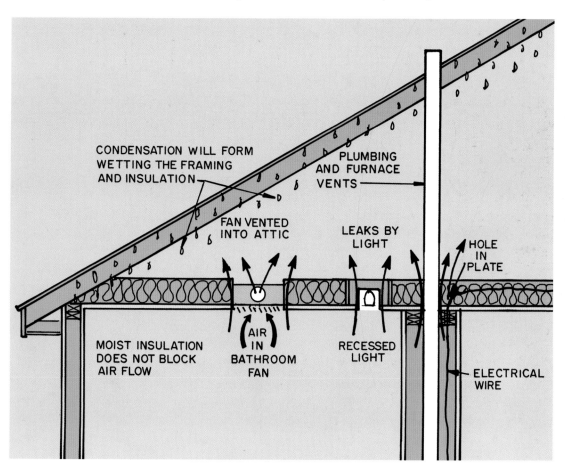

CONDENSATION WILL FORM WETTING THE FRAMING AND INSULATION

PLUMBING AND FURNACE VENTS

FAN VENTED INTO ATTIC

LEAKS BY LIGHT

HOLE IN PLATE

MOIST INSULATION DOES NOT BLOCK AIR FLOW

AIR IN BATHROOM FAN

RECESSED LIGHT

ELECTRICAL WIRE

2–9. Leaks in the ceiling and improper venting including leaking vent pipes will allow moisture-laden air to flow into the attic. It will most likely condense on the sheathing and rafters, freeze, and drip on the ceiling joists and insulation, destroying their effectiveness. Mold will also form.

walls and appliances in bathrooms and kitchens. Mold and mildew are microscopic fungi, which is a low level form of plant life. They live off organic matter and can grow on almost any surface. While the terms mold and mildew are often used interchangeably, mold is used to identify growths that are black, green, red and blue. Mildew appears white.

While material with what appears to be mold or mildew may be mistaken for dirt, an easy test is to place drops of a 5% solution of household bleach on it. If it bleaches out in a few minutes, it is mold or mildew. If the colored area remains, it is dirt.

Mold and mildew need moist, dark conditions to grow and spread. Leaks in exterior walls provide the moisture needed for mold to grow inside a wall. The same conditions exist for other parts of the house. If you find sources of leaks such as around windows and doors, pipes, and electric wires that are exposed to moist conditions, you can suspect mold may be developing. If it is really bad, you may be able to smell mold. It has a musty odor. This requires immediate action because mold can cause serious allergy problems such as stuffy, running noses, asthma, wheezing, fever, irritation of the eyes, skin rashes, and inflamed lungs.

In some areas there are companies that can test the house for mold and mildew. If mold is found in the structure, it will require tearing out drywall and exterior siding, removing insulation, and other rather drastic measures. If the wood framing or sheathing has deteriorated beyond just removing the mold, it will have to be replaced.

When a new house is being built, mold can form on the framing and sheathing if the weather is warm and there has been a lot of rain. Before applying the finishing materials inside and on the exterior, kill all the mold and mildew. Keep the surfaces dry until they are covered up.

A key to the situation in an existing house is to be certain there are no places water can enter the structure. It is very important to not forget to have a dry basement or crawl space. This may require waterproofing the outside of the foundation and grading the soil so exterior water drains away from the house.

Should mold or mildew be found and access is easy, it can be killed and the area cleaned using commercially available mold/mildew cleaners. A 5% solution of household bleach will also kill it.

■ Air Infiltration

For a house to provide economical energy costs and a comfortable living space, it must have an adequate **thermal envelope,** which is an insulated shell around the area that is impervious to air infiltration. This provides the boundary between the inside air and the outside air. Older houses frequently have little insulation and allow heavy air infiltration. New houses could also have these same conditions if improper attention was given to sealing the structure as the house was built. Locations of commonly existing air leaks are shown in **2–10**.

Air infiltration is the major reason a house has a large heat loss or gain and should receive attention before more insulation is added. While a house needs a regular supply of fresh air resulting in six to ten replacements per day, this should be provided by mechanical or planned natural vents. Air infiltration through cracks and defects in construction does not provide the clean, fresh air needed. It introduces moisture-heavy air into walls, floors, ceilings, and other places where it should not flow. This can cause mold and structural damage. For example, if the house has a damp basement, moisture-laden air can work up the wall cavities and floor openings into the house or the walls. Moist air in walls can not only cause mold and mildew and reduce the effectiveness of the insulation, it can also wet the drywall, causing stains to appear and the tape on the joints to come loose. Also, the exterior paint may start to peel and the sheathing might be damaged. The insulated envelope that surrounds the living area should be free of leaks.

If the house has leaks in the walls, floor and ceiling, the air that has been heated or cooled will not remain inside the building very long. It will flow out through openings in one area of the house as outside air is pulled in through leaks in other parts of the structure. In the summer, the hot air will flow into the house through leaks in the ceiling, while in the winter warm air will flow through ceiling cracks into the attic. Recessed lights, plumbing, electrical

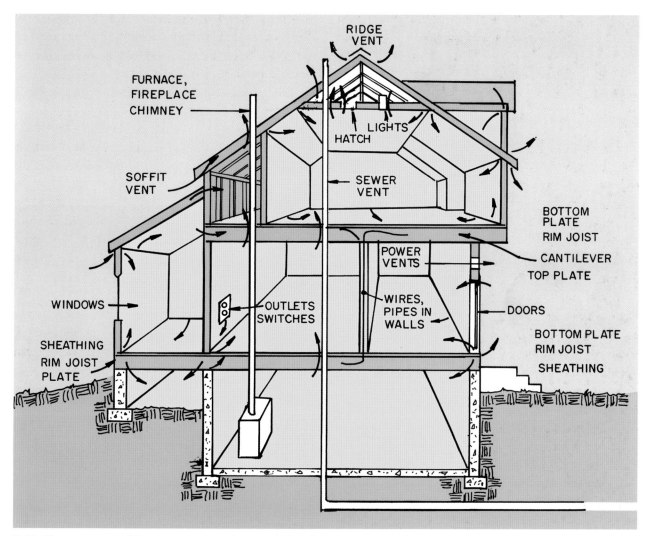

RIDGE VENT

FURNACE, FIREPLACE CHIMNEY

LIGHTS HATCH

SOFFIT VENT

SEWER VENT

BOTTOM PLATE
RIM JOIST

CANTILEVER
TOP PLATE

POWER VENTS

WINDOWS

OUTLETS SWITCHES

WIRES, PIPES IN WALLS

DOORS

BOTTOM PLATE
RIM JOIST

SHEATHING
RIM JOIST
PLATE

SHEATHING

2–10. Here are some of the most common places to look to find air leaks.

cables, pull-down stairs, and other ceiling penetrations provide the airways that rob the heated or cooled air from the interior. Openings along the foundation and in the floor provide low leaks, allowing the heated air in the house in the winter to flow up into the attic and off into space, wasting the energy it took to heat it.

■ Sealing Materials

The materials used to seal air leaks will vary, depending upon the situation. Most openings found in walls, ceilings, and floors can be sealed with caulking or a low-expansion foam.

Polyurethane and acrylic latex caulk is used to seal small openings up to about ³⁄₁₆ inch wide. It is difficult to get it to easily span wider openings. It also has difficulty sticking to surfaces that are dirty, which is a common situation in the attics of older houses (2–11). Read and follow the directions on the tube. For example, you do not caulk at temperatures below 40°, and it typically takes 7 to 14 days to completely cure.

Polyurethane low-expansion foams are available in canisters under pressure. Various size canisters are available. For small jobs, a small, inexpensive canister is available at local building supply dealers (2–12).

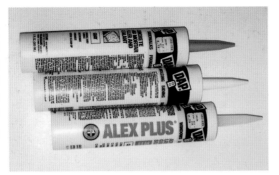

2–11. Polyurethane caulk is a widely used sealant for small cracks and openings.

2–12. Small canisters of polyurethane foam are great for small jobs where large quantities of foam are not required.

They are used up rather fast. Larger canisters with a gun-like control provide a large supply of foam. This is especially important when working in the attic or other hard-to-access spaces. Foams are used to seal all types of cracks such as around door and window frames, sill plates, plumbing and wiring penetrations, and wall junctions. Because the canisters consist of closed-cell polyurethane foam, which expands after being placed, they are used to fill wide gaps and cracks from ½ to 2 inches wide. Do not fill the gap or crack more than half full because the foam expands considerably.

Read the directions on the can. Since the flowing foam is flammable, do not smoke or use where flames, such as pilot lights, are near. Turn off all flaming burners. Shake the can vigorously between each squirt. Protect your face, hands, and especially your eyes.

Special adhesive tapes are available to place over areas such as the joint between sheets of sheathing. Pieces of rigid foam boards can be forced into areas

blocking airflow. Sometimes it is necessary to caulk the edges to ensure an airtight seal.

There are a variety of pre-formed foam gaskets that are installed around light switches and electric outlets after the drywall has been installed (**2–13**). Place the gasket behind the plate and tighten it. Other gaskets are available that are used as sill sealers and are installed along the sill before the carpenters raise the wall (**2–14**). Your building supply dealer will have a variety of these sealers.

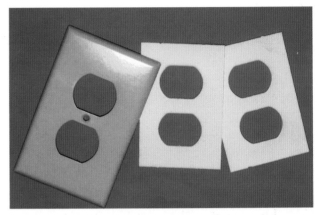

2–13. Pre-formed foam gaskets are installed on light switches and outlets to seal off any airflow that may be in the wall cavity.

2–14. The white polyethylene foam insulation is placed on the foundation and the frame wall is erected on the top of it. Then the adhesive flap is bonded to the sheathing and foundation, sealing any cracks below the wall bottom plate and the foundation. *(Courtesy the Protecto Wrap Company)*

■ Personal Safety

Before starting to work in various parts of the house, consider the possible dangers to your health by conditions in which you may have to work. For example, if you are in the attic and working around fibrous insulation and dust that has settled on it over the years, eye and respiratory protection will be needed. Detailed information on personal safety devices is in Chapter 4.

■ Sealing Leaks in the Ceiling

Leaks in the ceiling cause the greatest loss of heat in the winter and produce the greatest heat gain in the summer, so give them top priority. Following are repairs for some of the most frequently found ceiling leaks.

PLUMBING AND ELECTRICAL CABLE LEAKS

Possibly the most common source of leaks is from plumbing and electrical cables that penetrate the ceiling. Clean the area around the penetration, removing as much dust as possible. This helps the caulk or foam stick to the ceiling material and the pipe or electric wire. Lay in the caulk or foam so it fills the opening between the pipe or wire and the drywall or plaster ceiling (**2–15**). Then lay a ring around it again on top of the ceiling (**2–16**).

SUSPENDED CEILINGS

In older homes during a remodeling, an old, deteriorated ceiling is hidden by installing a suspended ceiling (**2–17**). As the house is checked for air leaks, remove some of the panels and look for possible air leaks in the old construction. This could include old lights that were removed, and wires extended to the new lights in the suspended ceiling. This could be a huge air loss since the suspended ceiling is not good about stopping air leaks. Many other problems can be hidden from view. Putting insulation on top of the ceiling does little to stop air leaks.

If the old ceiling is really bad and has large holes, it will be necessary to remove the suspended ceiling panels and install drywall over all the holes. Use foam to seal any edge joints or openings at the corners of the old ceiling.

2–15. The most common ceiling air leaks occur where a pipe or wire penetrates the ceiling. First seal the opening between the drywall and wire or pipe. Since the opening shown here was small, caulk was used.

2–16. Finish sealing a ceiling leak by laying a ring of foam around the wire or pipe on the attic side of the ceiling.

2–17. Suspended ceilings are an excellent way to cover an old deteriorated ceiling, but remember to seal all air leaks before installing one. They can conceal leaks in the old ceiling, but do not close them.

If the suspended ceiling is installed over an area that has no finished ceiling material, the joists and possibly some insulation are exposed. Insulation batts and blankets do not stop air leaks, so this is a huge leak. One solution is to remove the panels from the suspended ceiling and staple an air-barrier material such as 6-mil polyethylene film to the bottom of the joists. Seal all laps with a strong durable tape that bonds to plastic. Also bond the sheets to the walls. Seal the sheet at the wall with foam. There will be many wires that hold up the ceiling which will penetrate the polyethylene sheet. These need to be foamed and seam-taped as needed.

RECESSED INCANDESCENT LIGHTS

Recessed incandescent lights have the cover set flush with the ceiling (**2–18**). The shell is mounted with metal hangers that are nailed to the ceiling joists (**2–19**).

Before sealing and installing recessed incandescent lights, check the local building code. Typically, it will require that the recessed parts of newly installed fixtures be spaced at least ½ inch from any combustible material, such as wood ceiling joists. It will also require that there be a three-inch clearance between the fixture and any thermal insulation placed around it above the ceiling. Then seal the light at the ceiling with a noncombustible caulk (**2–20**). In this condition there will still be some heat lost or gained through the metal light enclosure and ventilation holes in it. This heat loss and gain can be controlled by installing a pre-formed metal or plastic rough-in box available at local building supply dealers. This is large enough to allow the heat developed to dissipate while it seals any direct air leaks (**2–21**).

When installing a new recessed light, buy one made with thermal protection. Fixtures marked 1C (insulation contact permitted) may be in direct contact with thermal insulation, making the insulation gap around them unnecessary.

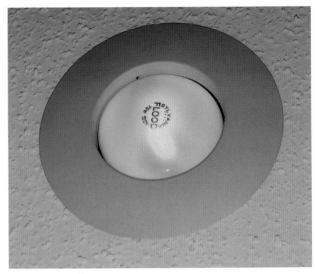

2–18. Recessed incandescent lights are set flush with the ceiling and do not visually distract from the flow of the ceiling.

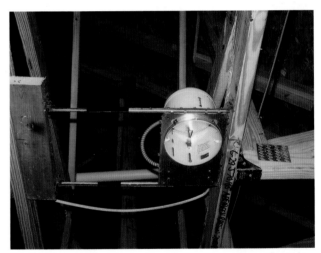

2–19. The recessed light is installed with metal hangers. It is set so the bottom edge will be flush with the drywall ceiling material.

2–20. Insulation should be kept three inches away from recessed lights that are not approved for insulation contact. Then seal the fixture to the ceiling material with a noncombustible caulk.

SURFACE-MOUNTED LIGHTS

Surface-mounted lights are mounted on the drywall ceiling and extend down into the room (**2–22**). They are mounted on standard octagonal electric outlet boxes, which are mounted with metal hangers that are secured to the ceiling joists (**2–23**). While the light fixture covers the box, it is not an airtight seal on the ceiling material. Seal the crack around the box and the drywall from the attic with foam (**2–24**). It could be sealed from the room. If the crack is small, caulk may be used.

Surface-mounted fluorescent lights (**2–25**) will have a small air leak where the electric wire penetrates the ceiling. Flow foam around the wire to seal this leak. Sometimes a fluorescent light is mounted on an electric box and the wire enters the light through a stud in the box. In this case, seal the edges of the box with foam (**2–26**).

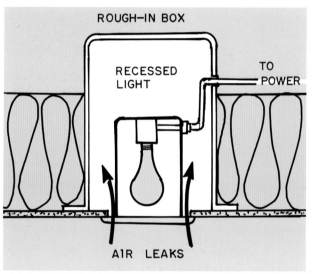

2–21. To reduce heat loss and gain in older recessed lights, install a rough-in box over them that seals air leaks and allows the generated heat to dissipate.

2–22. Surface-mounted lights are mounted on the drywall ceiling and extend down into the room.

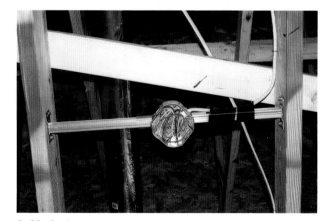

2–23. Surface-mounted lights are mounted on octagonal outlet boxes secured in place with metal hangers. They are set so the box is flush with the face of the drywall ceiling.

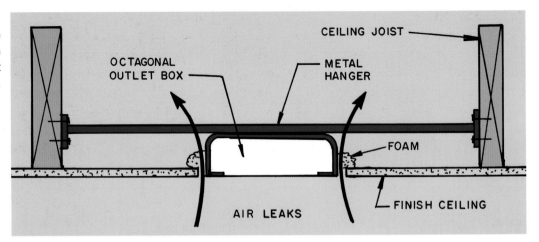

2–24. Seal the electric outlet box with foam in the attic where it fits along the drywall.

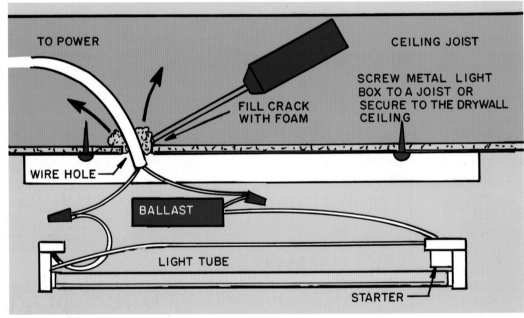

2–25. Other fluorescent light fixtures are screwed to a ceiling joist or secured to the drywall. The wires run through a hole in the drywall.

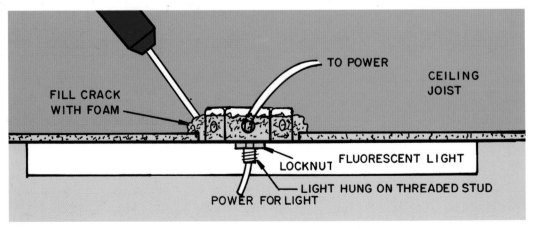

2–26. Some fluorescent light fixtures are mounted on an octagonal outlet box with a threaded stud through which the wires run.

SMOKE ALARMS

The best type of smoke alarm is one that is wired into the electric system. It is always on duty since it does not need batteries (**2–27**). These are mounted on electric boxes as shown for surface-mounted incandescent lights (refer to **2–23**). The crack around the box should be sealed with foam. A less-expensive alarm is battery-operated (**2–28**). It is mounted flush on the drywall ceiling with two screws, so does not present an air leakage problem.

2–27. This smoke alarm is wired into the house electric system and is mounted on an electric outlet box which should be sealed with foam at the ceiling.

2–28. This smoke alarm is battery-operated and is mounted flush on the ceiling with screws.

FANS

The ceiling fan in the bathroom, kitchen, or other rooms is another source of air leaks (**2–29**). While the fan case is airtight, it is necessary to seal the housing to the ceiling with foam (**2–30**). Wherever the pipe carrying away the exhaust air penetrates the roof or wall of the house is another place requiring sealing.

Ceiling-mounted fans (**2–31**) are mounted to electric boxes. They are secured to the box with brackets that come with the fan (**2–32**). Air leakage can occur around the electric box where it pierces the drywall ceiling. Seal this crack with foam.

2–29. Recessed ventilation fans pierce the drywall ceiling, giving the chance of a substantial air leak.

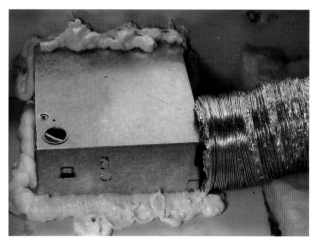

2–30. Seal the housing of the ceiling-mounted ventilation fan with foam.

2–31. Ceiling-mounted fans provide airflow within the living area.

2–33. Ceiling heat ducts pierce the drywall ceiling material, providing another source of air leaks.

2–32. Ceiling-mounted fans are secured to an electric box that pierces the ceiling. Seal the cracks around the box with foam.

HEAT DUCTS

Some houses have heating ducts in the ceiling (**2–33**). The hole in the drywall or plaster ceiling is larger than the duct and provides another source of leakage into the attic. Lay foam around the duct, filling the opening around the sides (**2–34**).

ACCESS HATCHES

Every house will have one or more small hatches in the ceiling, providing access to the attic (**2–35**). The hatches are openings between ceiling joists and are typically covered with a piece of plywood. They are loose-fitting covers and allow a major air leak into the attic. They also have a large heat loss or gain unless

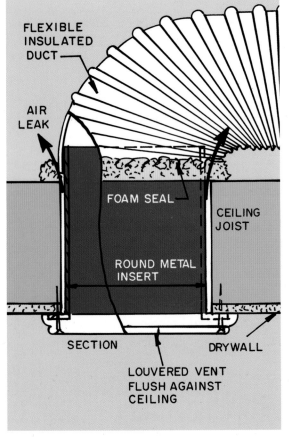

2–34. Caulk or foam around the metal insert of the duct. The flexible duct pipe connects to the insert in the attic, and the louvered outlet cover fits flush with the ceiling inside the room.

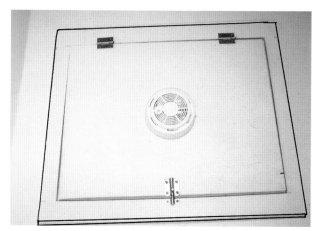

2–35. A typical plywood attic access door. Be certain to insulate it and seal the edges to close air leaks.

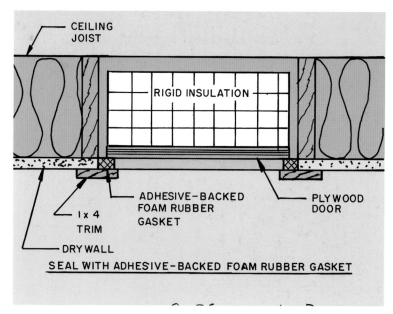

they are insulated. The leaks can be sealed by installing foam insulation strips on the wood strips that support the cover. Use a flexible plastic weather-strip on the edges of the cover that seals the space around the edge (**2–36**). While you are sealing leaks, add two inches of rigid foam insulation to the top of the hatch cover. If the old hatch cover is warped it will not seat properly, so install a new one using ½- or ¾-inch plywood.

FOLDING ATTIC STAIRS

Folding attic stairs are made with a completely assembled box that fits between the ceiling joists (**2–37**). The stair folds up on to a wood cover, which then folds flat with the ceiling. Air leaks around the edge of the cover can be sealed by installing some type of weatherstripping around the edges of the opening. The cover should firmly butt the weatherstripping, but it should not stop the cover from closing completely (**2–38**).

CHIMNEY AND FURNACE VENT-PIPE AIR LEAKS

Before starting to seal air leaks around a chimney, remember what is done must meet local codes. They typically require that it have at least a two-inch clearance from all combustible material. Anything used to seal a gap around a chimney must be rated as a non-combustible material.

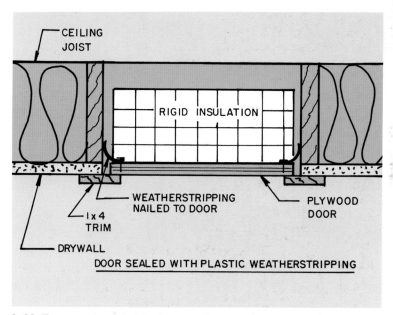

2–36. Two ways to seal air leaks around access doors to an attic.

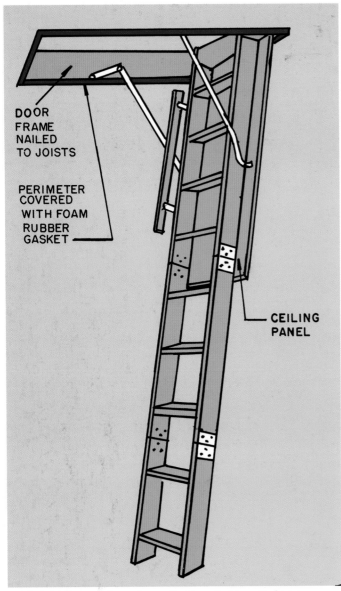

DOOR FRAME NAILED TO JOISTS

PERIMETER COVERED WITH FOAM RUBBER GASKET

CEILING PANEL

2–37. A folding stair has a frame that is nailed to ceiling joists.

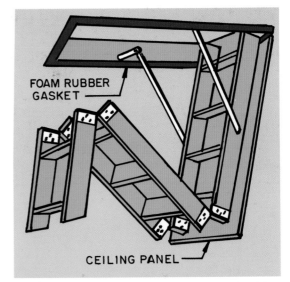

FOAM RUBBER GASKET

CEILING PANEL

2–38. As the stair folds up, the ceiling panel fits tight against a foam rubber gasket placed around the perimeter of the opening.

As the chimney is checked for possible air leaks, remember to check it in the basement or crawl space as well as at each floor above this and each ceiling. Sometimes the clear space around a chimney will run from the basement all the way to the attic. This forms a flue that moves a lot of air through the house (**2–39**).

Openings around a chimney can be sealed by installing aluminum or steel flashing or by laying non-combustible duct board against it. Then caulk with a high-temperature silicone caulk or seal with furnace cement (**2–40**).

Prefabricated metal flues used to vent furnaces and wood-burning stoves also require that the space between the flue and the combustible material, such as a wood floor framing, be blocked as described for masonry chimneys. They usually require a two inch or larger clear space from all combustible materials. Such chimneys usually are supplied with metal adaptors (**2–41**) that provide fire protection and meet codes wherever they pass through floors and ceilings (**2–42**). They also have metal liners that hold back the insulation as required by code.

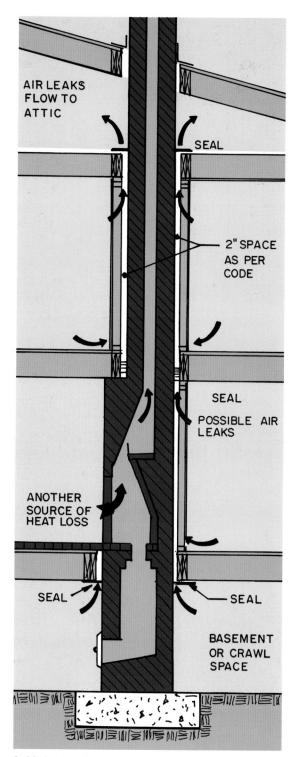

AIR LEAKS
FLOW TO
ATTIC

SEAL

2" SPACE
AS PER
CODE

SEAL
POSSIBLE AIR
LEAKS

ANOTHER
SOURCE OF
HEAT LOSS

SEAL

SEAL

BASEMENT
OR CRAWL
SPACE

2–39. Leaks along the chimney create a vertical stack, moving air from the rooms to the attic. A natural draft can be formed.

2–40. Seal openings around a chimney with metal flashing or fireproof duct board. Caulk to the chimney with high-temperature silicone caulk.

2–41. A typical installation of an adapter used to carry a double pipe smoke vent through wood framing.

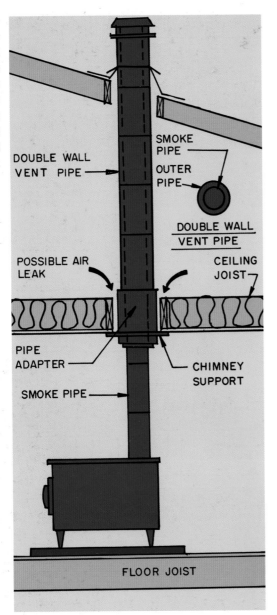

2–42. A typical smoke pipe installation used on wood-burning stoves and prefabricated fireplaces.

DOUBLE WALL VENT PIPE

SMOKE PIPE

OUTER PIPE

DOUBLE WALL VENT PIPE

POSSIBLE AIR LEAK

CEILING JOIST

PIPE ADAPTER

SMOKE PIPE

CHIMNEY SUPPORT

FLOOR JOIST

■ Air Leaks in Floors

One commonly neglected area is the crawl space or basement. If the basement does not have a drywall ceiling, it probably will not have insulation. If it has not been waterproofed, it will have high moisture content in the air, which will flow into the house through various air leaks in the floor. If the house was built with a crawl space, it too can be very wet unless the foundation was waterproofed and the soil floor covered with 6-mil polyethylene sheets. They keep the natural moisture in the soil from invading the air in the crawl space.

After the soil floor is covered, glue or tape the edges of the sheets together and secure them to the foundation. It is wise to seal the covering at the foundation with foam. If the crawl space has good control of humidity, seal the vents in the foundation wall by sliding the cover closed and installing blocks of two-inch rigid foam insulation. Then seal the edges with foam.

Common air leaks in floors include spaces around heat ducts (**2–43**), electric wire, and plumbing that penetrate the floor. Seal them with foam.

There may be air leaks in the basement or crawl space from the sill that is bolted to the foundation (**2–44**). Lay a bead of foam on top of the foundation, sealing the wood sill to it. Also insulate and seal the rim joist with foam.

If a house is built on a concrete slab, the main source of air leaks is where the exterior wall is joined to the slab. If the house is under construction, install a sill sealer and caulk the sill on the inside and outside (**2–45**). A **sill sealer** is a fibrous strip of insulation placed below the sill to seal air leaks due to irregularities in the surface of the concrete. (Refer to **2–14**.) If it is a remodel job, it can be caulked from the inside by removing the shoe molding and caulking and reinstalling the molding (**2–46**). If the floor has been carpeted, this is messy and difficult. It would require raising the carpet and caulking under the baseboard (**2–47**).

2–43. Anything that penetrates the floor produces an air leak. All cracks should be sealed with foam. While this pipe has been sealed at the floor, it would be good practice to also seal it with foam below the floor.

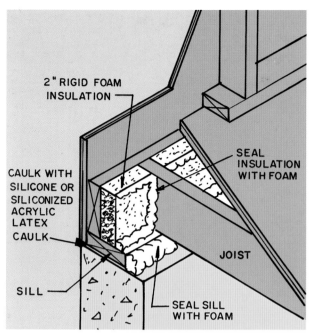

2" RIGID FOAM
INSULATION

CAULK WITH
SILICONE OR
SILICONIZED
ACRYLIC
LATEX
CAULK

SEAL
INSULATION
WITH FOAM

JOIST

SILL

SEAL SILL
WITH FOAM

2–44. Air leaks along the sill can be blocked by laying a bead of foam on the top of the foundation against the sill. Other leaks can be sealed by adding rigid foam insulation against the rim joist and sealing the edges with foam.

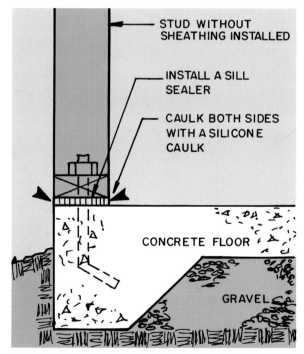

STUD WITHOUT
SHEATHING INSTALLED

INSTALL A SILL
SEALER

CAULK BOTH SIDES
WITH A SILICONE
CAULK

CONCRETE FLOOR

GRAVEL

2–45. With new construction using a concrete slab, install a sill sealer under the bottom plate and caulk both sides before installing the sheathing.

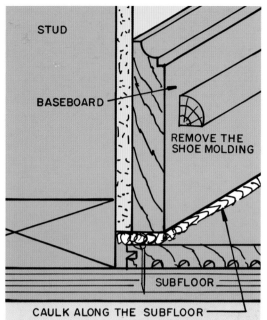

STUD

BASEBOARD

REMOVE THE
SHOE MOLDING

SUBFLOOR

CAULK ALONG THE SUBFLOOR

2–46. To seal air leaks along an exterior wall at the floor in existing houses with concrete floors, remove the shoe molding and caulk below the base-board.

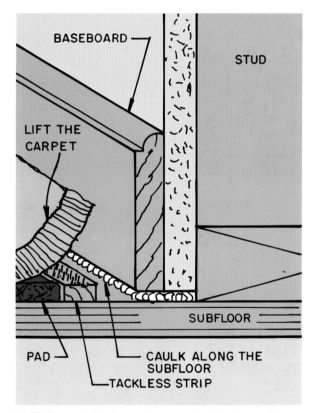

BASEBOARD

STUD

LIFT THE
CARPET

SUBFLOOR

PAD

CAULK ALONG THE
SUBFLOOR

TACKLESS STRIP

2–47. If an existing house has carpet, air leaks can be sealed along the exterior wall by lifting the carpet and caulking below the baseboard.

■ Air-Sealing Exterior Walls

Generally the exterior walls are quite tight and do not contain many air leaks. One common source of air leaks is where something penetrates the wall. Typically, this will be plumbing, electrical wires, and vents such as those used for clothes dryers and bathroom ventilators (**2–48**). These are easily sealed with caulk or foam.

2–48. Sources of air and water leaks in exterior walls.

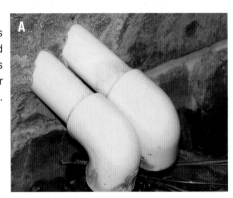

Another source of leaks is where some part of the exterior wall is interrupted by another part of the structure such as the soffit (**2–49**). Again, these unions are easily sealed with silicone caulking.

If there are air leaks into the exterior wall, one place they can cause air inflow and outflow is around cracks left in the drywall and insulation vapor barrier around electric boxes such as used for switches and duplex outlets. These can be sealed by caulking the cracks, but a total seal can be had by installing molded plastic air-vapor barrier boxes. They are nailed to a stud and the outlet or switch is installed inside. Then the vapor barrier is taped to the flange. Installation details are shown in **2–50**.

An important source of air leaks in a wall is the rough openings for doors and windows. If the house is under construction, the rough opening can be sealed with house wrap (**2–51**), which is wrapped around the framing and stapled to it on the inside. Then wrap plastic flashing material over the house wrap as shown in **2–52**. In mild climates, the window is nailed over the house wrap and the nailing flange is sealed to it with adhesive-backed window-wrap tape (**2–53**).

Exterior door rough openings have the house wrap installed around the framing and the sides are flashed with plastic flashing material as described for windows. A sill pan is laid on the floor of the door opening (**2–54**). This is essential to stop air leaks under the door.

2–50. The steps for installing air-vapor barrier boxes which seal all air leaks that occur around electric boxes:

A. Staple the air-vapor barrier box to the stud.

B. Insert the electric outlet box inside the air-vapor box and nail to the stud.

2–49. When the exterior wall is interrupted, such as by this soffit, most likely an air leak has been created.

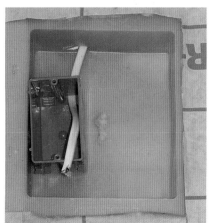

C. Install the wiring through the air-vapor box inlet into the outlet box.

2-50 continued

D. Caulk the opening in the top of the box after the wire is in place.

2–52. Wrap the black plastic flashing material around the rough opening and nail the window to the framing through the nailing flange.

E. Install the outlet or switch and seal the insulation vapor barrier to the edge of the box.

(Courtesy Low Energy Systems Supply Co., Inc.)

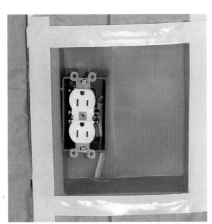

2–51. The house wrap is laid around the sides of the rough opening and stapled to the studs inside.

2–53. In mild climates, the window is nailed over the house wrap and the nailing flange is sealed with adhesive-backed window-wrap tape.

2–54. The door opening at the floor is sealed with a metal sill pan and a gasket mounted on the bottom edge of the door.

One place windows in older homes admit air is through the gap between the window frame and studs (**2–55**). While this space is normally filled with insulation, this will not stop airflow. If you can easily remove the window casing, do so and then compress the fibrous insulation an inch or so and fill this space with a foam insulation. If there is no insulation, slide a piece of rigid foam insulation in the gap, leaving a gap of one inch or so on the end for the foam. Do not try to fill the entire uninsulated space with the foam. Do not over fill or the window frame may bow.

If you do not want to remove the casing and can feel air flowing in around it, lightly caulk around the casing with a paintable caulk. Smooth it against the wall and edge of the casing so it will flow unnoticed around the window.

The old window sash may be worn and loose and leak air. They can be weather-stripped by installing a thin flexible, adhesive-backed vinyl weather-stripping material in the channels on the side jambs. They are bonded to the channels of the window frame (**2–56**). If the wood parting stops are worn, remove them and install new ones. This might be enough to reduce an air leak and make the window open easier (**2–57**).

FILL SPACE WITH FOAM INSULATION

2–55. In older houses, remove the door and window casing and fill the space between the studs and the door or window frame with foam insulation.

2–56. Worn window slides can have air leakage reduced by installing adhesive-backed vinyl weather-stripping to the channel. Cut the strip to length, peel off the paper backing, and press it in place against frame.

WOOD PARTING STOPS

2–57. Old windows have wood parting stops between which the sash fits. If they deteriorate, replace them to cut air infiltration.

INSTALLING STORM WINDOWS

Another solution is to install storm windows. Interior storm windows are available that have a vinyl frame holding a glass panel. They are designed to be mounted on the inside of the stops of the window. This seals the sash, so air infiltration is eliminated (**2–58**).

Exterior storm windows are mounted by their flanges to the window frame (**2–59**). After installing, caulk the edges to ensure an airtight seal.

Storm windows not only control air leaks, they also substantially reduce heat loss. They are inexpensive, but may detract from the appearance of the house. While they do move vertically like a double-hung window, they do make opening windows for natural ventilation difficult.

■ Replacement Windows

Older houses have double-hung windows that are balanced by weights hanging on a cord that runs over pulleys set in the window frame. These can cause a lot of trouble by binding or if the rope carrying the weight breaks. While new rope can be installed, this might be the time to consider installing replacement windows. While it is probably less expensive to replace the rope if the old sashes are in bad shape, replacement windows should be considered. They will give an airtight installation as well as improve the appearance of the house. Several kinds are manufactured.

KITS TO REPLACE THE SASH

A typical replacement kit has new sash and vinyl jamb liners with weatherstripping (**2–60**). Complete details for installing these are provided with the kit. The old window is removed and repairs to the old window frame are made. Then the vinyl jamb liners and original sash or new sash are installed into the channels in the liner (**2–61**). Once both sashes are in place, the original or new sash stops are reinstalled (**2–62**).

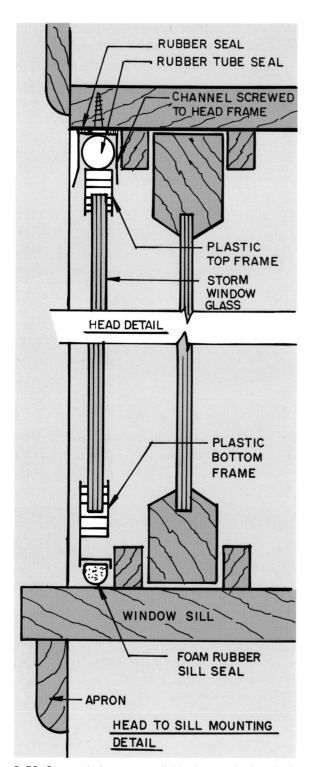

RUBBER SEAL
RUBBER TUBE SEAL
CHANNEL SCREWED TO HEAD FRAME

PLASTIC TOP FRAME
STORM WINDOW GLASS

HEAD DETAIL

PLASTIC BOTTOM FRAME

WINDOW SILL

FOAM RUBBER SILL SEAL

APRON

HEAD TO SILL MOUNTING DETAIL

2–58. Storm windows are available that can be installed on the inside of the windows.

2–59. Exterior storm windows are screwed to the frame through an aluminum flange.

2–60. This is a sash replacement kit. The jamb liners are installed on the inside of the old window frame and the new sashes are inserted into the jamb liners.

(Courtesy Kolbe and Kolbe Millwork Co., Inc.)

Replacement Windows **39**

2–61. Install the top sash in the liner track and raise it to the top of the frame. Then install the bottom sash.
(Courtesy Kolbe and Kolbe Millwork Co., Inc.)

2–62. After the sashes are in the tracks on the vinyl liner, reinstall the wood sash stops on the inside of the window.
(Courtesy Kolbe and Kolbe Millwork Co., Inc.)

INSTALLING ASSEMBLED REPLACEMENT WINDOWS

Completely assembled replacement windows have the frame with the sash installed (**2–63**). The old window is removed and the rough opening repaired if there is any damage. The installation instructions are available with each window. The window is slid into the opening and secured as directed. After it has been installed, caulk all seams inside and outside the house.

2–63. This fully assembled pocket window is installed from inside the house. The one on the wall behind the carpenter has already been installed.
(Courtesy Weather Shield Windows and Doors.)

■ Sealing Exterior Doors

New exterior doors are supplied installed in a door frame. They have excellent weatherstripping and a sweep and seal out all possible air leaks. Older doors may have warped or have deteriorated weatherstripping or frame. If the frame is bad, some carpentry work will be required to remove and replace it. Secure one into which the old door, if it is to be reinstalled, fits perfectly or with minor trimming. This might be the time to replace the old door and frame. This is a bit expensive but does add to the appearance of the house, both inside and outside (**2–64**).

If the old door and frame are sound and attractive and suit the architectural style of the house, work on sealing air leaks.

Begin by replacing old damaged weatherstripping. There are a variety of weatherstripping products available. Some will work better for your situation than others. Three excellent examples are shown in **2–65**, **2–66**, and **2–67**.

2–64. This new door and sidelights replaced an older door that had no glazing. In addition to letting light into the living room, it came with a new frame, rubber weatherstrip gaskets, and an airtight sill and rubber sweep.

2–65. This tubular-type weatherstripping provides considerable adjustment if the door or frame is slightly bowed.

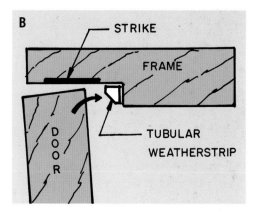

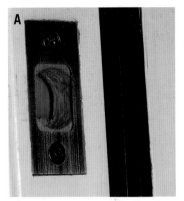

2–66. The accordion-type weatherstripping compresses, allowing a good airtight seal even if the door is slightly bowed.

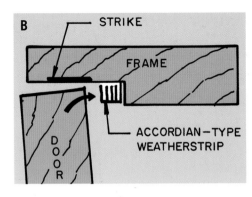

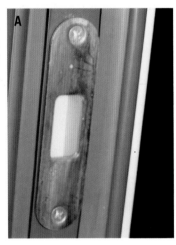

2–67. This double weatherstripping installation seals both corners of sliding doors.

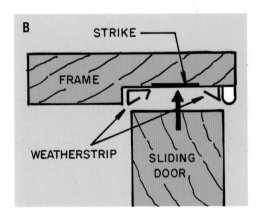

A lot of air can leak under a door. This can be controlled by installing a door sweep. There are a variety of designs available, so choose the one that seems to fit your situation (**2–68**).

The door frame is installed against the studs in the wall opening. There is a space between them that needs to be caulked or sealed with foam as described earlier for windows.

The old door can be covered with a storm door (**2–69**). They break the wind and keep the rain off the door. They have rubber weatherstripping and a sweep on the bottom to seal it at the threshold. Another important advantage is the security they provide. When you open the door in response to the doorbell, you have a strong panel of glass between you and visitor.

2–68. The door sweep along the bottom of the exterior door seals against the threshold, blocking air leaks. A number of designs are available.

2–69. Storm doors not only protect an expensive exterior door from the weather, but reduce air infiltration and heat gain and loss.

2–70. A typical house will have many leaks which must be sealed.

■ Inside Places to Seal Air Leaks

As you consider sources of air leaks, walk around inside the house and look for possible places that air on the outside could leak into the house. Any opening in the drywall is a source for a leak. Remove the cover plate on electric outlets and wall switches and caulk around the box (**2–70**). Also refer back to **2–13** and **2–50** for other sealing techniques.

If a vent penetrates the wall, caulk around the pipe. Check around the electric service entrance panel and caulk inside and outside. Look for openings in the drywall in closets and other places not clearly visible.

■ Finding and Sealing Chases

In some houses, the heat to second-floor rooms is run through vertical ducts if the house has hot-air heat or a series of pipes if hot-water heat was used (**2–71**). Also refer to **2–39** and **2–40**. Plumbing and electric wires may also be run up through these vertical chases. They provide a place where large amounts of air can flow from the basement all the way to the second floor rooms. Make provisions to seal these spaces at each floor and ceiling. A small run of plumbing or electric wire might be able to be sealed with foam. Larger areas will require additional materials. Repairs like those described for stopping leaks up chimneys would be appropriate.

■ Leaks in Attic Rooms

If livable rooms are planned for the attic, some prefer to insulate the entire floor while others will insulate the ceiling of the room below just up to where the floor begins. If there is no blocking placed at the kneewall, outside air can flow under the floor, making it quite cold in the winter (**2–72**). Since many kinds of insulation do not block the flow of air, wood blocking should be installed even if the ceiling below the floor is insulated (**2–73**). Additional information on insulating attic rooms is in Chapter 6.

2–71. Chases are open areas between floors in which plumbing, electric wires, heat ducts, ventilation ducts, and other systems are run. They must be sealed to prevent massive airflow between floors.

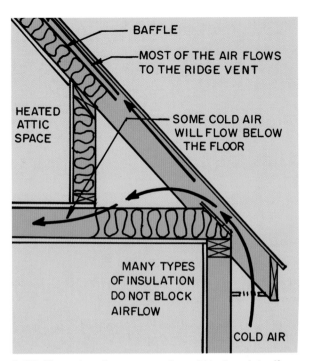

2–72. Floors in attic rooms can be cold in the winter if the insulation is run up to the kneewall and stopped there. Cold exterior air will pass through many types of insulation, chilling the floor of the heated room.

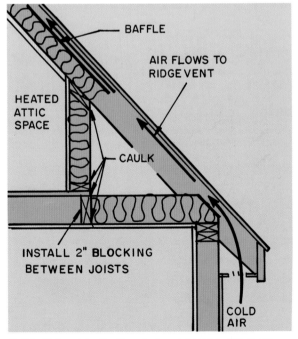

2–73. Airflow into the floor below a heated attic room can be stopped by installing blocking and caulking all the joints.

INSULATION MATERIALS

There are a number of insulation materials that have been used for many years and still are widely used and provide good service. However, in recent years there has been a change in the products available due to concerns about the health of the occupants of the house, changes in building codes, and environmental concerns. Some are more cost-effective. Adequate insulation for your geographic area is very important for an energy-efficient house (3–1).

3–1. Installing adequate insulation for the geographic area produces lower energy costs and a more pleasant living area. *(Courtesy Knauf Insulation)*

■ Choosing An Insulation

There are many types of insulation available and each has properties and installation requirements that make it important to review the choices available. Study the literature available from the insulation manufacturer. Visit with the local insulation contractor and get recommendations. While some will cost more, this is not as important as choosing the best type for the job.

One consideration is the needed R-value. R-values are a numerical measure of the resistance of a material to the flow of heat. The higher the R-value, the greater the insulating value. For a new house, the choice involves selecting insulation of the proper thickness. For a remodeling job, it is necessary to find out what insulation is in place and if it is still usable. Then the amount to be added can be decided. Another factor is the type of insulation—whether it is fibrous blankets, rigid foams, sprayed foam, or loose fill. If it is a do-it-yourself job, consider how the insulation is packaged, the ease of installation, and the physical problems of respiratory and skin irritations. Another limiting factor is that many local building supply dealers do not handle all types. Also some, such as sprayed foam or blown loose fiber, require special equipment and experience. Finally, consider the possibility of using more than one type of insulation.

■ Specifying Thermal Properties

Heat is the form of energy that is transferred by virtue of a temperature difference between two bodies, this transfer being from the warmer to the cooler body. The quantity of heat is measured in British thermal units

(BTU). One BTU is the amount of heat needed to raise the temperature of 1 pound of water 1°F. The terms used to describe the thermal properties of materials include thermal resistance (R), thermal conductivity (k), thermal transmittance (U), and conductance (C).

Thermal resistance (R) is a measure used to indicate the ability of a material to resist the flow of heat through it. The larger the R-value, the greater the material resists the passage of heat and has a better insulating value (**3–2**). Typical R-values for several widely used types of insulation are in **Table 3–1**.

3–2. The thermal resistance of an insulation product is indicated by its R-values.

(Courtesy Knauf Insulation)

TABLE 3–1.

TYPICAL R-VALUES OF SELECTED TYPES OF INSULATION

Type	Material	Approximate R-Value per Inch of Thickness
Loose Fill	Fiberglass and Rock Wool	2.2
	Cellulose	3.3
	Vermiculate	2.4
	Perlite	2.4
Batts	Standard Fiberglass	3.2
	High-Density Fiberglass	3.8 to 4.3
	Rock Wool	3.2
Rigid Foam Board	Expanded Polystyrene	4.0 to 5.0
	Extruded Polystyrene	5.0
	Expanded Polyurethane	3.0 to 4.0
	Polyisocyanurate	6.0 to 8.0
Sprayed-In-Place	Urea Formaldehyde	3.0 to 4.0
	Polyurethane	4.0 to 7.0
	Polyisocyanurate	7.4 to 8.0
	Urethane	4.0
Sprayed-In-Place	Wet Sprayed Cellulose	3.7
	Fiberglass	4.0

Actual R-values depend upon the density and the manufacturer.

Thermal conductivity (k) is a measure used to indicate the amount of heat that will be conducted through one square foot of area of a material per a specified unit of thickness. The lower the k-value of a material, the better are its insulating properties.

Thermal transmittance (U) is a measure of the amount of heat that would pass through an assembly of various materials, such as a floor or exterior wall. The smaller the U-value, the greater is the resistance of the assembly of materials to the transmission of heat.

Thermal conductance (C) is a measure used to indicate the amount of heat that will pass through a specified thickness of material. It is the reciprocal of thermal resistance. For example, C = 1/R. A large C-value indicates the material will transmit quite a bit of heat. Copper has a higher C-value than wood.

■ Sound-Deadening Materials

Sound deadening materials are rated by their sound-transmission class (STC) and sound-absorbing materials are rated by their noise-reduction coefficient (NRC).

Sound-transmission class (STC) is a number rating that indicates the effectiveness of a material or an assembly of materials to reduce the transmission of airborne sound through the material or assembly of materials. The larger the STC number, the more effective the material is as a sound-transmission barrier. Materials designed to reduce sound transmission will have the STC rating available from the manufacturer.

Mineral wool sound-attenuation and fire-resistant batts are made from inorganic fibers derived from basalt, a volcanic rock. Sound-attenuation, fire-resistant batts improve the Sound-Transmission Class (STC) ratings of interior partitions and suspended ceilings. They have a high melting point, in the range of 1500° to 2000°F. They are classified as noncombustible by many building codes. They can improve the STC ratings by up to 10dB. They can have fire ratings up to 2 hours.

Fiberglass sound-attenuation batts are widely used in interior partitions. They can improve the STC of the partition by 4 to 10dBs. They are made a little wider than the stud spacing, so can be installed by friction-fit methods. They are generally considered noncombustible.

The noise-reduction coefficient (NRC) is a number indicating the amount of airborne sound energy that can be absorbed by a material. The larger the NRC rating, the greater the efficiency of the material to absorb sound.

Installing carpet and vinyl composition floor covering reduces impact noise and dampens airborne noise. Carpeting is much more effective and is improved when installed over a carpet cushion. There are a variety of ceiling tiles available made from wood fibers, sugarcane fibers, mineral wool, and fiberglass that will absorb and deaden sound within a room. Wall panels made from these materials are also available and are generally used in commercial buildings such as restaurants. Draperies also are a good material to absorb and deaden sound.

■ Batts and Blankets

Batts and blankets are widely used to insulate walls, ceilings, and floors. They are a flexible insulation made from fiberglass, mineral wool, cotton fibers, and wood fibers. Batts are 48 inches long and blankets 8 feet long. Some thinner blankets are available in longer sizes. The most frequently used thicknesses range from 3½ to 12 inches. Thinner sizes are available for special uses such as a noise barrier.

Batts and blankets are available unfaced or faced on one side with moisture-resistant kraft paper that forms a vapor barrier. They are also available faced with an aluminum foil which reflects heat and cold and provides a fire-resistant facing.

Fiberglass is the most commonly used fiber insulation used in batts and blankets (3–3). Since there is some concern about possible health risks from the breathable glass fibers causing cancer, the U.S. Occupational Safety and Health Administration requires that warnings be placed on both fiberglass and mineral-wool insulation packing. To help home owners who do their own work, manufacturers make batts with the fiberglass confined within a perforated wrapping on both sides of a nonwoven polypropylene fabric. *Still, you should wear a respirator or mask when installing it.*

3-3. Fiberglass blankets and batts are available in a range of thickness and may have a kraft-paper vapor barrier or be unfaced. Unfaced blankets and batts can be laid over fiberglass insulation already installed, creating additional protection.

Another fiberglass insulation product is made by using two different types of glass which expand at different rates. As they cool, the fibers curl and link together without the use of the phenol formaldehyde binder used on other fiberglass products. The batts are stronger and more flexible than standard fiberglass batts and the fibers stay in place and do not get into the air, reducing the possible health hazard.

Some fiberglass batts have a flame-resistant foil-scrim kraft paper facing. These do not need to be covered with a fire-resistant material, such as gypsum wallboard.

Manufacturers of fiberglass insulation also product high-density batts. This provides a batt with a higher R-value per inch of thickness. The fibers are tightly packed together so the airspaces between them are smaller, thus reducing possible air circulation.

Mineral wool is made from inorganic fibers derived from basalt, a volcanic rock. The fibers are bonded and formed into flexible batts. Mineral wool is used to produce sound-attention batts and is used in boards that provide fire resistance and the passage of air through openings in the wall, ceiling, or floor assembly. It also provides excellent insulation.

Mineral wool resists heat better than fiberglass and has better acoustic properties. It is heavier than fiberglass and costs more.

Cotton insulation is made from recycled textile mill waste and polyester. It is produced in kraft-faced batts and as loose insulation that is treated with flame retardants. It is used on walls, ceilings, and floors. It does not produce the itchy feeling on your arms and the danger to your eyes as does fiberglass (**3-4**). Cotton insulation is formaldehyde and resin free and fire, fungi, and corrosion resistant.

3-4. Cotton insulation is used on walls, ceilings and floors and does not produce that itchy feeling when it gets on your hands and arms. *(Courtesy Bonded Logic, Inc.)*

Loose-Fill Insulation

Loose-fill insulation is available as a granular or loose, fibrous material. Granular insulation is poured while loose-fill fibrous insulation is machine blown into the areas to be insulated (**3–5**). Granular insulation includes perlite (expanded volcanic rock), vermiculite (expanded mica), cork and expanded polystyrene. These are available in different densities which influence the R-value.

Fibrous loose insulation is made by blowing a jet of air through molten glass, slag, or rock to form thin fibers that form a wool-like substance when gathered together. One type is made from cellulosic fibers obtained from wood chips, newsprint, and other organic fibers. Cellulose fibers must be fireproofed. Look on the label to be certain this was done.

Granular insulation is used to fill vertical cavities, as the cores in a concrete block wall. Fibrous insulation is used to insulate large areas, as ceilings, walls, and floors.

Cellulose insulation is primarily ground-up newspaper that has been treated with fire retardants (**3–6**). It is used as a loose fill insulation in walls and attics. Cellulose insulation tends to settle over time, however this can be reduced by treating it with a moisture-activated acrylic binder and water during installation. It can also be blown into wall cavities and will not settle if mixed with an acrylic binder and water. It is really a wet installation. Since it packs firmly in the cavity and has been treated with a fire retardant, it does not provide a major fire hazard.

Rigid Insulation

Rigid insulation sheets are made from organic fibers such as wood or cane, expanded and extruded polystyrene, polyurethane, polyisocyanurate, and some forms of cellular hard rubber. Rigid insulation is used in all parts of a house including walls, floors, ceilings, and roofs.

Expanded polystyrene (EPS), also known as beadboard, is made by expanding polystyrene beads in a mold. The block formed is then cut in the thickness desired (**3–7**). It does not use ozone-depleting substances and is favored by many because of this environmental property. Another type is made by extruding the

3–5. Loose-fill fibrous insulation is installed by using a special blowing machine to move it to the area where it is laid down from a hose. *(Courtesy Knauf Insulation)*

3–6. Cellulose insulation is made of ground paper products. It is treated with a fire-retardant chemical.

3–7. Expanded polystyrene insulation, often called beadboard, resembles the structure of the widely used styrene-foam coffee cups.

3–9. This extra-durable extruded polystyrene sheathing material has a tough reinforcing scrim facing on both sides which helps resist puncturing and a good base to hold staples.

material as the boards are formed. Extruded polystyrene is denser than expanded polystyrene and has a higher R-value per inch (**3–8** and **3–9**).

Polyisocyanurate rigid foam sheets have a white to yellow colored core. Some types are covered with aluminum foil (**3–10**). It is widely used for sheathing exterior walls. It typically has an R-value of 6.0 per inch.

Polyurethane rigid insulation board has high R-values, good moisture resistance, stops air infiltration, and is dimensionally stable. It resists fungi, mildew, and vermin. It is available with a variety of facing materials. It is used on walls, ceilings, and floors (**3–11**). Polyisocyanurate

3–10. Polyisocyanurate rigid foam insulation is widely used as the core of exterior wall sheathing panels. These panels may have aluminum foil coverings on one or both sides. Some have a non-reflective black-coated foil on one side.

3–8. This rigid foam material is a form of extruded polystyrene used for sheathing. It has low moisture absorption and an R-value of 5 per inch.

3–11. Polyurethane foam board is white or light yellow in color and has a higher R-value than polystyrene. Polyurethane is also applied in liquid form by spraying. This makes it possible to insulate in small, difficult-to-reach places as well as coat large flat and curved surfaces.

rigid foam sheets and polyurethane rigid insulation board are used on floors, walls, roofs, ceilings, and foundations. Some types are faced with aluminum foil.

Wood and cane fiberboard is asphalt-impregnated and is used for roof insulation and exterior sheathing. Granulated cork sheets are used for floor, wall, and roof insulation. Most rigid insulation panels are made from flammable materials; therefore, building codes require they be covered with a fire-resistant material, such as gypsum panels.

■ Sprayed-Foam Insulation

Sprayed-foam insulation is typically a form of polyicynene, polyurethane, or phenolic compound. It is mixed and pumped through hoses into cavities, such as wall cavities between the sheathing and drywall (3–12) and in the cores of concrete blocks. It is also sprayed in layers on roofs, ceilings, walls, and tanks. It has the advantage of being able to bond to irregular shaped and sloped surfaces. Fire-resistance can vary, so some types must be covered with a fire-resistant material.

Other sprayed foam compositions are available on the market. One example is an inorganic foamed magnesium-oxide cement. It has the advantage of not providing allergic problems for those who are sensitive to chemicals. Another uses a three-component system consisting of an aqueous plastic three-polymer resin.

The foam-blowing agent used for many years was CFC-11. It was damaging to the ozone layer and was replaced by HCFC-141b. While this is less damaging than CFC, other environmentally friendly blowing agents are being used. Among these are carbon dioxide, water, and compressed air. As you consider selecting a brand of foam insulation, not only consider ease of application and insulating properties, but be aware of the blowing agent to be used.

Sprayed-foam insulation has great air-sealing properties and, when sprayed into a framing cavity, it bonds to the framing and expands to fill every crack or opening. Some types are effective vapor barriers, so the polyethylene sheet vapor barrier is not needed in that case. It is more expensive than fiberglass batts and spray cellulose.

3–12. Sprayed foam insulation bonds to various materials and builds up in thickness as layer after layer is sprayed. *(Courtesy North Carolina Foam Industries)*

Foam insulation is available from a number of companies, so the properties and insulating values will differ. Most foams used in residential work weigh between .5 and 2.0 pounds per cubic foot. The denser the material, the greater the insulation value. A foam weighing .5 pounds per cubic foot will have an R-value of about 3.5 per inch thick. A 1.8 pound per-cubic-foot foam will have an R-value of about 7.0 per inch thick. The denser foams have more chemicals per cubic foot, so will cost more. Consult the manufacturers for specific data. The foam insulation must be applied by a certified insulation contractor. It requires special equipment and training.

Sprayed-foam insulation is a good vapor barrier for any climate, and especially useful in mixed climates. Here the house has a heating and cooling period; therefore, a vapor barrier is needed on each side of the insulation. While this can be done with fibrous insulations, sprayed foam, being a solid material, automatically resists the passage of water vapor from inside and outside the house.

Sprayed foam is used in walls, under floors, in ceilings, on foundations, and any other place where insulation is needed. It is especially useful to get into small and difficult-to-reach places (**3–13**).

■ Radiant Insulations

Radiant insulations are reflective materials that block the flow of radiant heat. Radiation is the transmission of heat through space by means of electromagnetic waves. The heat energy passes through the air between the source and the surface it strikes without heating the air between them. The heat, such as from the sun, passes through the roof or wall by conduction and, if radiant insulation is placed behind the surface hit by the sun, it will reflect the heat energy back through the material. In this way, the amount of heat through a roof or wall that hits the insulation is reduced, which lowers the temperature of the ceiling or wall materials. This increases the effectiveness of the dead air spaces behind the insulation. Radiant insulations also serve as vapor barriers.

Heat flow by radiation is indicated by its E-value. The lower the E-value, the more effective the material. E-values range from 0 to 1, with 0 indicating no radiation and 1 the highest measure of radiation. Various insulation materials can be compared on their E-value. Typically fiberglass, foam, and cellulose will have surface emittances (E-values) in excess of 0.70, while

3–13. Sprayed foam can be placed in difficult places and forms a tight air seal in any cracks in the structure.
(Courtesy North Carolina Foam Industries)

reflective insulations will have E-values around 0.03. As radiant insulation products are chosen, consult the data provided by the manufacturer for the effectiveness of its products.

While various radiant barriers reduce the flow of heat energy into an attic or wall, they are most cost-effective in the hot southern climates. In northern climates, the savings in the warm months would be small. In northern climates, it would most likely be best to install additional batt insulation on the ceiling and have good attic ventilation. This would save quite a bit in the winter heating season.

TYPES OF RADIANT INSULATION

There are three basic types of radiant insulation products. These are reflective insulation, radiant barriers, and interior radiation control coatings.

Reflective Insulation

Reflective insulation is made up of layers of aluminum foil, heavy papers, or sheet plastic. They can trap air and, therefore, reduce convective heat transfer. Materials used to make reflective insulation can reduce radiant heat transfer by as much as 95%. Reflective insulations will have E-values of 0.03, which is lower and therefore better than that of most other types of insulation. This means that reflective insulation is a superior material for reducing radiant heat. When reflective insulation is installed in building cavities, such as exterior walls, it traps air in the same manner as other types of insulation and reduces heat flow by convection. Reflective insulation must always be installed next to an air space.

There are several types of reflective insulation available. One type has multiple layers of aluminum foil separated by one or more layers of foam insulation (**3–14**) or plastic bubbles (**3–15** and **3–16**).

Reflective insulation blankets and batts are available in widths from 16 to 72 inches and up to 125 feet long. Board products are typically 16 and 24 inches wide and 48 and 96 inches long.

3–14. This reflective insulation blanket has a low-density flexible polypropylene foam core bonded between layers of aluminum foil.

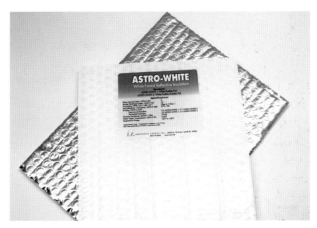

3–15. This reflective insulation blanket has polyethylene air bubble pockets sandwiched between thin layers of reflective aluminum foil. It has a class A fire rating and blocks the passage of moisture. *(Courtesy Innovative Energy, Inc.)*

3–16. This form of reflective insulation blanket contains layers of dead air space formed by installing air bubble insulation layers between the exterior foil surfaces. *(Courtesy Reflexfix, Inc.)*

Radiant barriers are aluminum-coated plastic sheets (**3–17**) or laminates consisting of aluminum foil laminated to a material such as plywood or oriented strand board (**3–18**), gypsum wallboard, and sheets of rigid foam insulation (refer to **3–10**). They are most commonly used on roofs and, when installed, the foil faces the attic. They can be used on walls. This requires special techniques recommended by the manufacturer.

Radiant barriers have a low E-value which is typically 0.03 to 0.04. They have a class-A fire rating. They have a water transmission rate of about 0.02, so make good vapor barriers. They are available in rolls 24 to 48 inches wide and up to 500 feet long.

Interior radiation control coatings (IRCC) are low E-value coatings applied by spraying or rolling on porous building materials such as wood, brick, oriented strandboard plywood, plaster, or gypsum wallboard. These coatings will typically have an E-value of 0.24 or less. IRCC only limits heat transfer of radiation and does not reduce heat transfer by conduction or convection. It is similar in function to a radiant barrier, but is less efficient.

3–18. The oriented strand-board sheathing has aluminum-foil reflective insulation bonded to the back. It is installed with the insulation facing into the attic. This forms a radiant barrier.
(Courtesy Norbord Industries, Inc.)

3–17. This single-layer reflective insulation has a reinforced polymer film sandwiched between two layers of pure aluminum foil. One type has small perforations, which allows moisture behind it to vent to the air on the outside.
(Courtesy Innovative Energy, Inc.)

■ Vapor Barriers

Vapor barriers are part of the job of insulating a building. A vapor barrier prevents water vapor generated inside a building from penetrating the gypsum wallboard and condensing as moisture inside the wall cavity. This damages the insulation. In climates where heating is the major consideration, it is installed on the walls and ceiling facing the room, which is the warm side. In hot humid climates, it may be installed on the outside of the framing, blocking moisture from the outside air or omitted entirely.

A commonly used vapor barrier is a heavy kraft paper coated with wax or asphalt. The insulation, such as fiberglass, is bonded on one side to this paper (**3–19**). If unfaced insulation has been installed, the area is covered with polyethylene film that is stapled to the framing (**3–20**). It is also used to cover the ground in the crawl space to prevent moisture from the ground from entering that area. It is laid on the ground before a concrete slab floor is poured. This keeps the slab free of moisture from the ground.

3–19. This fiberglass insulation has a kraft-paper vapor barrier. It is installed facing the warm room.

3–20. Unfaced insulation is covered with a polyethylene vapor barrier.

■ Building Code Fire Regulations

Building codes specify that insulation materials—including facings such as kraft paper, polyethylene vapor barriers, and mesh screens installed within floor-ceiling assemblies, roof-ceiling assemblies, wall assemblies, crawl spaces, basements, and attics—must have a flame-spread index not over 25 and a smoke-developed index not over 450. Manufacturers have their products tested following American Society for Testing and Materials (ASTM) procedures.

Flame-spread index ratings are numerical designations applied to a building material which are a comparative measure of the ability of the material to resist flaming combustion over its surface. Flame spread is the rate of flame travel which is based on a selected species of untreated wood. The wood flame spread is given the value 100. Noncombustible materials have a rating of 0.

Smoke-developed index ratings are relative numerical classifications of materials based on ASTM tests of the surface burning characteristics. The rating classifies materials by the amount of smoke they will give off as they burn. Tests are made using ASTM procedures. Most codes prohibit the use of materials having a rating of 450 or more to be used inside a building.

Before selecting an insulation, check the local building code and the manufacturer statements concerning the insulation under consideration.

Fiberglass insulation is inorganic and noncombustible. Unfaced fiberglass insulation is accepted in many codes, such as a fire blocking material in a wall that is equal to a solid wood, gypsum board, or mineral fiber insulation. Unfaced fiberglass blankets typically have a flame-spread rating of 10 and a smoke-developed rating of 10. Faced blankets will have a flame-spread rating from 25 to 75, and a smoke-developed rating from 50 to 150.

The kraft and foil vapor retarder facing on fiberglass and other blankets is flammable, so they must be covered with a fire-retarding material such as ½-inch gypsum wallboard. The fire-resistant rating is sometimes shown on the insulation packaging. Some fiberglass batts have a flame-resistant foil-scrim kraft-paper facing and can be left exposed.

Cellulose insulation is made from recycled paper products, which are flammable. They are treated with chemicals to reduce their flammability. This adds fire-resistance, but the material is not noncombustible or smolder-resistant. If the insulation is exposed to fire that smolders in the insulation, the fire is difficult to extinguish. Cellulose insulation should be covered with a fire-resistant material such as ½-inch gypsum wallboard. It will typically have a flame-spread rating of 25 and a smoke-developed rating less than 50.

Mineral-wool insulation is made of inorganic fibers derived from basalt, a volcanic rock. Mineral wool has a melting point of 2000°F and is classified as noncombustible. When installed in approved wall systems, it will typically have up to a two-hour fire endurance rating. Unfaced insulation has a flame-spread rating of 5 and a smoke-developed rating of 0. Faced mineral-wool insulation has a flame-spread rating of 25 and a smoke-developed rating of 50. Consult the manufacturer for specific data pertaining to their product.

Reflective insulation is fire-retardant, and most types will have a low flame-spread rating and a low smoke-developed rating.

Cotton insulation is made using natural cotton fibers, which are flammable. When properly treated, some types have a flame-spread rating of 5 and a smoke-developed rating of 35.

Expanded polystyrene rigid insulation and sprayed foam insulation have a flame-spread rating of 10 to 25 and a smoke-developed rating of 60 to 200.

Polyrethane and polyisocyanurate sprayed foam and rigid insulations are lightweight and have high R-values. Typically, they have a flame-spread rating no greater than 75 and a smoke-developed rating no greater than 450.

Mineral-wool insulation is made from mineral slag and is spun into a soft, flexible material used for blankets and batts and as a loose fill insulation.

Slag is the residue left from blast furnaces. It is a noncombustible material with a flame-spread of 5 and a smoke-developed rating of 0.

■ Insulation Hazards

Vermiculite is a granular material that has been used for many years (**3–21**). One typical installation consists of filling the cores of a concrete block wall. Some older types contained asbestos, so it is a dangerous material to remove. If it must be removed, have the building inspector recommend a contractor certified to remove hazardous materials. If possible, leave it in place.

An early foam insulation used was urea-formaldehyde. It was eventually banned because of the possibility of releasing toxic formaldehyde gas as it aged. Over many years, this emission gradually decreases and may no longer present a hazard. Since it is old and dry, it will break into a powdery material, so a hazardous dust will be formed if you try to remove it.

Fiberglass insulation is known to release formaldehyde emissions; however, it appears they are minimal. Consult the insulation manufacturer for technical data.

3–21. Vermiculite is a granular insulation made from expanded bits of mica. It is poured into cavities.

INSTALLING INSULATION AND VAPOR BARRIERS

Once all air leaks in the walls, ceilings, and floors have been found and sealed, it is time to consider the insulation. Insulating a house under construction is much easier than upgrading insulation in an older house (**4–1**). The areas to be insulated are easier to access and the areas do not contain the dust that collects over the years in older houses. In both cases, there will often be areas that are difficult to reach but must be insulated if a totally satisfactory job is to be done.

The insulation forms a complete shield around the living area of the house, helping it stay warm in the winter and cool in the summer. If you are upgrading an older house and areas such as the ceiling have insulation, do not assume nothing needs to be done. Check them for thickness and a vapor barrier. What kind of insulation was used years ago? Is it worth saving? What is the recommended thickness for your geographic area?

As you consider upgrading existing insulation, evaluate the ventilation of the roof. If the amount is inadequate for the area, now is the time to rework the attic ventilation as discussed in Chapter 7.

Finally, all air leaks which allow exterior air to filter into the house uncontrolled should be sealed. A good insulation job can be less effective if natural air leaks, such as those around old doors and windows, are not sealed. Review Chapter 2 for information on air leaks.

■ The Thermal Envelope

The thermal envelope, also referred to as the thermal boundary, includes the parts of a house that protect the interior living area from the outside climatic conditions and from parts of the house that are not heated or cooled (**4–2**). The interior living area is heated and cooled to

4–1. Insulation and vapor barriers can be easily installed in new construction. *(Courtesy Ark Seal, Inc.)*

temperatures comfortable for day to day living. This is sometimes referred to as a conditioned space.

There are parts of the house that protect the interior from the weather but are not part of the thermal envelope. Generally, the roof protects the interior from the weather and is not part of the thermal envelope; however, if a house has cathedral ceilings, part of the roof serves as the weather protection shell and as a thermal boundary. The weather protection shell breaks winds

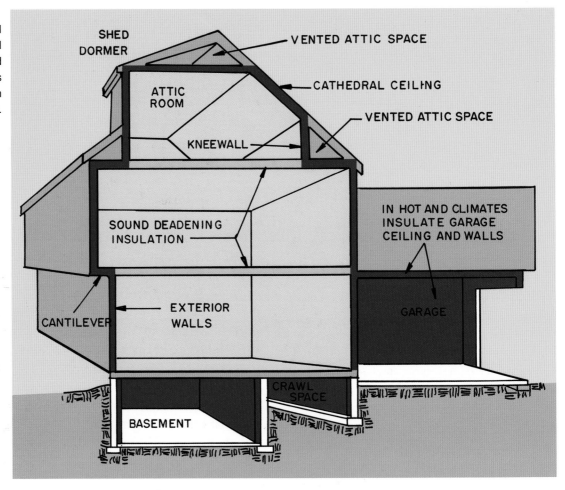

SHED DORMER

VENTED ATTIC SPACE

ATTIC ROOM

CATHEDRAL CEILING

VENTED ATTIC SPACE

KNEEWALL

SOUND DEADENING INSULATION

IN HOT AND CLIMATES INSULATE GARAGE CEILING AND WALLS

GARAGE

CANTILEVER

EXTERIOR WALLS

CRAWL SPACE

BASEMENT

and resists rain and snow. The ceilings of rooms that have unheated spaces above and the wall separating a garage from the living area are other examples of areas that are part of the thermal envelope.

The materials making up the thermal envelope each have insulating value in addition to that provided by the insulation itself. For example, an exterior wall on a wood-framed building will typically consist of the interior drywall, a dead air space into which insulation is placed, some type of sheathing, house wrap or builder's felt, and some form of siding (4–3). A typical R-value picture of this wall is shown here.

The thermal envelope can have unusual locations where a decision must be made as whether to require insulation. For example, if a basement is under part of a house and a crawl space under the rest, the crawl space should not open on to the basement. If it does, the basement foundation will need to be sealed and insulated where it meets the crawl space. Where dormers meet the roof is another place requiring special attention. These and other locations are frequently found and are created by the method of framing.

An example of where insulation should be placed to form an unbroken thermal envelope is shown in 4–2. This includes walls, ceilings, and floors, as well as the foundation. In two-story houses, some prefer to not insulate the first floor ceiling because the second floor rooms are heated and cooled. It is a good place to place sound-attenuation batts, which will also provide thermal insulation. Vented spaces such as a crawl space

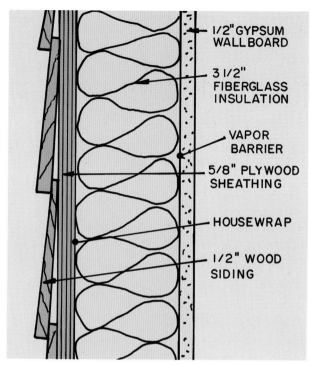

4–3. Typical frame wall construction which will give a normal R-rating to the complete assembly.

| ½" GYPSUM WALLBOARD |
| 3 1/2" FIBERGLASS INSULATION |
| VAPOR BARRIER |
| 5/8" PLYWOOD SHEATHING |
| HOUSEWRAP |
| 1/2" WOOD SIDING |

TABLE 4–1.

R-VALUES SUMMARY

	R-Value
Outside Air Film	0.2
½" Wood Siding	1.0
Housewrap	0.0
⅝" Plywood Sheathing	2.0
3½" Fiberglass Insulation	13.0
Vapor Barrier	0.0
½" Gypsum Wallboard	0.5
Outside Air Film	0.2
Total R-Value of the Wall	16.9

Table 4–1. A summary of the R-values of the materials in the wall assembly shown in 4–3.

should have insulation between the floor joists. Unvented spaces, such as basements, should have insulation around the foundation, extending at least two feet below grade. In cold northern climates, this would be extended four to six feet below grade to get below the frost line.

■ Determining the Amount of Insulation Needed

The amount of insulation depends upon such things as the cost of fuel, the climate, the desired interior temperatures, and the type of construction. The thickness needed will depend on the kind of insulation to be used. Types of insulation and their R-values are discussed in Chapter 3. The R-value is a number used to indicate the ability of a material to resist the flow of heat. The higher the R-value, the better the material resists heat.

A major consideration is the geographic location. In **4–4** are shown typical recommended R-values for various parts of the country. You can also get recommendations from the local building inspector and insulation contractors as to what is typical for your area. Notice that even in southern climates the ceiling should have an R-value of 30 because of the long months when the house is air-conditioned. See **Table 4–2** on page 60.

■ Personal Protection

Some types of insulation are made with fibers that tend to get into the air and can inflame the eyes and lungs and cause arms and other exposed skin to itch and become irritated. Often it is necessary to work in tight places where insulation is very close to the face and body. In older homes, when additional insulation is added or the old insulation removed and replaced, considerable dust will be encountered. Since the attic is open to exterior air, this is a special problem in hot, dry areas where dust blowing in the air is common. These conditions require the use of various personal protection devices.

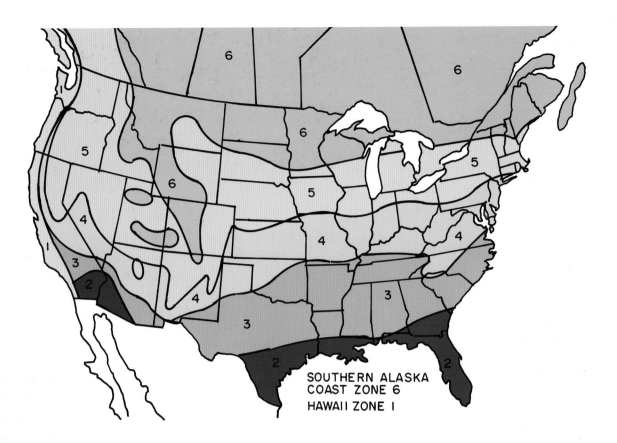

4–4. Typical recommended R-values for various parts of the United States and Canada. Check local codes for specific recommendations.

SOUTHERN ALASKA
COAST ZONE 6

HAWAII ZONE I

TABLE 4–2.

TYPICAL RECOMMENDED R-VALUES BY ZONES

Zone	Exterior Wall	Ceiling with Unheated Area Above	Floor with Unheated Area Below
1	R–11	R–19	R–11
2	R–13	R–26	R–11
3	R–19	R–26	R–13
4	R–19	R–30	R–19
5	R–19	R–33	R–22
6	R–19	R–38	R–22

EYE PROTECTION

Eyes should be protected with impact goggles (**4–5**). These must fit tight against the face so particles and fumes do not reach the eyes. Regular eyeglasses provide little protection. Safety glasses protect from the front and sides, but not from the top or bottom (**4–6**). They can be used when conditions are mild and the area has good ventilation. However, goggles are the best choice for all conditions. If there is danger to your face, wear a full face shield (**4–7**). The polycarbonate window can be replaced when an existing window gets scratched or broken.

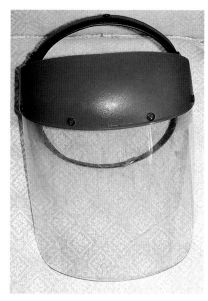

4–7. A face shield provides protection for the entire face. It is useful when working on insulation overhead.

4–5. Tight-fitting eye-protection goggles are important to keep fibers and fumes away from the eyes.

RESPIRATORY PROTECTION

Breathing particles in the air can cause health problems, so at least a disposable paper dust mask must be worn (**4–8**). If the job is small or in an open area with good ventilation, such as insulating exterior walls in new construction, this mask may be adequate. However, purchase the type that is certified by the National Institute for Occupational Safety and Health (NIOSH) which has a rating of N95 or better. As soon as it begins to collect particles, throw it away and use a new one. Read the instructions on the container holding the masks. The mask in **4–8** cannot be used for

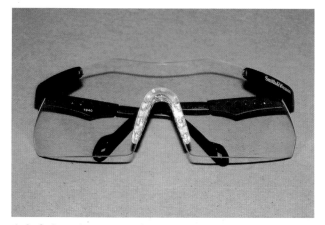

4–6. Safety glasses are often used when conditions are such that there is little particle float in the air and no noxious fumes exist.

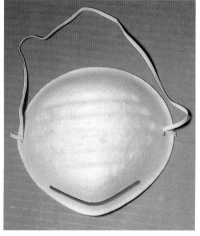

4–8. This paper mask is useful in situations where there is little dust or fibers in the air and the area has natural or power ventilation. Any paper mask used for insulation installation should be NIOSH approved.

protection against toxic and other hazardous dusts such as lead, asbestos, paint sprays and pesticides, and all fumes, gases, and vapors. Do not use it for protection for sanding or the installation of fiberglass, which are likely to generate dusts above the nuisance level. Masks must fit tightly against the face. Some types are suitable for use against non-toxic dusts such as fiberglass and sawdust.

Another type of respiratory device is referred to as a comfort mask (4–9). These are often not NIOSH-approved. If used for insulation work, wear only those indicated as being approved. They have replaceable filters, so buy a supply when you buy the respirator.

The respirator in 4–10 has several filters/cartridges. It is recommended for use when organic vapors or particles are present. These are typically from spray-painting and non-asbestos insulation.

Use a High Efficiency Particulate Arresting (HEPA) respirator when working in dusty attics or in close quarters where fibers will be in high density in the air. Also use it with foam insulation to filter fumes developed by the foaming and placing process (4–11). These types of respirators provide the very best respiratory protection. They protect against paints, pesticides, vapors, asbestos,

dust, fiberglass, and other air pollutants. The manufacturer supplies the required replacement cartridges.

Respirators should be cleaned and disinfected regularly. Discard any damaged respirators. If you find it getting difficult to breath, leave the work area immediately.

4–10. This respirator is recommended for use to protect against organic vapors such as those generated when spray-painting.

4–11. High Efficiency Particulate Arresting respirators provide the best protection from particles in the air and should be worn under difficult conditions. Keep several replacement cartridges available. (Courtesy Aearo Company)

4–9. This is a typical nonapproved comfort mask. They are generally used to protect against pollen, mowing, and dust from sweeping.

CLOTHING

Clothing should suit the weather and working conditions. Torn or loose clothing, loose cuffs, and neckwear are hazardous. Never wear rings or any other type of jewelry. Wear long pants and shirts with long sleeves and a cuff that can be buttoned. Wear hard-sole work shoes with metal toe protection. Never wear soft sole shoes, sandals, or other light shoes.

Some jobs require the use of overalls designed to protect the entire body (**4–12**). Companies supplying safety equipment offer disposable coveralls and tough types made from Tyvek.

Wear light gloves to keep the fibers off your hands and wear shirts with long sleeves that are tied at the wrists (**4–13**). This will protect the skin on your hands and arms. Finally, you need to cover your hair. A light-weight hard hat is recommended. If fibers get in the hair and down the neck of your shirt, it gets very uncomfortable and will cause skin irritation.

When working in places where falls can occur, be certain to use approved scaffolds, guardrails, safety nets, and personal fall arrest harnesses, lanyards or lifelines, as shown in **4–1**.

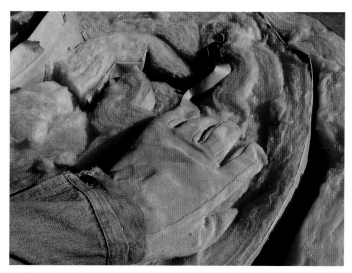

4–13. Wear light gloves and shirts with long sleeves. Tie the sleeves over the gloves so fibrous particles cannot get to the hand and arm.

HEARING PROTECTION

If you have to work in an area where the noise level is so high you have to shout to talk to someone next to you, wear approved ear plugs. These are soft plastic and sold in containers protecting them until they are needed (**4–14**). These are disposable, so discard them when they get dirty or damaged. Under very dirty conditions, wear them to keep particles in the air from entering the ear canal.

4–12. This foam insulation is being installed by a trained technician who has his body and head completely covered and is wearing a high efficiency particulate arresting respirator. *(Courtesy Icynene Inc.)*

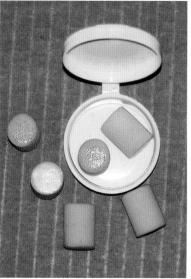

4–14. Disposable ear plugs help protect against excess noise and air heavily contaminated by hazardous particles.

OTHER SAFETY RECOMMENDATIONS

Also watch for things that could cause physical injury. Electric wires that are frayed or have the insulation completely gone in places can cause a fatal accident. Such a case is not unusual in very old homes with wiring that does not have the protective coverings available on current wire products.

There are numerous other things to watch out for, such as nails sticking out of the framing and roof sheathing. If the attic has some floorboards installed, be certain they are nailed to the joists. If not, they could slip and you could put a leg through the ceiling. Stay on the alert.

■ Vapor Barriers

Vapor barriers are moisture-impervious materials or films that will prevent the passage of water vapor in the air. Water vapor moves from areas where it is in high concentration to areas having a lower concentration. As the temperature of the air decreases, air can contain less water vapor. As the air temperature increases, air can contain more water. When moisture-laden air strikes a colder surface, the water vapor will be deposited on that surface as liquid water.

Materials commonly used for vapor barriers include special paints that are placed on the interior surface of the drywall, plastic films, aluminum foil, and asphalt-laminated paper.

Vapor barriers are compared on their perm ratings. The perm rating is a measure of the material's resistance to vapor penetration. Codes require vapor barriers to have a perm rating of 1.0 or less. For example, kraft paper has a rating of 1.0, 6-mil polyethylene has a perm rating of 0.06, and aluminum foil vapor barriers are rated at 0.00. This indicates that aluminum foil is impervious to penetration, while plastic sheeting is next best (**Table 4–3**).

Since most vapor barriers are flammable, codes require they be covered with a fire-resistant material such as drywall or plaster.

TABLE 4–3.

TYPICAL PERM RATINGS OF VAPOR BARRIER MATERIALS

Vapor Retardant Paint	0.5
Latex Primer	6.0
15-lb. Building Felt	4.0
1-inch Expanded Polystyrene Bead Board	2 to 5.8
1-inch Extruded Polystyrene Board	1.2
Kraft Paper Insulation Facing	1.0
6-Mil Polyethylene Sheet	.06
1 Mil Aluminum Foil	0.0

LOCATING VAPOR BARRIERS

In geographic areas where heating is the major factor, if the warm, moisture-laden interior air is allowed to leak into the wall cavity it will strike the cold sheathing and change to liquid water. Under these conditions, mold and rot can develop. This is why moisture barriers are installed on the warm side of an exterior wall in climatic areas where heating is a major factor (**4–15** and **4–16**).

In climates where cooling the interior air is the major factor, the reverse occurs. Warm moisture-laden outside air flowing into the house and penetrating the exterior wall will condense on the cooler drywall surfaces, forming liquid water and wetting the interior of the wall. The vapor barrier in cooling climates is placed under the sheathing on the outside of the wall. In other words, the vapor barrier is always placed on the warm side of the wall.

In an area where heating and cooling are about of equal importance, the area is called a mixed climate. In these areas, neither heating or cooling is dominant. The need for low permeance vapor barriers in most buildings in a mixed climate is less pronounced than in other climates. In a mixed climate, the vapor barrier should be placed to protect against the more serious condensation, be it winter or summer. Consult the local building inspector for recommendations if the house is in a mixed climate. If there is no code requirement, consult an insulation contractor to see what is typically done in this area.

4–15. These fiberglass blankets have a kraft-paper vapor barrier that has been installed facing the inside of the house.

4–16. These are unfaced fiberglass blankets. They have been covered with a 6-mil polyethylene vapor barrier.

INSTALLING VAPOR BARRIERS

Unfaced blown and fiberglass blanket insulation, foam insulation, and cellulose insulation are all covered with a 6-mil polyethylene vapor barrier (4–16). The vapor barrier should be lapped and stapled to the studs and floor and ceiling joists (4–17) or the seam taped with a special tape. Pull the sheet tight so it does not form air pockets. Staple it to the top and bottom plates, providing a tight

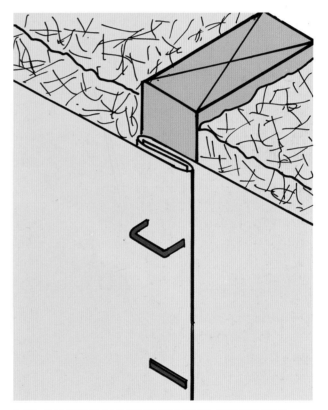

4–17. One way to seal the butting edges of polyethylene vapor barriers.

seal at the ceiling and subfloor (**4–18**). Pay special attention to installing it around doors, windows, and other wall openings (**4–19**). Be certain to work the vapor barrier behind electrical outlets, plumbing, and other things mounted in the wall, ceiling, or floor (**4–20**).

When installing blankets with the vapor barrier attached, the flanges on the blanket should be stapled to the studs, top, and bottom plates (**4–21**). Also seal around doors and windows as shown in **4–19**.

Sometimes during installation or later on during construction, the vapor barrier may be torn. Always check it and tape any damage before installing the drywall. Check around places where plumbing or wiring may have been run after the insulation has been installed. Tape or seal it with foam insulation.

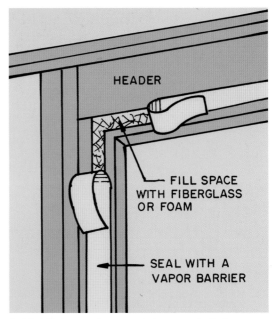

4–19. Fill the cracks around doors and windows with insulation and staple a vapor barrier over the wood framing.

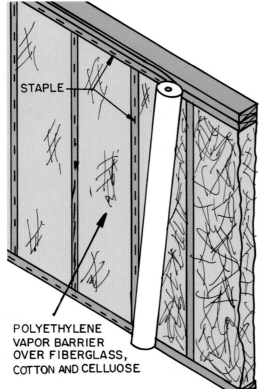

4–18. Pull the polyethylene vapor barrier tight and staple it to the studs and top and bottom plates.

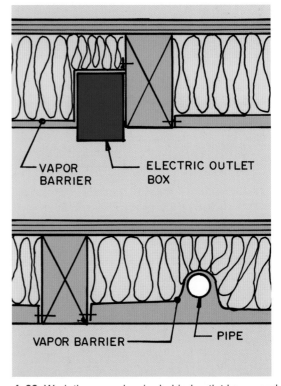

4–20. Work the vapor barrier behind outlet boxes and plumbing.

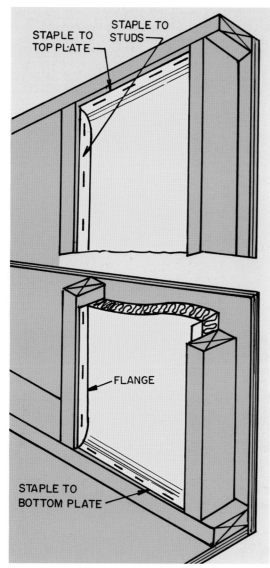

STAPLE TO TOP PLATE

STAPLE TO STUDS

FLANGE

STAPLE TO BOTTOM PLATE

4–21. Insulation blankets with the vapor barrier attached should be stapled tightly against the studs and top and bottom plates through a flange.

TABLE 4–4.

TYPICAL R-VALUES FOR SHEATHING

½" Plywood	0.62
½" Oriented Strandboard	0.62
1-inch Polystyrene Foam or Beads	5.00
1-inch Extruded Polystyrene	4.0
¾" Expanded Urethane	1.2

It is common practice to increase the amount of insulation in a ceiling by laying on additional blankets over the old insulation. This new layer must not have a vapor barrier. Lay unfaced blankets or batts perpendicular to the joists on top of the old insulation. If the old insulation does not have a vapor barrier, it should be removed and a new blanket with a vapor barrier be placed with the vapor barrier side down against the ceiling material. In heating climates, the vapor barrier always faces the side of the ceiling, wall or floor that is warm in the winter. Then place the old unfaced insulation over the new. If the old has deteriorated, throw it away.

Aluminum foil is installed in the same manner as polyethylene sheeting. Be careful it does not get torn. Repair any tears in the vapor barrier. The damaged area may be covered with a piece of vapor barrier material glued or taped to the surface. Polyvinyl tape is available for repairs.

Another form of vapor barrier is the paint put on the inside wall. A typical interior wall primer will have a perm of around 6.0. A vapor retarding paint will have a perm of around 0.5. This is a good and easy way to upgrade walls and ceilings with the least effort.

Rigid foam insulation panels also retard vapor transmission; however, their perm ratings are often above the required 1.0 minimum.

■ Sheathing Exterior Walls

Sheathing can make a difference in the insulation value of the exterior wall assembly. Typical R-values of sheathing available are shown in **Table 4–4**. The installations of a sheathing material with a high R-value will reduce the amount of heat gained or lost through the studs and other uninsulated parts of a wall. This heat flow is referred to as **thermal bridging.** It will also reduce the passage of heat through the total wall assembly and help control air infiltration.

When using some type of foamed plastic sheathing on wood-framed walls, the stud framing will need some extra bracing. Check the local codes. Typically, the ways this is done are to let in 1 × 4 inch wood members (**4–22**), install metal bracing straps (**4–23**), or place plywood panels at each corner (**4–24**) and in

4–22. Wood bracing is placed at the corners and other places along the wall as needed to provide the bracing.

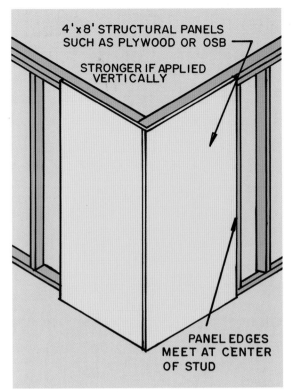

4–24. Plywood and OSB structural sheathing produces a strong, rigid wall.

4–23. Stud framed walls can be braced with diagonal metal strapping.

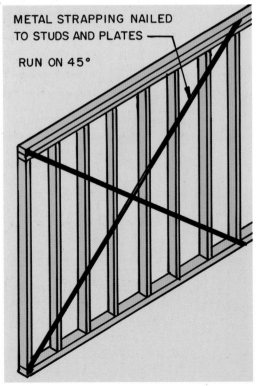

between the corners of long walls, as shown in **4–25**. The type of bracing greatly affects the strength of the wall. Plywood and oriented strandboard sheathed walls provide the strongest material load capacity.

■ Installing Faced Blankets and Batts

In new construction, the insulation is relatively easy to install because the wall studs are exposed and the wiring and plumbing is in place. Cut the blankets or batts to length by compressing it with a straight edge and cutting it with a sharp knife (**4–26**).

The following discussion is the procedure used when installing faced blankets and batts in areas where heating is the major factor. The vapor barrier has been placed facing the heated room.

There are three commonly used methods for installing faced insulations: inset-stapling, face-stapling, and pressure-fitting the insulation.

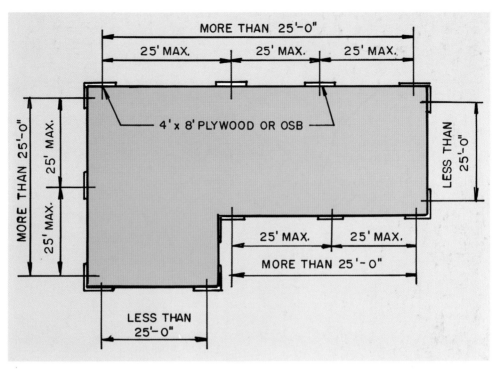

4–25. Typical examples of locating 4 × 8-foot plywood or OSB structural sheathing panels when used for bracing. While this provides adequate bracing, the wall is stronger if completely sheathed with these panels.

4–26. To cut fiberglass blankets, place the vapor barrier side up, line up the cut with a board, and slice with a sharp, long-bladed knife.

INSET-STAPLING

Fold out the flanges and carefully press the blanket in the cavity between the studs until the flange is flush with the face of the stud (**4–27**). This provides a ¾-inch airspace behind the drywall. Staple the flange to the studs, top and bottom plates as shown in **4–21**. Use enough staples to firmly hold the blanket in place and avoid air gaps between the flanges and the framing (**4–28**). Usually if they are 8 inches apart the flange will stay flat.

FACE-STAPLING

Some people prefer to staple the flange to the face of the stud. This has the advantage of providing an unbroken vapor barrier. Gently press the insulation between the studs. Make sure it fits tight against the top and bottom plates. Lay the flange on the framing and staple (**4–29**). Be certain it fits flat again the framing. When the next cavity has the blanket placed in it, overlap the flanges and staple. Use enough staples to get the lapped flanges flat on the framing.

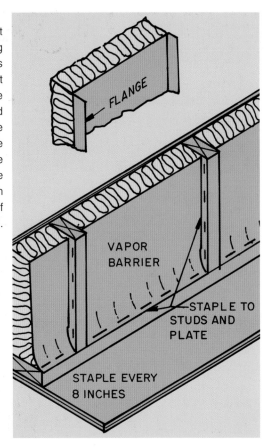

4-27. Bend out the stapling flanges, press the blanket against the sheathing and staple the flange to the stud. The edge of the flange should be flush with the face of the stud.

FLANGE

VAPOR BARRIER

STAPLE TO STUDS AND PLATE

STAPLE EVERY 8 INCHES

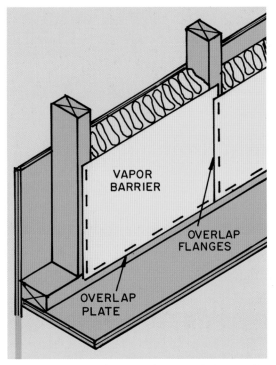

VAPOR BARRIER

OVERLAP FLANGES

OVERLAP PLATE

4–29. The stapling flange on faced insulation can be laidover the surface of the wood framing and stapled to it. This provides an unbroken vapor barrier.

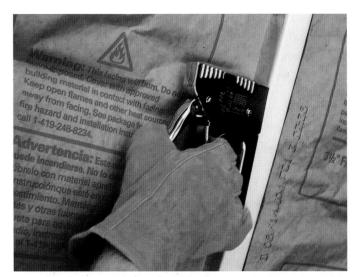

4–28. Use enough staples to keep the flange tight to the framing.

PRESSURE-FITTING THE INSULATION

Generally, high-performance batts have sufficient density so that they are stiff enough to stay in place by pushing them into the cavity space. Before doing this, make certain the manufacturer recommends that the pressure-fit techniques be used. Keep the face of the blanket flush with the face of the studs and top and bottom plates (4–30). Be certain the ends butt firmly against the framing and the end of the blanket against which it will butt.

■ Installing Unfaced Insulation

Unfaced insulation is carefully placed in the cavity between the framing members (4–31). It must be cut the proper size so it fits snugly at the sides on the framing and butts on the ends tightly (4–32). Make it an inch longer than the space, so it can be worked in place. It is held in place by friction on each side. Short lengths, such as in kneewalls or below windows, sometimes must be held in place with wire laced across the surface so that the insulation does not fall out (4–33).

4–30. High-density insulation batts are installed using the pressure-fit technique in a cathedral ceiling. *(Courtesy CertainTeed Corporation)*

4–31. Unfaced insulation is cut to the correct size and gently worked in the cavity between the framing. *(Courtesy Knauf Insulation)*

4–32. This unfaced ceiling insulation is very poorly installed. It does not firmly butt the framing, and the thickness varies.

4–33. Sometimes short lengths of unfaced insulation need wire strapping to hold it in place. In this example, the polyethylene vapor barrier was installed right after the insulation was put in place.

4–34. After pressing the unfaced insulation in the cavity, use a wide-blade wall scraper to tuck in the corners of the batts to keep them from forming a rounded corner.

As the unfaced insulation is pressed into the cavity, use a wide-blade wall scraper or a drywall joint knife to tuck the edges and ends neatly into the cavity (**4–34**). This makes it fit firmly against the framing, increasing its effectiveness.

■ Butting Blankets

When butting blankets and batts end to end, be certain they are forced tightly together (**4–35**). Gaps are easy to leave and do not obstruct heat flow in that area. If faced insulation is used, the gap also is a break in the vapor barrier (**4–36**). If necessary, the batt can be secured with tape.

■ Insulating Narrow Cavities

Frequently a wall, ceiling, or floor cavity will be narrower than the common 14½-inch space between framing members. To insulate this narrow space, cut the faced insulation about one inch wider than the width of the cavity. Leave one side with the existing flange. Pull about one inch of the facing loose from the insulation and staple it as you did the first flange (**4–37**).

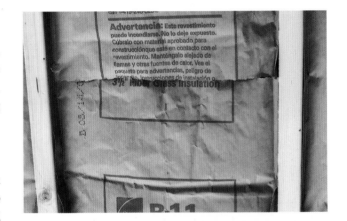

4–35. End butts between batts should be very tight. Seal them with tape if necessary.

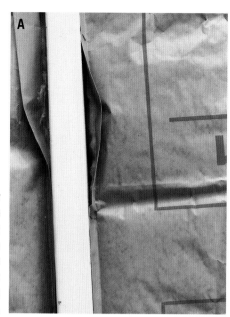

A

4–36. Any gaps in the insulation provide a place for heat loss and also a break in the vapor barrier.

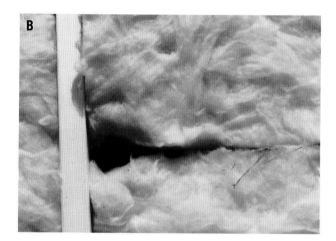

B

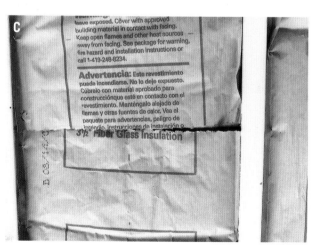

C

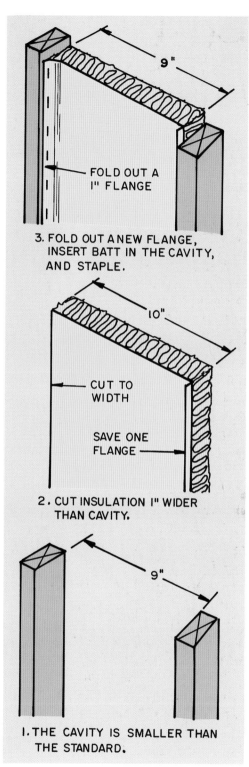

FOLD OUT A 1" FLANGE

3. FOLD OUT A NEW FLANGE, INSERT BATT IN THE CAVITY, AND STAPLE.

9"

10"

CUT TO WIDTH

SAVE ONE FLANGE

2. CUT INSULATION 1" WIDER THAN CAVITY.

9"

1. THE CAVITY IS SMALLER THAN THE STANDARD.

4–37. When insulating cavities narrower than standard with faced batts, cut the batt one inch wider than the cavity and form a new flange on the cut side.

■ Insulating the Ceiling

Blankets are easiest to install in a ceiling if the drywall is in place; however, they can be stapled to the ceiling joists just like they are to studs (**4–38**). Blankets have to be compressed with a baffle at the outside wall so the air from the soffit can flow into the attic (**4–39**). If unfaced pressure-fit blankets are used, wedge them between the joists and let it overlap the top plate (**4–40**). Then staple a 6-mil polyethylene vapor barrier over the ceiling.

4–40. Ceilings can be insulated before the drywall is in place by using pressure-fit blanks. *(Courtesy CertainTeed Corporation)*

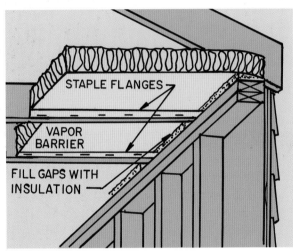

4–38. Ceilings can have faced insulation installed before the drywall is in place by stapling the flanges to the joists.

If the drywall ceiling is in place, lay the blanket between the ceiling joists with the vapor barrier down against the drywall. It will have to be cut to fit around ducts, pipes (**4–41**), wiring, and bridging (**4–42**). Fit it tight so there is no heat loss due to a gap.

When the ceiling joists overlap on a load-bearing wall, it is difficult to get a single batt to flow through the area and fit snugly against the joists. Gaps occur which make a break in the vapor barrier on faced insulation and provide a place for heat to leak into the attic (**4–43**). To get a tight fit, cut the batt at this point flush

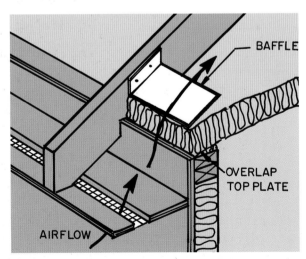

4–39. Be certain to leave several inches of air space at the exterior wall so the soffit vent airflow will move into the attic. Use a baffle when necessary.

4–41. Fit insulation firmly against pipes and other things that pierce the ceiling.

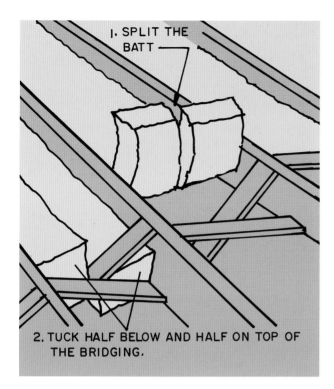

1. SPLIT THE BATT

2. TUCK HALF BELOW AND HALF ON TOP OF THE BRIDGING.

3. CUT AND BUTT THE JOINING PIECE.

4–42. To insulate where cross-bridging occurs, cut the batt to length and split it. Run part of the batt under and part on top of the bridging.

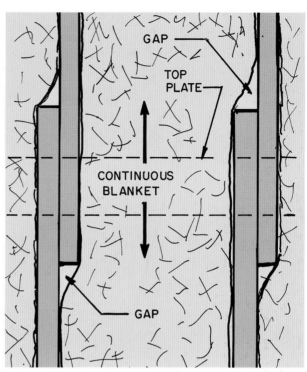

GAP

TOP PLATE

CONTINUOUS BLANKET

GAP

4–43. If the insulation batts are laid through areas where the joists are closer together than standard, gaps in the protection will occur.

with the end of one joist as shown in **4–44**. Then cut a filler piece the proper width and fit it snugly in place. Then start a new batt on the other side.

The most effective way to insulate a ceiling with blankets is to lay blankets the same thickness as the width of the joists between them, filling the cavity full. Then lay a layer of unfaced blankets on top and perpendicular to the joists (**4–45**). This gives the best protection when using batts and blankets. It is also a good way to increase the amount of insulation in an existing house.

If a room has a cathedral ceiling, the insulation can be stapled to the rafters (**4–46**) or pressure-fit insulation can be used (refer to **4–30**). However, it is necessary to provide a 1½-inch space between the sheathing and the insulation so air can flow from the soffit vent into the attic and out the ridge vent (**4–47**). Baffles are available that can be stapled to the roof sheathing, forming an air passage (**4–48**). They also protect the

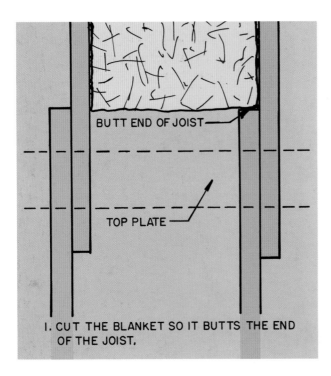

I. CUT THE BLANKET SO IT BUTTS THE END OF THE JOIST.

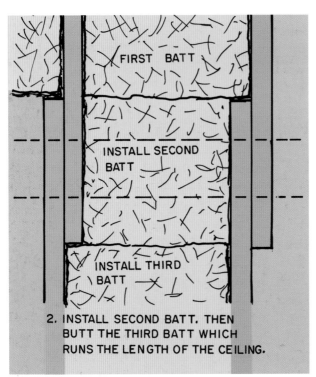

2. INSTALL SECOND BATT. THEN BUTT THE THIRD BATT WHICH RUNS THE LENGTH OF THE CEILING.

4–44. Cut batts to the width of areas between joists that are narrower than standard so a tight fit is produced.

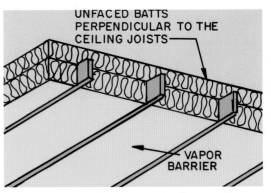

4–45. The most effective way to insulate a ceiling with blankets or batts is to lay one between the joists equal to their width and lay an unfaced blanket over this perpendicular to the joists.

4–46. This insulation batt has a vapor-barrier facing and is being stapled to the rafters, forming a cathedral ceiling.

(Courtesy Knauf Insulation)

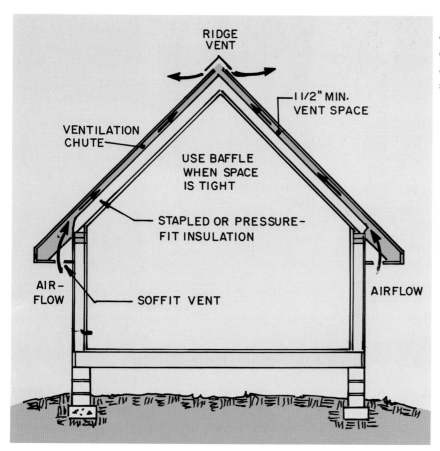

RIDGE
VENT

1 1/2" MIN.
VENT SPACE

VENTILATION
CHUTE

USE BAFFLE
WHEN SPACE
IS TIGHT

STAPLED OR PRESSURE-
FIT INSULATION

AIR-
FLOW

SOFFIT VENT

AIRFLOW

4–47. Insulation in cathedral ceilings must leave a 1½-inch air space between it and the sheathing.

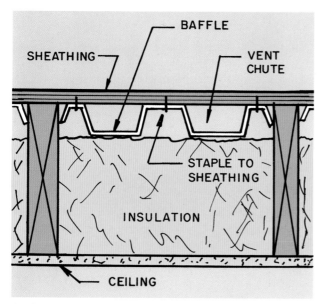

BAFFLE

SHEATHING

VENT CHUTE

STAPLE TO SHEATHING

INSULATION

CEILING

4–48. Baffles help maintain the required air space between the sheathing and insulation on cathedral ceilings.

insulation from condensation that may form on the sheathing. The size of the typical rafter minus the 1½- to 2-inch air space limits the thickness of insulation allowed. If the recommended minimum R-value is 30 to 38, this will require fiberglass batts 10 to 12 inches thick. There is not enough room for them.

One solution is to use high-performance fiberglass batts. R-30 high-performance batts typically are 8½ inches thick. Another solution is to consider using sprayed-foam insulation.

Cathedral ceilings with a vapor barrier require a vent area of one square foot for every 300 square feet of ceiling area. If a vapor barrier is omitted, this vent area has to be doubled. In cold parts of the country, the vapor barrier faces the winter heating area. In some southern climates, the requirements are different. Check local codes.

Flat and low-slope roofs have the same difficulty in getting the desired minimum insulation in the roof or ceiling. In flat-roofed houses, the ceiling joists also are the roof rafters.

When insulating a ceiling, there will be times when it is pierced by a chimney, which creates a fire hazard if combustible materials are in contact with them. Codes typically require that all wood structural members be two inches from a masonry chimney (**4–49**). The space can be insulated by sealing it with aluminum or metal flashing, gypsum drywall, or fire-resistant rigid insulation (**4–50**). Nail this to the framing and caulk the edge along the chimney with furnace cement or high-temperature silicone caulk. Additional layers of rigid insulation can be laid over this first application.

Light fixtures should be installed so that combustible material near them will not be subjected to temperatures in excess of 194°F (90°C). This is generally interpreted to mean that combustible insulation should not be installed within three inches of a recessed light-fixture enclosure, wiring compartment, or ballast and should not be installed above the fixture so it traps heat generated and prevents the free circulation of air (**4–51**). Install wood or metal blocking to hold back the insulation. There are recessed lighting enclosures that are suitable for insulation to be in direct contact with

4–50. Seal the two-inch air space around the chimney to block airflow which, during a fire, could let the flames move up inside the house. Also add some fire-resistant insulation.

4–51. Older recessed lights that are not insulation-contact (I.C.)-rated must have the insulation kept at least three inches away.

4–49. All combustible materials should be kept at least two inches away from a fireplace or chimney.

TILE FLUE LINERS

MIN. 2" CLEARANCE ON ALL SIDES

them. Be certain the fixture is clearly marked as meeting insulation contact (IC) requirements. Some codes require that the fixture be airtight. Airtight retrofit covers are available to cover older recessed lights. See Chapter 2 for more information.

■ Other Installation Situations

The walls, ceiling, and floor will contain wiring, outlet boxes, plumbing, heat ducts, and other systems that must have the insulation fit around them. While most conditions are typical, there will be unusual occurrences. When considering how to handle a specific situation, remember the purpose of the installation is to block heat flow around or from going through the obstruction. It must also protect any parts of the mechanical system involved.

■ Windows and Doors

Fill the spaces around windows and doors with insulation. Refer to **4–19**. While fibrous insulation is commonly used, foam seals it better and reduces airflow through the space. If foam is used, fill only an inch or two deep. Do not overfill because as the foam expands it may bow the window frame, making the window difficult to open.

PLUMBING IN CAVITIES

The insulation should be placed between the plumbing pipes and the sheathing (**4–52**). It is best the insulation is in place before the pipes are installed. Avoid placing water pipes and drains in exterior walls in cold climates because even with an inch or two of insulation they can freeze on very cold days. Never place insulation between the plumbing and the warm side of the wall (**4–53**).

ELECTRIC SYSTEMS

Electric wiring outlet boxes and lights are commonly found in wall, ceiling, and floor cavities. Place insulation between the outlet boxes and the sheathing and cut the insulation to fit around the box (**4–54**).

The electrical codes for some states require that one- and two-family dwellings have all electrical boxes and openings that penetrate the thermal envelope be sealed

4–52. Insulation is placed behind plumbing in exterior walls. It helps keep it from freezing in cold weather.

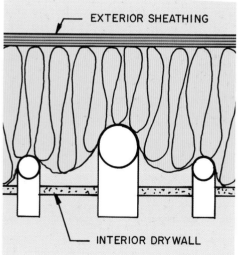

EXTERIOR SHEATHING

INTERIOR DRYWALL

4–53. Insulation is never placed between the warm side of a wall and the plumbing. It needs the heat from the room to help prevent freezing.

4–54. Fit the insulation and vapor barrier behind the outlet box and cut and fit it around the sides.

4–55. The air-vapor barrier box provides an airtight surround for installing electric outlets and any other items that may penetrate the thermal barrier.

(Courtesy The Low Energy Systems Supply Company, Inc.)

airtight. One way to accomplish this is to install an air-vapor barrier box. This installation must pass the blower door test so cold air infiltration and warm air exfiltration are blocked (**4–55**). The barrier box is installed on a stud and the electric outlet is installed inside it. The wires are introduced into the box and the wire opening is caulked. The wall is insulated in the normal manner surrounding the barrier box. The vapor barrier is taped to the flanges of the barrier box (**4–56**). More information is given in Chapter 2.

Electric wires are run through studs and joist as they are installed to reach various outlet sources. If the wiring has been placed at the center of the stud or joist, cut a slit in the insulation and fit it around the wire (**4–57**) and press it carefully down between the wire and the sheathing. If the wire is near the top or bottom plate, the insulation can be split across the width and the wire covered by the flap (**4–58**).

Recessed light fixtures have to meet code installation requirements. See **4–49** and Chapter 2 for details.

AIR DUCTS

Typically air ducts that run in an attic, crawl space, or other area that is not insulated are usually the insulated type. Insulated air ducts deliver conditioned air to the rooms with little loss to the air in the unconditioned space. If a duct runs in an exterior wall, blanket insulation should be placed between it and the sheathing.

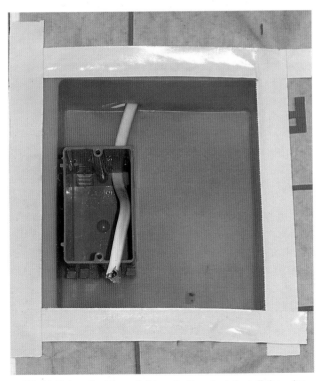

4–56. Nail the electric outlet box to the stud, install the wire, place insulation and a vapor barrier around the air-vapor box, and seal the box to the vapor barrier with tape. Now the duplex outlet or switch can be installed.

(Courtesy The Low Energy Systems Supply Company, Inc.)

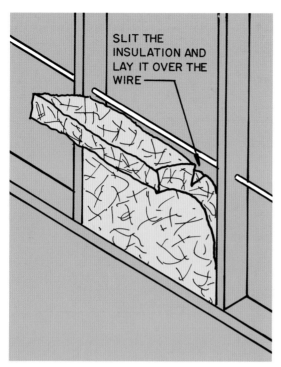

SLIT THE INSULATION AND LAY IT OVER THE WIRE

4–57. Electric wires can be worked into the insulation by cutting a slit in it and wrapping it over the wire.

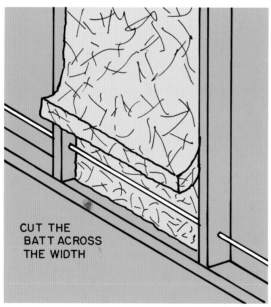

CUT THE BATT ACROSS THE WIDTH

4–58. If the wire is near a plate, the insulation can be cut across the width and the inside flap laid over the wire.

■ Insulating Floors

Floors over crawl spaces and unheated basements are insulated much like ceilings. Some people do not insulate the floors if the foundations are insulated.

The bottom of the floor for crawl spaces and basements is easily accessible. A common way to insulate is to place faced fiberglass batts between the joists. Make certain the vapor barrier is firmly against the subfloor and the batt is not compressed. To be effective, it must be open to its full width. Hold the insulation in place with rigid, springy wire fasteners that are especially for this purpose. Place them so the batts are secure but not compressed (4–59). Place a wire every 18 to 24 inches or as needed in special circumstances.

In the floor are a wide range of obstructions such as electric wires, plumbing, and bridging. Handle these as explained for insulating ceilings earlier in this chapter. Some floors are built with solid bridging (4–60) rather than cross bridging, as shown in 4–42. Lay the insulation up firmly against the bridging so no gaps exist.

As the floors are insulated, the headers and band joists must be insulated. The insulation should be pushed against the subfloor and header so there are no leaks. In 4–61, the joists run perpendicular to the header. In 4–62, they run parallel with it. Should the insulation not be thick enough to fully cover the header, install blankets cut wide enough to fill the entire height

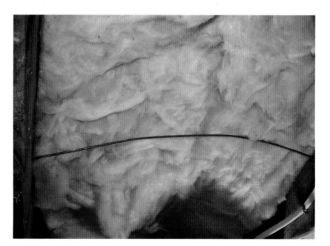

4–59. Insulation in floors over unheated areas can be held in place with rigid wire fasteners. Cut the wire to length so it holds the insulation almost flat.

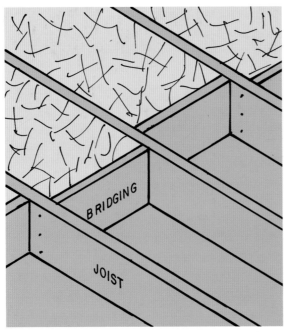

4–60. Solid bridging is often used in floor construction. Butt the insulation firmly against it.

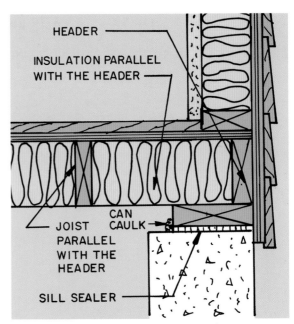

4–62. These joists are running parallel with the header. The insulation runs parallel with the header.

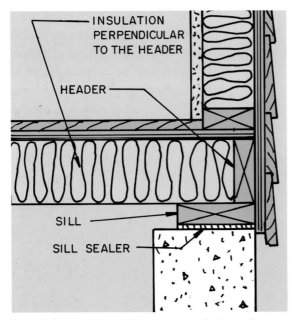

4–61. When the floor joists run perpendicular to the header, the insulation must butt firmly against it.

(4–63). Notice that the sill was installed over a sill sealer. A sill sealer is a thin strip of insulation that is placed on top of the foundation before the sill is installed. It fills any gaps that occur in the top of the foundation. If this has been omitted, lay a bead of caulk or foam along the top of the foundation next to the sill to seal any air leaks.

Floors can also be insulated with blown fiberglass, cellulose, and sprayed foam as discussed later in this chapter.

Concrete floors present special insulation problems. With new construction, the perimeter of the slab can be insulated as shown in 4–64. If an existing house has a concrete floor and the edges get very cold in the winter, this can be helped some by bonding rigid insulation to the foundation and running it down to the frost line. The frost line is the depth at which frost penetrates the earth in your geographic location. To keep the insulation from being damaged, it can be covered with a hard durable material such as cement board (4–65).

See Chapter 5 for information on insulating existing concrete floors.

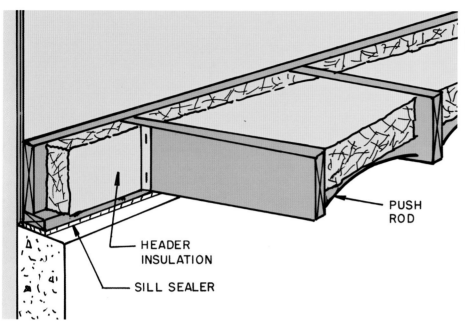

4–63. The header should be fully insulated.

PUSH ROD

HEADER INSULATION

SILL SEALER

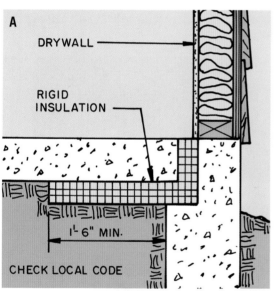

A

DRYWALL

RIGID INSULATION

1'-6" MIN.

CHECK LOCAL CODE

4–64. Two ways used to insulate a concrete slab floor in new construction. Check local codes.

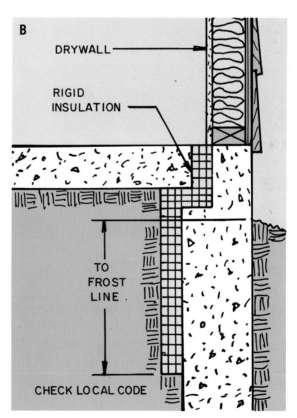

B

DRYWALL

RIGID INSULATION

TO FROST LINE.

CHECK LOCAL CODE

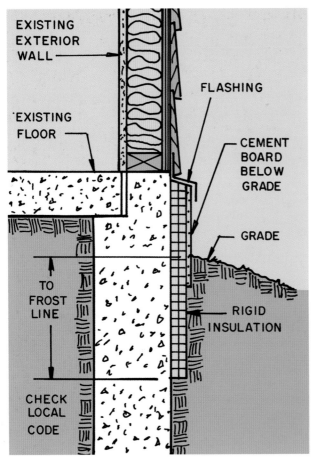

EXISTING EXTERIOR WALL

EXISTING FLOOR

FLASHING

CEMENT BOARD BELOW GRADE

GRADE

TO FROST LINE

RIGID INSULATION

CHECK LOCAL CODE

4–65. An existing house with a concrete floor can have perimeter insulation added by bonding it to the outside of the foundation.

■ Installing Blow-in Fibrous Insulation

Blow-in fibrous insulation, such as fiberglass, is used to insulate exterior walls, ceilings, and difficult-to-reach places. It is moved into the cavities with a blowing machine. It is installed by insulation contractors authorized to do this work. Special preparation and machine adjustments must be performed correctly. **Personal protection from loose fibers is very important.**

Blown loose-fill insulation is commonly used to insulate in new construction and when upgrading the insulation in existing houses. Any voids in the ceiling such as the opening above the kitchen cabinet soffit or other openings should be sealed with gypsum wallboard. Use baffles at the eaves so the airflow from the soffit vents is not blocked. Prepare recessed lights as described earlier for blanket insulation. Also remember that if loose-fill insulation is blown over the top plate of the exterior wall, it will flow out and fill the area over the soffit. To prevent this, wood or rigid insulation can be nailed along the edge and butt the baffle, or a strip of fiberglass insulation can be laid along the top plate (4–66). The entire attic must be sealed and ready before starting to blow the insulation.

The trained installer will keep the hose parallel with the ceiling and lay the insulation about 10 feet in front of them (4–67). They will work the area in sections and complete one section before starting another. Many unusual situations will arise which must be overcome. Some attics provide very little headroom and there are often obstructions in the way. The operator and the hose must be moved over, under, or around these obstructions (4–68). It is important that the person operating the blowing machine makes certain the settings are

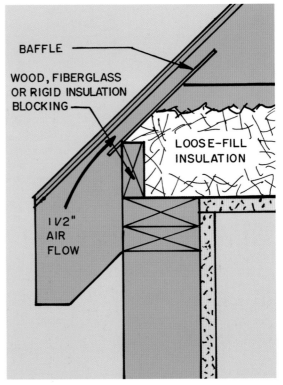

BAFFLE

WOOD, FIBERGLASS OR RIGID INSULATION BLOCKING

LOOSE-FILL INSULATION

1 1/2" AIR FLOW

4–66. Use some form of blocking along the top plate on the exterior walls to keep the loose-fill insulation from flowing into the soffit.

4–67. Keep the hose parallel with the ceiling and lay out the insulation 10 feet or so in front of the operator.

(Courtesy CertainTeed Corporation)

4–68. This operator has to work in a tight area, which makes laying in a uniform thickness more difficult. Be certain to run in plenty of light so no area is overlooked or underinsulated.

(Courtesy Knauf Insulation)

adjusted to provide the required flow of insulation. Be certain to level out any high or low spots so a uniform thickness is produced.

BLOW-IN FIBERGLASS IN WALLS IN NEW CONSTRUCTION

Blow-in insulation completely fills the wall cavities, leaving no gaps or air spaces. It has both thermal and acoustic properties.

The studs are covered with a special fabric available from the manufacturer of the fiberglass blowing insulation. The insulation is blown into the cavities through holes in this fabric (**4–69**). As the cavity fills, the hole is covered and the hose is moved up. Blown loose fill will work easily around wires and pipes in the wall (**4–70**). As it comes to objects such as electric outlet boxes, it fills behind them and firmly on all sides (**4–71**). While plumbing in exterior walls should be avoided in cold climates, blown loose-fill fiberglass will seal behind the pipes and completely surround them, providing good protection (**4–72**). Under these conditions,

4–69. Blown fiberglass insulation is installed behind a special fabric which allows it to fully fill and seal the cavity.

(Courtesy CertainTeed Corporation)

4–70. As the blown fiberglass fills the cavity, it surrounds wires and other things running through the wall cavity.
(Courtesy CertainTeed Corporation)

4–71. Outlet boxes are covered with the insulation retaining fabric, which allows the blown fiberglass to completely surround them.
(Courtesy CertainTeed Corporation)

4–72. Plumbing in exterior walls is completely surrounded by the blown fiberglass insulation.
(Courtesy CertainTeed Corporation)

the exterior wall should be framed with 2 × 6-inch studs, which provide an extra two inches of insulation behind the plumbing. Fiberglass-blown insulation has high R-values and provides some sound control. It is installed by certified insulation contractors.

■ Installing Mineral Wool Insulation

Mineral wool insulation is a form of glass fiber insulation made when air or steam is blown through molten rock or slag. The fibers are formed into blankets and batts and are also available as loose wool.

While mineral wood insulation was for years the major form of insulation, it has been largely replaced in residential construction by fiberglass, cellulose, and foam. The type available is held in wall, roof, and floor cavities by pressure against the framing. It requires no stapling flanges.

■ Insulating with Sprayed-Foam Insulation

Insulating foams have through the years gone through many changes that have influenced their properties. Before choosing them, secure information about the types of foam available and their cost. Generally, foamed insulation will cost more per square foot than fiberglass or cellulose. It will also vary in density and insulating properties. See Chapter 2 for detailed information.

If you are designing a new house, often the exterior studs used are 2 × 6 inches rather than 2 × 4 inches. This gives more strength than needed, and permits the addition of two additional inches of insulation. If you plan to use a high-density foam, the extra width is not needed because it has a very high R-value. If you plan to use a low-density foam, the R-value will be about the same as fiberglass. In some climates, the wall cavity need not be filled completely full to get the required amount of insulation. For example, using a 1.8 pound foam in a 2 × 4–inch wall will give an R-value of about 24. Some people prefer to use 2 × 6 studs and only fill the cavity partway, which leaves a clear space for locating plumbing and wires (**4–73**).

Another factor is that foam is resistant to water vapor, and in many climates the installation of a polyethylene or kraft paper vapor can be omitted. Check local codes to see if this is an acceptable practice. In climates where air-conditioning dominates, this gives a vapor barrier next to the sheathing as is required. In climates where heating dominates, this gives a vapor barrier toward the warm (interior) side of the wall. In mixed climates where air-conditioning and heating are of equal importance, foam insulation provides protection from moisture in both seasons because it resists the passage of water vapor from outside and inside the house.

4–73. When 2 × 6 studs are used, the wires and plumbing will fall in a small, open space between the foam and the drywall. *(Courtesy North Carolina Foam Industries)*

4–74. As the foam is sprayed into the cavity, it bonds to the sheathing and framing and begins to expand.
(Courtesy North Carolina Foam Industries)

Foam insulation is installed by manufacturer-certified contractors. They arrive on the job with drums of the chemicals, a pumping machine, and a hose. The pumping machine is adjusted to meter the exact amount of the two chemicals; heats them, which speeds up the chemical reaction, causing the foam to develop; and pumps the mix through separate hoses to a single hose. This hose connects to a nozzle, where the two components mix, flow from the nozzle, and instantly foam into a thin, creamy material. As this leaves the nozzle, it rapidly expands into a thick foam, which quickly sets into a solid material (**4–74**).

A word of caution should be made at this point: The person regulating the pumping machine and the person placing the foam should observe the safety recommendations made by the manufacturer. Those not involved in the operation should be kept out of the area. Notice the protective body, head, face, hand and respirator in **4–75**. As sprayed foam is applied, respiratory protection is essential to avoid the inhalation of atomized material. After it cures, there are no levels of any emission which could cause adverse health effects.

When using small handheld pressurized cans of foam, observation of safety recommendations is also important. Some types warn that it should not get on your skin. It is very difficult to remove. Other foams are water-soluble and can be washed off if it is done shortly after it gets on the skin. Wear rubber gloves to avoid any problems. Also, foams are very flammable when being sprayed. Any source of possible ignition should be removed and the area should have good ventilation.

As cavities are being filled, the technician knows how much the foam being used will expand. This varies considerably, so it takes experience to know how thick a layer should be sprayed to fill the cavity (**4–76**). Low-density foams expand a lot more than high-density foams and will typically overfill the cavity (**4–77**). After the foam has hardened, the excess is cut flush with the frame with a saw that has a long, flexible blade. Then the ceiling and wall finish materials can be applied. The foam should be

4–75. The installation technician is advised to take protection against atomized material as it is sprayed. *(Courtesy Icynene Inc.)*

applied behind and around outlet boxes (**4–78**), plumbing, and heat ducts in the walls, ceiling, and floor.

Foam insulation sticks firmly to the framing and sheathing and does not sag as do blanket-type insulations. This makes it very useful for ceilings and floors. Floors over unheated spaces, such as a crawl space, can be easily and quickly insulated with the foam against the subfloor and joists. Since it resists the passage of water vapor, it also forms the vapor barrier (**4–79**).

When foam insulation is being used on cathedral ceilings, polystyrene baffles are usually installed along the entire length of the ceiling and foam from there to the edge of the rafter (**4–80**). This provides a path for airflow from the soffit to the ridge. Some people foam

4–76. As the foam is sprayed into the cavity, it will expand many times thicker than the original layer. The technician knows from experience how much foam should be laid in the cavity. *(Courtesy North Carolina Foam Industries)*

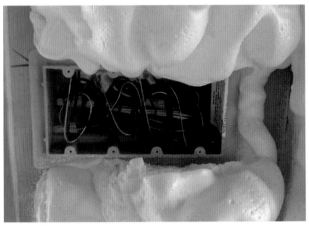

4–78. The foam has been applied behind and around this outlet box. The excess will be trimmed flush with the face of the stud. This forms an airtight seal around the box. *(Courtesy Icynene Inc.)*

4–77. When cavities are filled to the full depth some overfill occurs. This is cut away with a long thin saw blade. *(Courtesy Icynene Inc.)*

4–79. The floor in this attic room has been insulated with foam insulation. It is ready for the subfloor to be installed. The rafters forming the sloped side wall have also been foamed. *(Courtesy North Carolina Foam Industries)*

the ceiling without allowing for airflow to the ridge vent. This could void the warranty on the shingles due to possible heat buildup.

Truss-framed roofs can provide another insulation challenge. In **4–81**, two-inch framing was installed between the trusses and the foam laid in the cavities formed.

An attic room is shown in **4–82**. The foam insulation forms a tight unbroken layer sealing out all air leaks and water vapor from the ceiling through the kneewall to the floor.

Since the foam bonds to the framing and sheathing, it makes insulating unusual ceiling shapes an especially good choice (**4–83**). The foam easily fills the triangular cavities. No cutting and stuffing is required as when batts are used.

Rim joists are difficult to seal to block air leakage below the sill and the subfloor above. An easy way to seal this area and provide insulation at the same time is to spray a layer of foam insulation over it (**4–84**). This also resists the passage of moisture through the area.

■ Installing Cotton Insulation

Cotton insulation is available in blanket form and is held in cavities by pressure against the framing (**4–85**). The natural fiber does not cause itching and the insulation contains no harmful irritants, making it safe to handle and install without the need for protective gear or clothing. It contains no harmful airborne particles. After the blankets have been installed, they are covered with a 6-mil polyethylene vapor barrier.

See Chapter 3 for detailed information about cotton insulation.

■ Installing Cellulose Insulation

Cellulose insulation can be installed in walls, ceilings, and other places in a house where insulation is required. It is used on new and existing residential structures. It is installed as a dry, blown loose-fill material or a wet sprayed product.

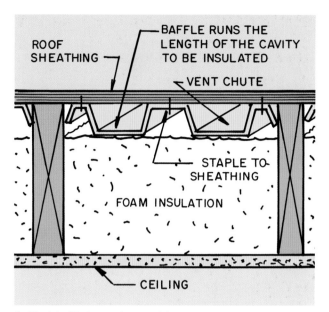

4–80. A baffle is used to provide an airspace between the roof sheathing and the foam insulation on cathedral ceilings.

4–81. The cathedralized truss frame roof has rafters installed between the trusses and the cavities insulated with foam. This produces a large, smooth finished ceiling between the massive trusses. *(Courtesy Icynene Inc.)*

4–82. This attic room is fully insulated with sprayed foam forming an airtight, water-resistant and energy-conserving living area. *(Courtesy North Carolina Foam Industries)*

4–83. This unusual ceiling has been fully sealed and insulated with sprayed foam insulation. *(Courtesy Icynene Inc.)*

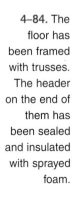

4–84. The floor has been framed with trusses. The header on the end of them has been sealed and insulated with sprayed foam.

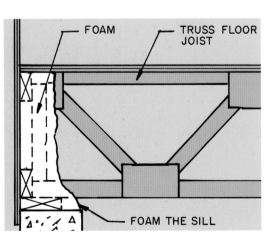

FOAM   TRUSS FLOOR JOIST

FOAM THE SILL

4–85. Cotton insulation blankets are pressure-fitted between the framing. Notice that the installer has no protective gear. The manufacturer indicates the fibers are bonded firmly, so no dust or loose fibers get into the air. *(Courtesy Bonded Logic, Inc.)*

■ Installing Dry, Blown Cellulose

Dry, loose-fill cellulose can be installed in attics, side-walls, ceilings, and floors by blowing with a pneumatic blowing machine (4–86). The insulation is supplied in plastic-wrapped bales (4–87). Cellulose blowing machines range in size from a small unit to a large container mounted on a truck (4–88). They have a mixing device that loosens up the fibers in the material, which is fed into a blower and sent through a hose to the point of application. The air-to-fiber mixture can be regulated by adjusting the amount of air admitted. Larger, more powerful machines are needed if the insulation is to be packed densely in closed cavities.

Cellulose insulation has to meet the same installation precautions as fiberglass. Review the fiberglass section of this chapter. Basically, it must not cover recessed lights unless they are insulation-contact (IC)-rated. It is kept three inches from non-rated lights (refer to 4–51). It should have at least three inches clear of chimneys and other heat-related devices (refer to 4–49). Ceiling insulation requires that blocking and a baffle be installed on the top plate to keep the blown insulation from flowing into the soffit (refer to 4–64). Since it is fibrous, the installer must wear eye and respiratory protective devices. Always refer to the local building code for guidance.

4–86. A cellulose-insulation blowing machine mounted on a truck. *(Courtesy Greenfiber)*

4–88. The cellulose insulation bale is opened and poured into the blowing machine. It has a mixing device that loosens up the fibers. *(Courtesy Greenfiber)*

4–87. Cellulose insulation is shipped in plastic-wrapped bales.

Installation procedures are much the same as described earlier for blown-in fibrous insulation. The dry, blown cellulose can be installed behind a mesh netting or reinforced polyethylene stapled to the framing. The cellulose is blown through slits in the mesh. The cellulose should be packed at a minimum density of 3.0 pounds per cubic foot. Some pack it tighter, but caution must be observed so it does not cause the mesh to bulge out beyond the framing. making it difficult to install the drywall.

Another technique is to use a manufacturer-supplied barrier, The Story Jig. It is clamped to the framing, and the cellulose can be installed to a density of 3.5 pct to 4.0 pct. The jig is strong enough to withstand the pressure and, when removed, the cellulose remains flat with the face of the framing.

Exterior walls are filled with dry, blown cellulose by preparing an opening at the top of the mesh or Story Jig, as shown in **4–89**. Move the tube to the bottom of

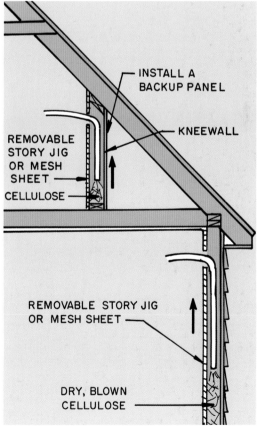

INSTALL A
BACKUP PANEL

KNEEWALL

REMOVABLE
STORY JIG
OR MESH
SHEET

CELLULOSE

REMOVABLE STORY JIG
OR MESH SHEET

DRY, BLOWN
CELLULOSE

4–89. The cellulose is blown into the wall cavities formed by covering the studs with a special mesh or a Story Jig.

the cavity and raise it as the cellulose fills the space. Notice that kneewalls need a backup panel on the back side to enclose the wall cavity.

Cathedral ceilings and attic rooms with sloped rafters forming part of the wall can be insulated after the drywall has been installed by moving the fill tube down the cavity to the blocking at a kneewall (**4–90**) or the top plate (**4–91**). This requires that access from the attic be available. Codes may require baffles be used to provide airflow to the ridge vent. If necessary, the cavity could be filled by boring holes in the drywall ceiling and blowing the cellulose through them. This is described later in this chapter. Sometimes the soffit and, if necessary, the fascia can be removed and the cellulose blown into the cavity from

there (**4–91**). Run the hose to the top of the area to be insulated and work down. The ridge board will serve to block the flow starting at the top.

The sloped roof insulation is a high-density installation giving a greater R-value in the space available.

Remember to shut down the blowing machine before you pull the hose out of the cavity. If you do not do this, it will spray cellulose all over the place.

Ceilings with an attic above are insulated by blowing the dry, loose-fill cellulose starting at an outside wall and moving the hose along, filling the cavity (**4–92**). Observe the code requirements mentioned for working around recessed lights, fireplaces, furnace vent pipes, and other heat-generating devices. Blow carefully, so too much

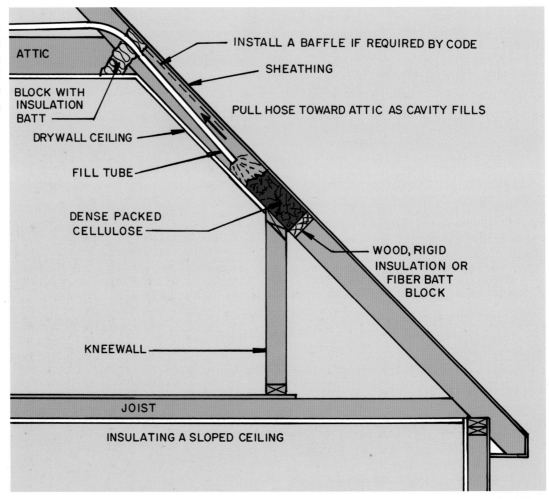

4–90. The sloped ceiling in attic rooms can be filled from the attic by running the fill tube down the cavity and moving it up as the area is filled.

ATTIC

INSTALL A BAFFLE IF REQUIRED BY CODE

SHEATHING

BLOCK WITH INSULATION BATT

PULL HOSE TOWARD ATTIC AS CAVITY FILLS

DRYWALL CEILING

FILL TUBE

DENSE PACKED CELLULOSE

WOOD, RIGID INSULATION OR FIBER BATT BLOCK

KNEEWALL

JOIST

INSULATING A SLOPED CEILING

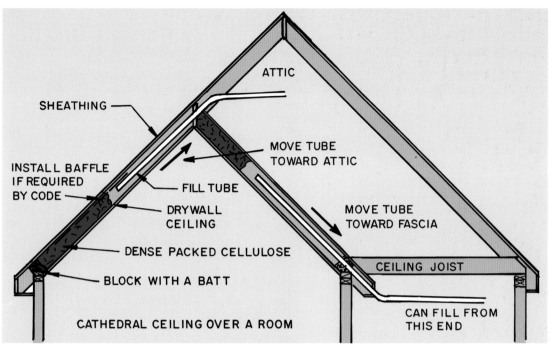

4–91. A cathedral ceiling can be insulated by blowing cellulose into the cavity from the attic. Should attic access not be available, it can be filled from the end of the rafter at the exterior wall.

ATTIC

SHEATHING

MOVE TUBE TOWARD ATTIC

INSTALL BAFFLE IF REQUIRED BY CODE

FILL TUBE

DRYWALL CEILING

MOVE TUBE TOWARD FASCIA

DENSE PACKED CELLULOSE

BLOCK WITH A BATT

CEILING JOIST

CATHEDRAL CEILING OVER A ROOM

CAN FILL FROM THIS END

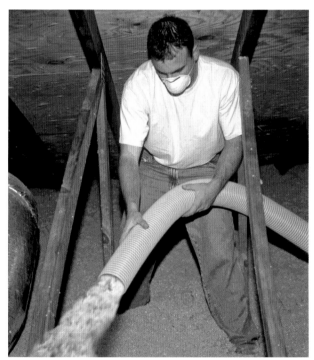

4–92. Ceilings with attics above can be insulated by blowing the cellulose between the joists starting at an outside wall and moving toward the center of the house.

(Courtesy Greenfiber)

fiber dust does not get into the air. Keep the hose low and move it so the cavity fills uniformly. When necessary, switch off the blowing machine to let things settle down. Generally, the initial lay of the cellulose is about 1½ to 2 inches thicker than the desired final thickness. This allows it to slowly settle over time.

■ Installing Wet, Sprayed Cellulose

Sprayed cellulose wall-cavity insulation is shredded newspaper mixed or treated with various chemicals to reduce its flammability. It is installed in conjunction with water spray and an adhesive that enables it to bond to the open wall cavity. After it dries, it is covered with a vapor barrier and the finish wall material. It is installed by qualified insulation personnel.

Before spraying, cover anything in the room that may be contaminated by any overspray such as windows, doors, and electric outlet boxes.

The cellulose is placed in a blower machine, which can be mounted outside the building or in a central location inside the building. A pump is located on top of a water barrel. The blower supplies a constant supply of cellulose that mixes with water under pressure at the nozzle. A moisture meter monitors the moisture content as it is being sprayed. The nozzle is located on the end of a long hose and mixes the cellulose and water in the proper liquid-to-fiber ratio. Adjust the blower and pump as recommended by the manufacturer. Of importance is to get the proper pressure settings for the nozzle. Typically, the liquid-to-fiber ratio is in the range of 0.3 to 0.4 pounds of water per pound of fiber. This will give a moisture content of 30 to 40 percent in the sprayed cellulose.

It takes some experience to spray the wet cellulose insulation. The angle of the nozzle and laying it on in layers produce the fill that forms into a solid mass. Typically, the angle of the spray is downward, about 5 to 10 degrees. Keep the nozzle about four feet from the wall. Spray from the bottom of the wall and work from one side to the other of the cavity. As the top plate is reached, it will be necessary to turn the nozzle facing up under it. After laying in the first layer, go back and spray the next layer over it in the same way.

After spraying the cellulose insulation in place, wipe off any excess that may extend beyond the face of the studs. A power-operated rotary brush is available for this job. It is often referred to as a wall scrubber (**4–93**). This leaves a flush uniformly filled cavity (**4–94**).

The vapor barrier and finish wall material are not installed until the insulation has dried. This is checked with a moisture meter. When the moisture content is less than 25 percent, the wall can be enclosed. Normal drying requires 24 to 48 hours, depending on the depth of the insulation, the amount of moisture used to make the mix, and the air temperature. Do not trap wet, sprayed cellulose between an interior vapor barrier and an exterior vapor barrier. The high moisture content in the trapped area can eventually cause problems. Some leave off the interior vapor barrier. Some foam sheathings have a low perm rating and can serve as an exterior vapor barrier.

■ Vapor Barriers

There are different opinions regarding the use of a vapor barrier over **blown, dry cellulose insulation.** First, check the local building codes. Very likely, they may require a

4–93. After the wet cellulose has filled the wall cavity, the excess beyond the face of the studs is removed with a rotary brush. *(Courtesy Greenfiber)*

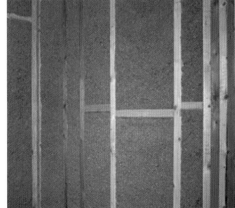

4–94. After the excess cellulose is scraped off, the result is a flush, fully filled wall cavity. *(Courtesy Greenfiber)*

vapor barrier, such as 6-mil polyethylene sheeting, be stapled over the insulation as described earlier for unfaced fiberglass. You can also check with the manufacturer to see what they recommend. One recommendation that is being made is that a vapor barrier is not required on the ceiling if the attic space above has the recommended ventilation. If the attic is not ventilated, a vapor barrier is required on the cold side of the ceiling.

Manufacturers' recommendations for applying a vapor barrier of **wet, sprayed cellulose** state that you should follow the recommendations of the local building code. Many people recommend leaving off the interior vapor barrier because at 25 percent moisture there is a lot of dampness in the cellulose.

■ Installing Reflective Insulation, Radiant Barriers, and Interior Radiation-Control Coatings

These products reduce the amount of radiant heat flow into a building. They do not contribute measurably to the total R-value of a wall or roof. It is usually more cost-effective to add additional thermal insulation to an existing house than add a radiant barrier to the roof. If you are replacing the roof deck on a house in a hot climate, it is a good time to install sheathing with the radiant barrier bonded to it.

Reflective products have the advantage of being nonfibrous; therefore, the installer need not wear a respirator. They do not irritate the eyes or skin as do fibrous insulation.

Reflective insulation has flanges that are used to staple it in place. They can be overlapped and stapled to the face of wood framing or set inside and nailed to the sides of the framing. The overlaps are sealed with a special tape supplied by the manufacturer. Some are single-thickness aluminum sheets, while other types have an airspace filled with a foam insulation. These are available in 48- and 60-inch widths. Another type consists of several layers of foil which open up and provide dead air spaces between the layers. Samples of reflective products are shown in Chapter 3.

REFLECTIVE INSULATION

Reflective insulation may be made of multiple layers of aluminum foil, paper, or plastic. The layers of aluminum foil may be separated by ¼- to ½-inch air spaces, plastic bubble insulation, or foam such as polypropylene. It is designed to be installed between, over, or under framing members. Common locations include roofs, walls, basements, ceilings, floors, and crawl spaces (**4–95**). Be certain to install as directed by the manufacturer.

These multiple-layer foils are installed between wood rafters (**4–95**), wood studs (**4–96**), furring strips on masonry walls (**4–97**), floors (**4–98**), and ceilings (**4–99**). Another way some prefer to install reflective insulation is to nail wood furring strips to the studs and staple it to them. Then nail wood furring strips over the reflective insulation and nail the drywall to it (**4–100**).

Reflective insulation must be installed with the reflective material next to an air space, such as the air in an unheated attic or a living area (**4–101**). Since aluminum conducts heat at a high rate, if it is trapped between two other materials, such as sheets of plywood, it would conduct heat from one sheet to the next.

When installing reflective insulation, make sure that the air spaces between the layers of foil are kept open. Some types have a foam in the air space, so crushing the insulation is not as major a problem. If this is not done, the product will not have the designed R-value.

Reflective insulation is stapled to the face of the stud or rafter. The edges of each piece are butted or overlapped and stapled with ¼-inch staples placed every five or six inches. The joint is then covered with a manufacturer-supplied tape.

4–95. This reflective insulation has a ¼-inch-thick polypropylene core and has been installed between the rafters. It is stapled to the rafters. *(Courtesy Refectix, Inc.)*

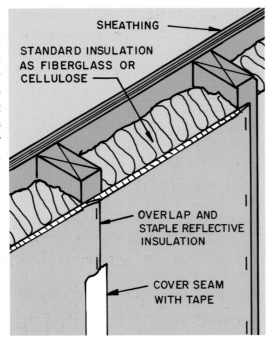

4–96. Reflective insulation is installed by stapling it to the studs. It also serves as a vapor barrier.

SHEATHING

STANDARD INSULATION AS FIBERGLASS OR CELLULOSE

OVERLAP AND STAPLE REFLECTIVE INSULATION

COVER SEAM WITH TAPE

4–98. Reflective insulation is stapled to the floor joists. The flanges overlap and are sealed with a special tape. Notice the piece that has been stapled to the header between the joists and extends down over the foundation to the crawl space or basement floor. *(Courtesy Reflectix, Inc.)*

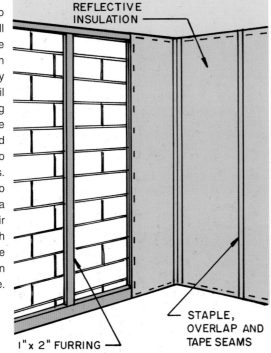

4–97. To install reflective insulation on masonry walls, nail wood furring strips to the wall and staple it to these strips. This also creates a dead air space, which has some insulation value.

REFLECTIVE INSULATION

STAPLE, OVERLAP AND TAPE SEAMS

1" x 2" FURRING

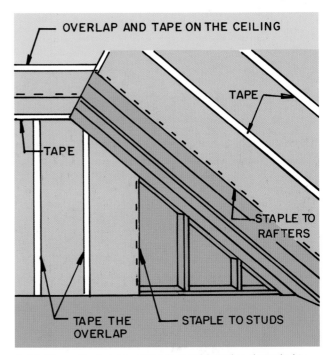

OVERLAP AND TAPE ON THE CEILING

TAPE

TAPE

STAPLE TO RAFTERS

TAPE THE OVERLAP

STAPLE TO STUDS

4–99. The reflective insulation is overlapped and stapled to the faces of the rafters on sloped ceilings and the ceiling joists on horizontal ceilings. The overlaps are sealed with a special tape.

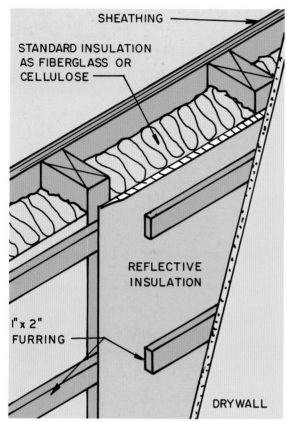

SHEATHING

STANDARD INSULATION AS FIBERGLASS OR CELLULOSE

REFLECTIVE INSULATION

1" x 2" FURRING

DRYWALL

4–100. Another way to install reflective insulation is to use wood furring strips to give it support and form two additional dead air spaces, which increase the insulation value.

4–101. The reflective insulation is installed on the room side of an exterior wall.
(Courtesy Reflectix, Inc.)

RADIANT BARRIERS

Radiant barriers are made by bonding an aluminum foil to kraft paper, plastic films, or oriented strand board or plywood used for roof sheathing. They are most often used to control heat energy flow into attics. A system used both on new construction and to upgrade the insulation in an existing house consists of stapling the barrier to the face of the rafters (**4–102**) or the top cord of a roof truss (**4–103**). Overlap the edges of the sheets so they form a tight vapor barrier.

If the roof uses ridge vents for ventilation, run the radiant barrier from the top plate on the wall to the ridge board. Air from the soffit vent will flow between the barrier and the sheathing, eliminating heat buildup.

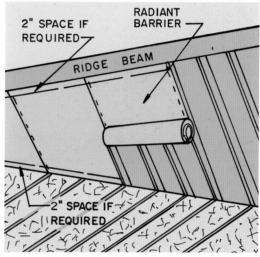

2" SPACE IF REQUIRED

RADIANT BARRIER

RIDGE BEAM

2" SPACE IF REQUIRED

4–102. This radiant barrier is installed from the ridge to the top plate. It can be installed horizontally. Leave a two-inch space at the ridge board and top plate if ridge vents are not used.

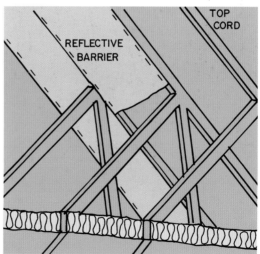

REFLECTIVE BARRIER

TOP CORD

4–103. Radiant barriers are stapled to the face of the top chord of roof trusses.

If other roof venting, such as gable end vents, is used, leave a two-inch gap at the top plate and ridge vent to allow the heat built up to exit into the attic and be vented through existing roof vents. Never block any attic venting with a radiant barrier.

On new construction, the radiant barrier can be draped over the rafters, as shown in **4–104.** Staple it to the rafters as needed to hold it in place as the roof sheathing is nailed over it. It is important to let it drape down a little. This forms an air space on the top side, allowing heat buildup to escape. The back side faces the air space created by the attic.

Radiant barriers can be stapled to the roof sheathing before it is nailed to the rafters. Since radiant barriers are available in 48-inch widths, they cover the sheathing without trimming.

Perforated radiant barriers can be laid over the ceiling joists in the attic. The perforations allow any moisture that may penetrate the ceiling to move into the attic and be vented to the outside. The barrier is laid over the joists and lapped three inches, but is not stapled to the joists (**4–105**). This radiant barrier deflects solar-generated heat that flows through the roof assembly into the attic away from the ceiling insulation, which will over time gradually absorb the heat and move it to the drywall ceiling. The radiant barrier provides a cooler ceiling, reducing energy costs and making occupancy more comfortable. It also reduces heat transfer into any air-conditioning ducts in the attic.

In crawl spaces and unfinished spaces, staple the radiant barrier to the bottom of the floor joists. Overlap the sheets and tape the joints with the manufacturer-supplied tape.

INTERIOR RADIATION-CONTROL COATINGS

Interior radiation-control coatings limit heat transfer by radiation and are not specifically intended to reduce heat transfer by conduction or convection. They consist of a coating of a special paint product that is sprayed on a building surface. It can also be applied with a paint roller. Do not brush it on.

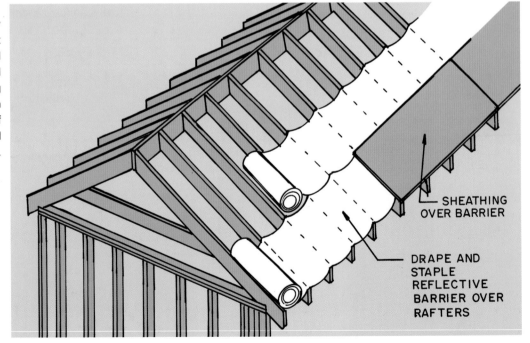

4–104. On new construction, radiant barriers can be laid over the rafters and allowed to sag several inches. Then staple it to the top of the rafter and install the sheathing over it.

SHEATHING OVER BARRIER

DRAPE AND STAPLE REFLECTIVE BARRIER OVER RAFTERS

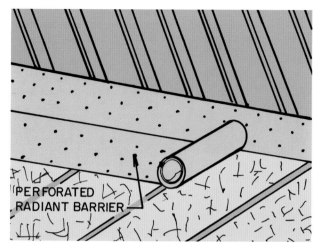

4-105. Perforated radiant barriers allow moisture that may pass through an assembly, such as a ceiling, to vent into the attic and to the outside. The perforated vapor barrier is laid loose on top of the ceiling joists and lapped three inches.

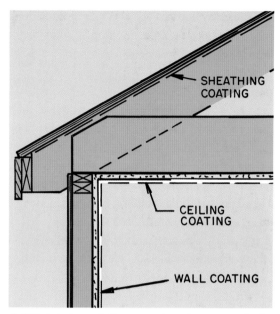

4-106. Interior radiation-control coatings are typically used in residential construction on the roof sheathing and interior wall surfaces.

The coating can be applied to surfaces already in place, such as the underside of roof sheathing or the interior surface of a wall. In new construction, it is usually sprayed on the building material before it is installed. Any surface with this coating should have at least a two-inch air space. In residential construction, the most commonly coated surfaces are the roof sheathing and the interior wall surface (**4–106**). There are many other uses in commercial construction.

■ Sound Control

When planning a new house or a remodeling job, it is important to consider actions to control sound transmission. This includes sounds generated outside the house, such as automobile traffic, and the many sounds created inside, such as conversation or the television, washing machines, and furnaces. Bathroom privacy is especially important.

Sealing the house as described in Chapter 2 will prevent sounds from moving between living areas through cracks in the walls and ceiling. Just upgrading the insulation will also help. Additional improvements can be made to provide a quieter living area than is provided by normal construction.

TYPES OF SOUND

Three types of sound must be considered as you plan to reduce its effect on the living spaces. These are direct sound, airborne sound transmission, and vibrations.

Direct Sound

Direct sound is sound that reaches the ear without being reflected, such as sound from passing automobiles entering through an open window. Acoustic materials within the living space will help reduce the reflections of this sound as it hits interior walls but have no effect on sound that directly strikes the ear. This airborne sound also can enter through cracks around doors and windows. A major passage is through single-glazed windows and hollow-core doors. Solid-core doors have the mass needed to reflect this sound. Double-glazed windows help.

Airborne Sound

Airborne sound developed within a room, such as a washing machine in operation, can be reduced by treating the ceilings with acoustical tiles, by hanging draperies, and carpeting the floor. While these actions do muffle the sound, they do not stop it from being transmitted to adjoining rooms.

Vibrations

Sound is transferred long distances when a device, such as a furnace, produces vibration in structural members, such as a wood floor. Other vibration-creating devices are ceiling fans, washing machines, dryers, exhaust fans, and various ventilation devices. These have to be secured to some part of the building structure. Through normal use, sounds are transmitted through the structure and frequently can be heard all over the house. To control these vibrations, each device must be mounted on vibration control pads made to dampen and restrict vibration. While there are a variety of products available, rubber isolation mounts and pads are useful in residential applications (4–107). Other materials used are neoprene, cork, and fiberglass.

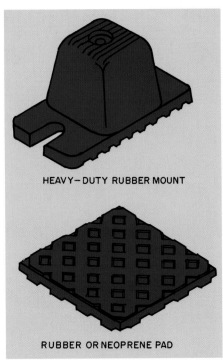

4–107. Rubber and neoprene vibration isolators provide high resistance to the transmission of high-frequency vibrations.

HEAVY–DUTY RUBBER MOUNT

RUBBER OR NEOPRENE PAD

■ Sound Rating Indicators

As designs and materials are selected, it is necessary to consider the sound rating features involved. These include Sound Intensity, the Noise Reduction Coefficient (NRC), Sound Transmission Class (STC), and the Impact Isolation Class (ICC).

SOUND INTENSITY

Sound intensity depends upon the strength of the force that sets off the sound vibrations. Sound intensity is measured in decibels (dB). A decibel rating of 0 is just below the lowest audible sound which can produce a feeling of vibration in the ear. High intensities can cause damage to the human ear and structural damage to a building. Sound levels in decibels for various situations are in **Table 4–5**.

NOISE-REDUCTION COEFFICIENT (NRC)

The indication of the ability of a material to absorb sound is indicated by its noise reduction coefficient (NRC). This measure is the average of sound reduction

for a material over a range of frequencies of 250, 500, 1000, and 2000 Hz (hertz). The larger the NRC number, the greater the efficiency of the material to absorb sound. Some examples are in **Table 4–6**.

SOUND-TRANSMISSION CLASS (STC)

The ability of a wall or ceiling to block the transmission of airborne sound is indicated by its Sound-Transmission Class (STC). The higher the rating number, the better the wall or ceiling blocks sound transmission. Residential partitions for bedrooms should have an STC of 40, but higher is recommended. Living rooms and kitchens should usually have an STC of at least 45, and an STC of 50 is recommended for bathrooms. A general STC rating system is shown in **Table 4–7**.

The STC rating for a wall assembly will depend upon the arrangement of the studs, the thickness of the gypsum wallboard, and the thickness and type of sound-deadening board and sound-attenuation insulation used. Some use standard fiberglass or rock wool insulation.

TABLE 4–5.

SOUND INTENSITY LEVELS OF SELECTED SOUNDS

Sound Levels (Decibels)	Source of Sound	Sensation
140	Near a jet aircraft	Deafening
130	Artillery fire	Threshold of pain
120	Elevated train, rock band, siren	Threshold of feeling
110	Riveting, air-hammering	Just below threshold of feeling
80–100	Power mower, thunder close by, symphony orchestra	Very loud
60–80	Noisy office, average radio or TV, loud conversation	Loud
40–60	Conversation, average office, quite radio or TV	Moderately loud
20–40	Average residence, private office, quiet conversation	Quiet
0–20	Whisper, normal breathing	Very faint

TABLE 4–6.

NOISE REDUCTION COEFFICIENTS FOR SELECTED MATERIALS

Material	Coefficient
Acoustical tile	0.55–0.85
Fiberglass	0.50–0.85
Carpeting with pad	0.45–0.75
Mineral wool	0.45–0.85
Lightweight concrete block	0.45
Acoustical plaster wall	0.21–0.75
Wood paneling	0.10–0.25
Gypsum wall	0.01–0.04
Standard plaster wall	0.01–0.04
Vinyl floor covering	0.01–0.05
Glazed clay tile	0.01–0.02

TABLE 4–7.

RECOMMENDED SOUND-TRANSMISSION VALUES FOR VARIOUS LIVING AREAS

Area	STC
Bedroom	48–55
Bathroom	52–59
Kitchen	52–58
Living Room	50–57
Halls	48–58
Furnace/Utility Room	50–60

The basic way used to reduce sound transmission in partitions is to insulate them with sound-attenuation blankets (**4–108**). This will give an STC rating of at least 40, which is satisfactory for most residences. Some partition designs with higher ratings are shown in **4–109**. Some feel it is best to use ⅝-inch-thick gypsum wallboard rather than ½ inch, which is typically used. This does increase the STC rating because it adds mass to the wall assembly. Products with mass, such as concrete or solid gypsum, provide excellent sound blocking.

Suspended ceilings have very little sound control. Sound-attenuation blankets can be placed on top, increasing the rating (**4–110**). If there is a partition to any ceiling that is below a floor or old ceiling in a remodeled house, the sound will go into the next room (**4–111**). This can be corrected by extending the partition up to the overhead floor or ceiling (**4–112**) or laying sound-attenuation blankets over the ceiling (**4–113**).

Sound control on old ceilings can also be controlled by gluing acoustical tile directly to it (**4–114**) or stapled to wood furring strips nailed over the old ceiling. They are nailed into the joists. If there is no existing ceiling, the furring is nailed directly to the joists (**4–115**).

Exterior walls can have the same sound control techniques used as described for interior partitions. One difference is that one side or the wall will have some form of siding. For example, walls constructed with the same technique, except one has a brick veneer and the other wood siding, have different resistance to airborne sound transmission. Brick veneer provides a wall with good-to-excellent sound-blocking properties, while the one with wood siding is rated poor-to-fair (**4–116**).

4–108. Insulating interior partitions with sound-attenuation blankets greatly reduces the transmission of sound.
(Courtesy CertainTeed Corporation)

4–109. Some commonly used partition designs which reduce the transmission of sound into the next roof. The STC ratings are typical for that type of construction. Actual ratings depend upon the thickness of the gypsum drywall and the type and thickness of sound-deadening board or sound-attenuation insulation used.

4–109 continues on the next page.

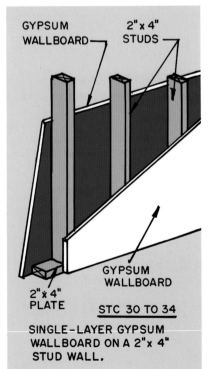

GYPSUM WALLBOARD

2" x 4" STUDS

GYPSUM WALLBOARD

2" x 4" PLATE

STC 30 TO 34

SINGLE-LAYER GYPSUM WALLBOARD ON A 2"x 4" STUD WALL.

A

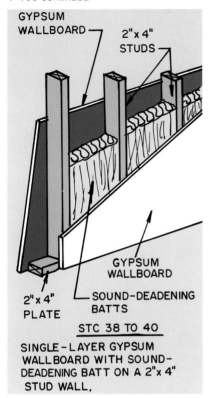

GYPSUM WALLBOARD — 2"x 4" STUDS

GYPSUM WALLBOARD — SOUND-DEADENING BATTS — 2"x 4" PLATE

STC 38 TO 40

SINGLE-LAYER GYPSUM WALLBOARD WITH SOUND-DEADENING BATT ON A 2"x 4" STUD WALL.

B

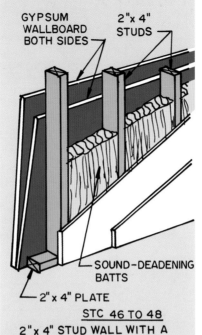

GYPSUM WALLBOARD BOTH SIDES — 2"x 4" STUDS

SOUND-DEADENING BATTS — 2"x 4" PLATE

STC 46 TO 48

2"x 4" STUD WALL WITH A DOUBLE-LAYER GYPSUM WALLBOARD AND SOUND-DEADENING BATTS.

C

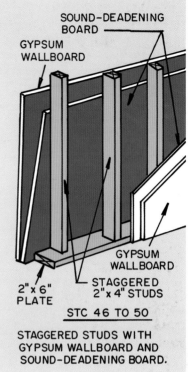

SOUND-DEADENING BOARD — GYPSUM WALLBOARD

GYPSUM WALLBOARD — STAGGERED 2"x 4" STUDS — 2"x 6" PLATE

STC 46 TO 50

STAGGERED STUDS WITH GYPSUM WALLBOARD AND SOUND-DEADENING BOARD.

D

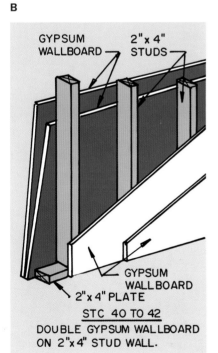

GYPSUM WALLBOARD — 2"x 4" STUDS

GYPSUM WALLBOARD — 2"x 4" PLATE

STC 40 TO 42

DOUBLE GYPSUM WALLBOARD ON 2"x 4" STUD WALL.

E

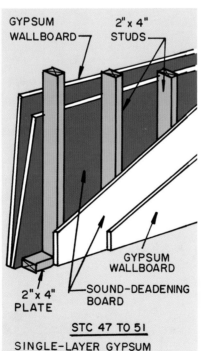

GYPSUM WALLBOARD — 2"x 4" STUDS

GYPSUM WALLBOARD — SOUND-DEADENING BOARD — 2"x 4" PLATE

STC 47 TO 51

SINGLE-LAYER GYPSUM WALLBOARD AND SOUND-DEADENING BOARD ON 2"x 4" STUD WALL.

F

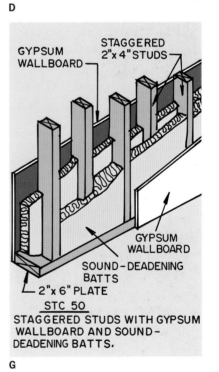

GYPSUM WALLBOARD — STAGGERED 2"x 4" STUDS

GYPSUM WALLBOARD — SOUND-DEADENING BATTS — 2"x 6" PLATE

STC 50

STAGGERED STUDS WITH GYPSUM WALLBOARD AND SOUND-DEADENING BATTS.

G

4–110. Sound-attenuation blankets placed over a suspended ceiling reduce sound transmission into the open area above the ceiling. *(Courtesy CertainTeed Corporation)*

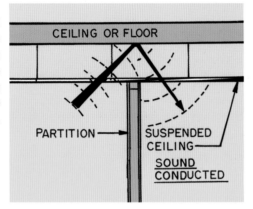

4–111. Sound will pass through the suspended ceiling and reflect off the overhead ceiling or floor into the adjoining room.

4–113. Sound transmission through suspended ceilings can be blocked and absorbed by installing sound-attenuation blankets over the ceiling.

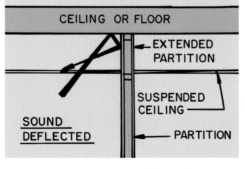

4–112. Sound transmission over suspended ceilings can be blocked by building the partition to the ceiling or floor overhead.

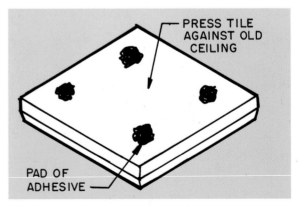

4–114. Airborne sound within a room can be controlled somewhat by gluing acoustical ceiling tile to the old ceiling.

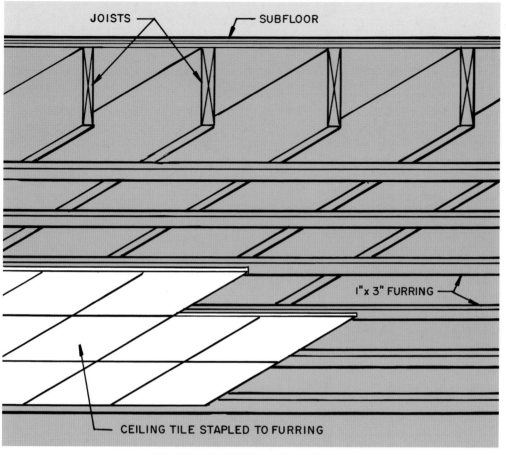

JOISTS
SUBFLOOR
I"x 3" FURRING
CEILING TILE STAPLED TO FURRING

4–115. Acoustical ceiling tile can be stapled to wood furring strips nailed to the floor joists. They can also be nailed over an old ceiling material.

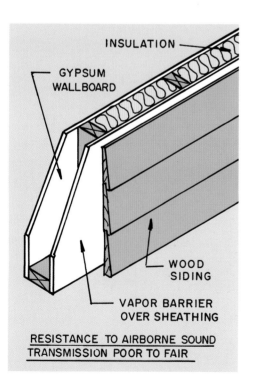

INSULATION
GYPSUM WALLBOARD
WOOD SIDING
VAPOR BARRIER OVER SHEATHING

RESISTANCE TO AIRBORNE SOUND TRANSMISSION POOR TO FAIR

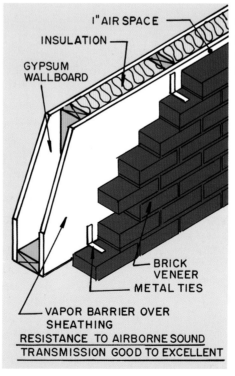

I" AIR SPACE
INSULATION
GYPSUM WALLBOARD
BRICK VENEER
METAL TIES
VAPOR BARRIER OVER SHEATHING

RESISTANCE TO AIRBORNE SOUND TRANSMISSION GOOD TO EXCELLENT

4–116. The materials used in the construction of the exterior wall greatly influence the resistance to airborne sound penetrating it.

■ Impact Isolation Class (IIC)

Another rating, the Impact Isolation Class (IIC), rates floors' or walls' ability to block the transfer of impact noises, such as walking or dropping things on the floor or bumping against the wall. Building codes typically require floor/ceiling assemblies to have an IIC rating of at least 50. Some typical code recommendations are in **Table 4–8**.

Several typical floor/ceiling assemblies and their IIC and STC ratings are shown in **4–117**.

Several of the floor/ceiling assemblies use resilient channels to suspend the gypsum wallboard ceiling panels. This is a metal strip that is secured to the bottom of the joists, and the wallboard is screwed to it (**4–118**). This separates the wallboard from the joist, reducing the transmission of sound that flows through the joist to the area below. This can also be used on walls where high sound controls are needed.

TABLE 4–8.

RECOMMENDED IMPACT ISOLATION RATINGS FOR SELECTED FLOOR/CEILING ASSEMBLIES

Area	IIC
Bedroom	48–55
Bathroom	48–55
Kitchen	52–65
Living Room	48–55
Halls	48–60
Furnace/Utility Room	40

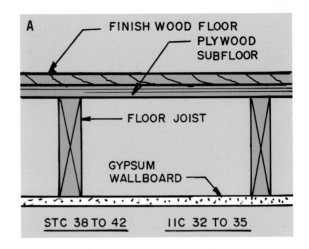

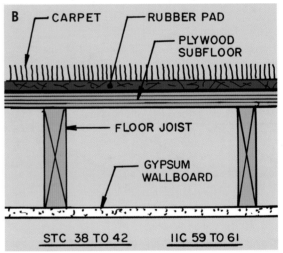

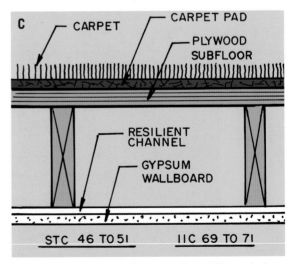

4–117. Impact Isolation Class and Sound Transmission Class ratings for some commonly used floor/ceiling assembles. The actual rating depends upon the thickness and types of materials used.

4–117 continues on next page

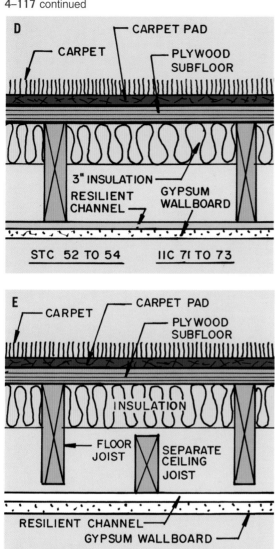

D

CARPET

CARPET PAD

PLYWOOD SUBFLOOR

3" INSULATION

RESILIENT CHANNEL

GYPSUM WALLBOARD

STC 52 TO 54   IIC 71 TO 73

E

CARPET

CARPET PAD

PLYWOOD SUBFLOOR

INSULATION

FLOOR JOIST

SEPARATE CEILING JOIST

RESILIENT CHANNEL

GYPSUM WALLBOARD

STC 49 TO 51   IIC 78 TO 80

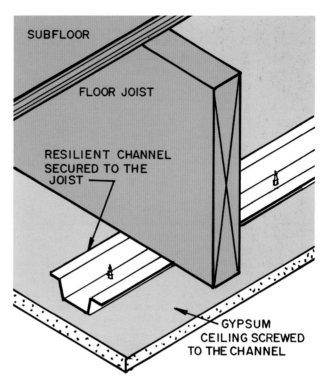

SUBFLOOR

FLOOR JOIST

RESILIENT CHANNEL SECURED TO THE JOIST

GYPSUM CEILING SCREWED TO THE CHANNEL

4–118. Metal-resilient channels are secured to the bottom of the floor joist, and the gypsum ceiling is screwed to it. They are also used on partitions.

5

ADDING INSULATION TO AN EXISTING HOUSE

Existing houses frequently have little or no insulation or insulation that has been damaged by water leaks and needs to be replaced. Following are some of the frequently used procedures to upgrade the existing insulation.

■ Determining the Thickness of the Existing Insulation

Before making decisions on how much insulation to buy to upgrade the walls, ceiling, and floor, find out how much insulation is in place and if it still is in good condition. Some areas of the house are easily accessible, such as that in an unfloored attic or in the floor over a crawl space or basement. Measure the thickness with a rule and note the kind and condition.

Insulation in finished walls is more difficult to check. One way is to open up a narrow slot along an electric outlet box. Turn off the electricity to that outlet. Remove the cover plate and make an opening on one side. This should be about ¼ inch wide (**5–1**). Peer inside to see if there is any insulation. You may need a light. Probe inside with a wire to see if it hits insulation. A hook in the end of the wire can grasp a sample of the insulation and pull it into the room for examination (**5–2**). Notice if the wire had to be pushed through a vapor barrier. If no evidence of a vapor exists, it is possible to produce one by painting the drywall or plaster with a moisture-resistant paint made for that purpose.

If the wall had been insulated with loose fibrous insulation, it may have over the years settled, leaving the

5–1. After turning off the electricity to the outlet, cut an opening along one side and probe into the cavity with a wire to see if there is insulation and, if any exists, what kind.

5–2. Run a wire with a hook inside the wall cavity and try to hook a sample of the insulation.

top part of the wall uninsulated. You can get a rough idea about this by touching the wall at the ceiling and noting its degree of coldness. Do this in the winter. Work your way down the wall to see if you notice any change in the warmth of the wall. Should this appear to be the problem, insulation can be blown in the wall from inside or outside the house as discussed later in this chapter.

If the insulation pulled out is wet or deteriorated, possibly the only recourse is to remove the drywall and replace the insulation. If it is wet, examine the studs and sheathing. They may be rotten and the cavity full of mold. This requires removal of the exterior siding and sheathing and replacing all rotted framing. When these areas are rebuilt, be certain to seal all possible leaks. Review Chapter 2 for some tips.

After making the wall check, be certain to fill any cracks around the outlet box with caulk. If this is a difficult check, you may want to remove a larger piece of drywall to get a better inspection. This can easily be repaired by using drywall repair clips available at a

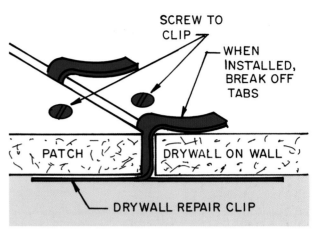

5–4. The clip fits over and is screwed to the drywall in the existing wall and the patch is screwed to the extended part. The tabs are broken off after the screws are tight.

building supply store (5–3). They hold the patch in place and are installed as shown in 5–4 and 5–5.

If you have a heated room over an unheated area, such as a garage that has a square-edge-floorboard wood floor installed, you may be able to raise one of the floorboards and examine the insulation. Removing a square-edge floorboard without damaging it is difficult. Possibly you can get a small pry bar under the edge of a piece along the wall and lift it in several places until the nails pull up. Then hammer it back down. The nails will remain sticking up and can be pulled (5–6). Do this enough to get an opening large enough for you to measure the thickness of the insulation and examine the condition.

If the floor is tongue-and-grooved boards or plywood sheets, drill a hole in an unconspicuous place and lower a stiff wire probe down until it touches the insulation. Mark the rod, remove it, and subtract the thickness of the floor. This will give the distance from the top of the joist to the insulation. Subtract this from the joist size to get the insulation thickness (5–7).

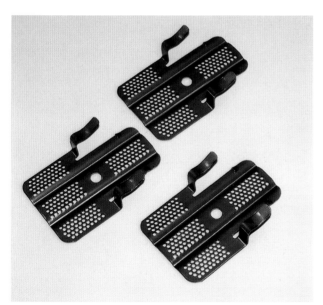

5–3. If it is necessary to cut open a large hole, a repair can be made using drywall clips.

5–5. Typical installation procedure for repairing a hole in drywall using drywall repair clips.

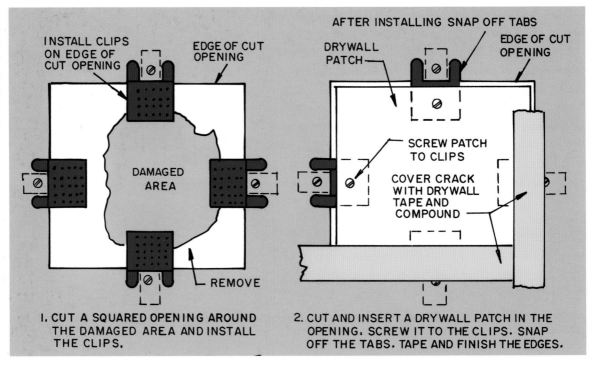

INSTALL CLIPS ON EDGE OF CUT OPENING

EDGE OF CUT OPENING

DAMAGED AREA

REMOVE

1. CUT A SQUARED OPENING AROUND THE DAMAGED AREA AND INSTALL THE CLIPS.

AFTER INSTALLING SNAP OFF TABS

DRYWALL PATCH

EDGE OF CUT OPENING

SCREW PATCH TO CLIPS

COVER CRACK WITH DRYWALL TAPE AND COMPOUND

2. CUT AND INSERT A DRYWALL PATCH IN THE OPENING. SCREW IT TO THE CLIPS. SNAP OFF THE TABS. TAPE AND FINISH THE EDGES.

5–6. Sometimes it is possible to raise floorboards and measure the thickness of the existing insulation with a wire. Also check the condition of the insulation to see if it is still usable.

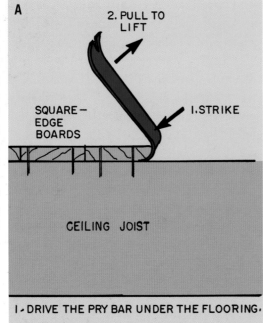

A

2. PULL TO LIFT

SQUARE-EDGE BOARDS

1. STRIKE

CEILING JOIST

1. DRIVE THE PRY BAR UNDER THE FLOORING.

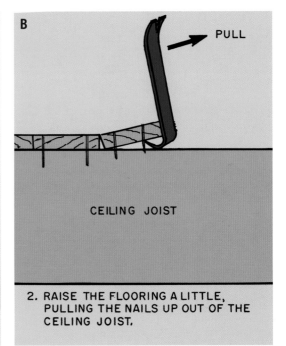

B

PULL

CEILING JOIST

2. RAISE THE FLOORING A LITTLE, PULLING THE NAILS UP OUT OF THE CEILING JOIST.

5–6 continues on next page

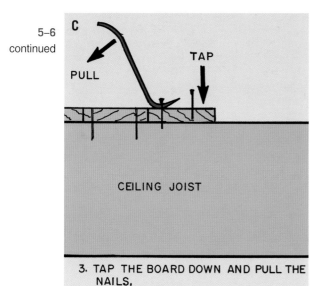

5–6
continued

3. TAP THE BOARD DOWN AND PULL THE NAILS.

Increasing Ceiling Insulation

Possibly the most commonly found situation is to add additional insulation in the ceiling. Check the existing insulation. See if it has a vapor barrier next to the drywall ceiling. If it does not and the old insulation is in good condition, remove it, install a polyethylene vapor barrier, and reset the old insulation.

If the old insulation has a vapor barrier and it still in good condition, lay new unfaced blankets over it perpendicular to the ceiling joists (**5–8**).

Loose-fill blown insulation can be installed in the attic by first installing baffles around areas where the new depth could cause clogging of ventilation areas.

If the attic is to be used for storage and a subfloor is to be installed, the unfaced batts should be placed between 2 × 4- or 2 × 6-inch members placed on top of the existing joists (**5–9**). Nail them to the joists and space them 15½ inches on center so the unfaced blankets will fit snugly between them. After the insulation is in place, install the subfloor.

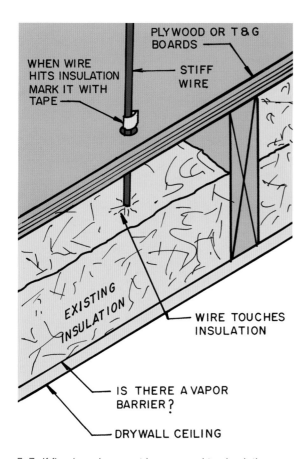

5–7. If floorboards cannot be removed to check the thickness of the insulation, a wire probe can be inserted through a small hole drilled through the floorboards.

5–8. If the existing attic insulation is still usable, the additional coverage should be unfaced and laid perpendicular to the ceiling joists.

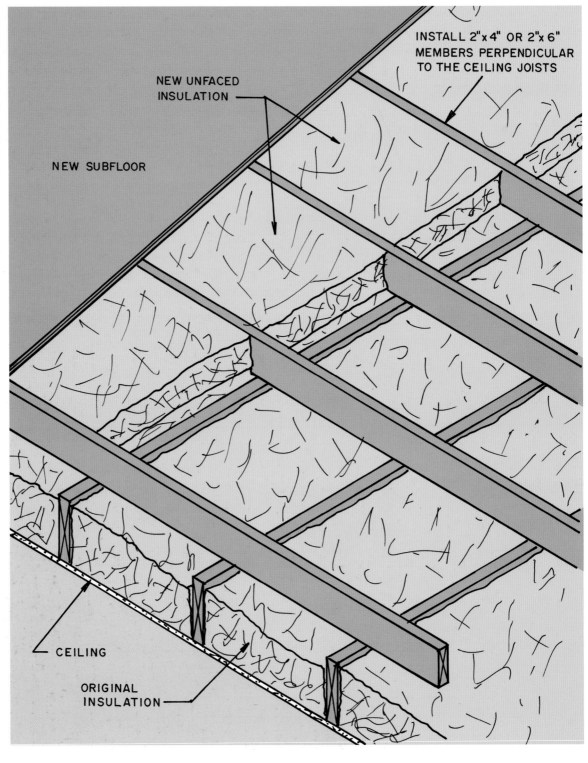

5–9. To add a floor and more insulation in an attic, install 2 × 4 or 2 × 6-inch members perpendicular to the ceiling joists and insulate between them.

NEW UNFACED INSULATION

INSTALL 2"x 4" OR 2"x 6" MEMBERS PERPENDICULAR TO THE CEILING JOISTS

NEW SUBFLOOR

CEILING

ORIGINAL INSULATION

When installing this new insulation, observe all the code requirements discussed earlier in this chapter. For example, do not put insulation over recessed lights unless they are insulation-contact approved. Observe restrictions around chimneys.

■ Insulating Disappearing Stairs

Disappearing stairs are installed in an opening framed in the ceiling, as shown in **5–10**. One type folds in three pieces which lay on a panel that forms a closure over the opening when the stairs are folded up (**5–11**). While this panel fits against a wood frame, considerable air leakage can occur. If the stair is in an unheated garage and provides access to unheated attic storage, there is little problem. If the stair is in a heated and cooled living area and provides access to an unheated attic storage area, it should be insulated. One way to do this

is to build an insulated wood frame and cover over the stair opening in the floor.

Begin by nailing a two-inch-thick wood frame around the stair opening in the attic. It should be high enough so the plywood cover to be put over them clears the folded ladder (**5–12**). Typically a 2 × 4- or 2 × 6-inch-wide frame will be adequate. Leave a 12-inch-wide flat area at the top of the stair inside the frame. This gives a place to put your feet as you ascend or descend before you hit the first step of the stair.

Cut a ¾-inch plywood panel that will cover the frame. Secure it to the frame on the long side with hinges (**5–13**). Place a rubber gasket on the inside edge of the frame that will seal the panel when closed. Then install two inches or more of rigid foam insulation on the top of the panel. Also install it on the sides of the frame (**5–14**).

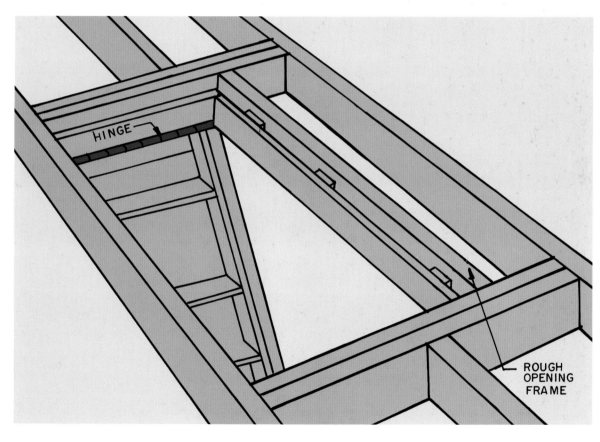

5–10. This disappearing stair has been installed in the opening framed in the floor.

HINGE

ROUGH OPENING FRAME

5–11. Many disappearing stairs fold into three parts and lay against the ceiling panel when the stair is closed.

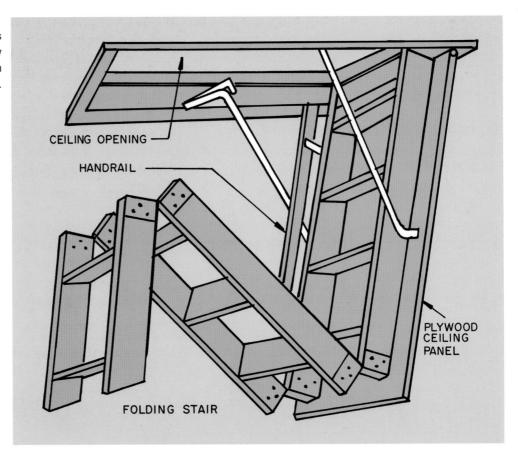

CEILING OPENING

HANDRAIL

FOLDING STAIR

PLYWOOD CEILING PANEL

5–12. Nail a frame around the stair opening in the attic.

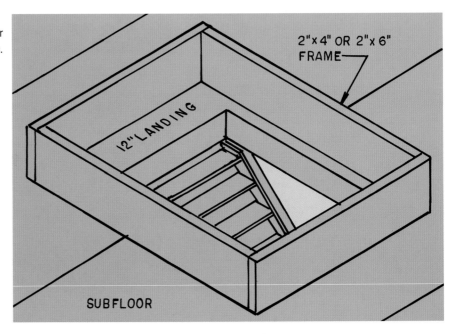

2"x 4" OR 2"x 6" FRAME

12" LANDING

SUBFLOOR

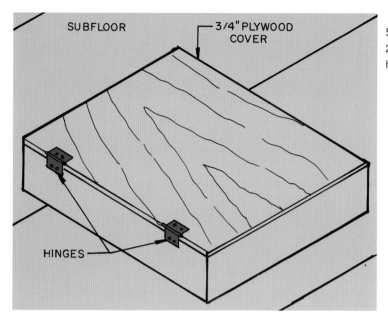

5–13. Fit a ¾-inch plywood panel over the 2 × 4-inch framing and secure it to the frame with hinges on the long side.

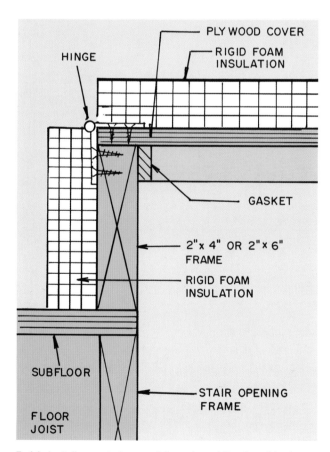

5–14. Install a gasket around the edge of the 2 × 4-inch frame and nail or glue two inches of rigid foam insulation to the top of the panel.

Put one or more handles on the bottom of the panel where they can be easily reached by someone going up the stairs. Install a chain on the end of the panel to hold it in an open position and keep it easy to reach when you are ready to go down the stair (**5–15**). As you descend, you can lower the cover by grasping one of the handles. This is a bit cumbersome, but since this attic storage is not frequently accessed the savings in heat and air-conditioning are worth the trouble.

■ Insulating Existing Exterior Walls

If you found there is little or no insulation in the walls, additional insulation can be added. In some older houses the wall insulation may have settled, leaving the top part of the wall uninsulated.

It is difficult to insulate exterior walls on existing houses. Generally, it is best to have it done by a qualified insulation contractor.

The wall cavity is filled with blown fiberglass or cellulose insulation. There is available a loose-fill blowing fiberglass insulation which fully fills the cavity and does not settle over the years.

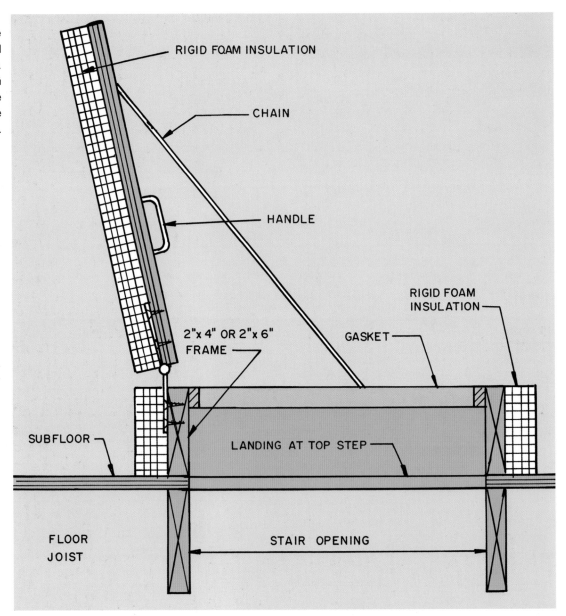

5–15. Install a handle to help to open and close the cover. A length of chain is used to hold the cover back while it is open.

RIGID FOAM INSULATION

CHAIN

HANDLE

RIGID FOAM INSULATION

GASKET

2"x 4" OR 2"x 6" FRAME

LANDING AT TOP STEP

SUBFLOOR

FLOOR JOIST

STAIR OPENING

OPENING EXTERIOR WALLS

Exterior walls can be insulated with blown-in insulation from the outside of the house. This requires that a number of bricks or pieces of siding be removed, holes drilled through the sheathing, and the insulation blown into the wall cavity at different levels. (See **5–16** to **5–22**.) The exact requirements can be had from the company doing the job and the type of blowing equipment used. A good carpenter is needed to remove wood, vinyl,

and aluminum siding to ensure that damage is minimal. It is often difficult to replace the pattern of the damaged siding. Also, the finish on vinyl and aluminum will often fade over the years and any new pieces required will be very noticeable. Likewise, it may not be able to get the exact style of wood siding. Stucco siding will have to be bored through and the hole repaired after the installation is completed. Brick-veneer houses require that individual bricks be removed.

PREPARING THE WALL

To insulate the exterior wall from the outside of the house, it is necessary to remove rows of siding and bore holes through the sheathing in the center of the cavities between the studs. Begin by removing strips of the siding at several levels up the wall and below the windows (**5–16**). The location of the strips removed may vary some but, if using a spray nozzle, locate one row about three feet from the bottom plate, a second strip four feet above this, and a third strip one foot below the top plate. These locations will vary depending upon whether fiberglass or cellulose is being installed.

As you work around windows and doors, you will find that typically over the rough opening is a solid load-bearing header, which means there is no need for insulation (**5–17**). In other cases, the header may be topped with cripples (**5–18**). These small areas can be filled with insulation. Older houses often have different framing systems. For years, balloon framing was popular on two-story houses. Details are shown in **5–19** to **5–21**. As you examine these drawings, you will see a number of additional factors that need to be considered. A knowledge of carpentry is a big help when insulating existing houses.

Once the strips of siding have been removed, locate and mark each stud. The studs can usually be located by noticing the nails in the sheathing holding it to the studs. Another technique is to drill a hole and then slide a piece of wire in the hole until it hits the next stud. Remove it and mark the distance to the next stud. Studs are typically spaced 16 inches on center.

Next, bore holes the required diameter through the vapor barrier and sheathing into the cavities between

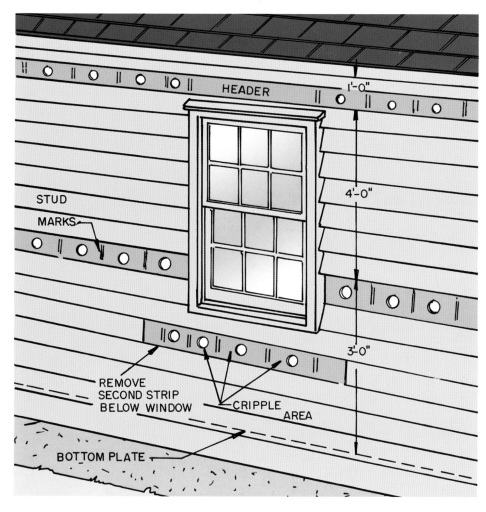

5–16. Remove strips of siding at each location where holes are to be bored for blowing in the insulation. This is one plan for locating the strips of siding to be removed. Contractors will often have a slightly different plan based on their experience and the construction of the house.

5–17. Typical framing around a window. Door framing is similar. Notice that the spaces between studs will vary on each side of the window. The area below the sill also needs insulating. Notice that this detail has a solid header. Also notice the framing uses firestops.

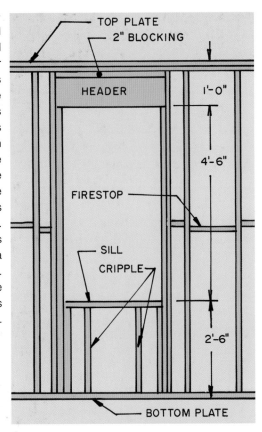

TOP PLATE
2" BLOCKING
HEADER
1'-0"
4'-6"
FIRESTOP
SILL
CRIPPLE
2'-6"
BOTTOM PLATE

5–18. This framing plan has cripples above the header as well as below the sill. Notice the firestops. If they are in the wall, their location can change the location of the holes.

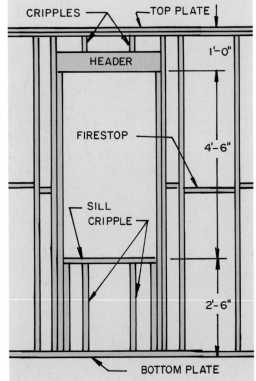

CRIPPLES
TOP PLATE
HEADER
1'-0"
FIRESTOP
4'-6"
SILL
CRIPPLE
2'-6"
BOTTOM PLATE

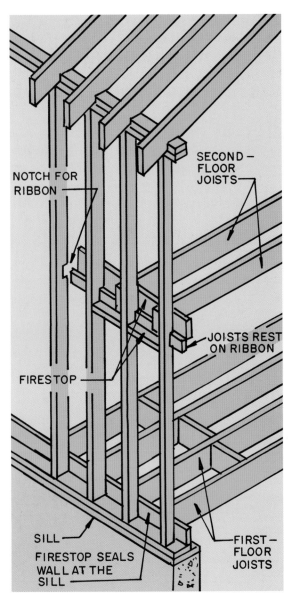

NOTCH FOR RIBBON
SECOND-FLOOR JOISTS
FIRESTOP
JOISTS REST ON RIBBON
SILL
FIRESTOP SEALS WALL AT THE SILL
FIRST-FLOOR JOISTS

5–19. Balloon framing was widely used on older two-story houses. Explore the construction at the first and second floors to see if it has the indicated firestops. If it does not, the blown-in insulation in the wall could flow out under the floor. The end of the floor would have to be blocked.

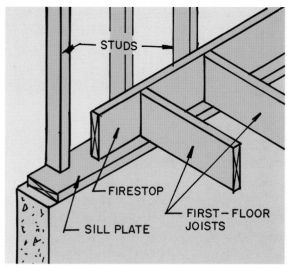

5–20. A sill detail for the first floor of a balloon-framed wall. See how the firestop seals off any opening to the floor joists.

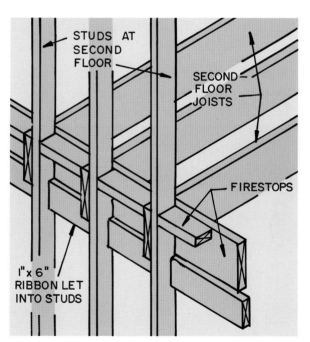

5–21. A detail for the framing at the second floor of a balloon-framed wall. Notice the horizontal and vertical firestops.

the studs. A hole saw in an electric drill is a good way to bore the holes (**5–22**). There may be electric wiring and plumbing in the wall. Bore carefully, so the hole saw does not jamb into the cavity, cutting a wire or pipe. It is recommended that the electricity to the wall be turned off. The hole diameter should be large enough to allow the nozzle of the blowing tube to enter.

BLOCKAGES IN THE WALL

If the wall already has some insulation, such as blankets, but it is inadequate, blowing in insulation will be difficult and probably not add much to the insulating value of the wall. Walls also contain wiring, plumbing, firestops, vents (**5–23**), and other things that block the flow of blown-in insulation. In some cases, it may work past the wire or pipe. Usually, a new siding strip above or below the obstruction will have to be removed and a new hole bored in order to fill the vacant part of the wall cavity.

5–22. A hole saw is a good tool to use to bore the holes.

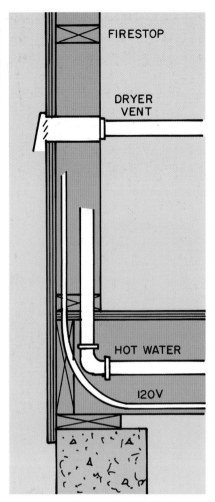

5–23. There are many obstructions in the wall which must be located and holes bored to fill around them.

FIRESTOP

DRYER VENT

HOT WATER

120V

makes certain the lower cavities have been filled. Then move up to the next row of holes. Finally, top off the fill at the top row of holes. Many contractors use a swivel nozzle because it can be turned to direct the insulation to the sides of the cavity and upwards as the top row of holes is filled.

The pressure required for the blowing machine to operate will vary depending upon the circumstances on the job. The manufacturer will also have recommendations (**5–24**).

The blowing machine should have a pop-off valve so that when the wall cavity is full the pressure will be diverted at the machine. This prevents the insulation from continuing to flow into the filled cavity. This could build up pressure inside the wall cavity and possibly force loose the drywall on the interior of the wall. Walls with drywall interior wall finish must be filled using a lower blowing pressure than stronger finishes such as lath and plaster or wood paneling.

It is important to keep moving the blowing nozzle back and forth to fill the entire width of the cavity. A typical between-studs distance is 14½ inches, and the cavity is 3½ inches deep.

FILLING THE CAVITIES

Now fill the cavities with insulation. Insert the nozzle in the holes on the lowest level and fill until the insulation reaches the level of the hole. If insulation dust tends to blow out around the nozzle, wrap a cloth around it and press the nozzle against the sheathing. Be certain to wear a respirator, eye protection, and gloves.

To see if the cavity between the studs is open to the bottom plate, lower a plumb line into the cavity from a hole high on the wall. The length of the chalk line used before the bob hits something will show where an obstruction exists.

The actual blowing procedure varies depending upon the experience of the contractor and the equipment. Generally, the lower holes are filled first, which

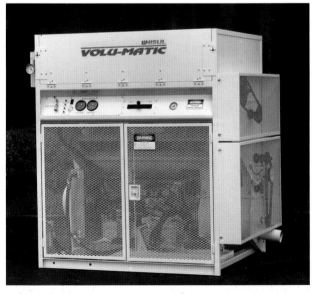

5–24. This fiberglass blowing machine is designed to blow in a product called Optima, a special fiberglass insulation manufactured for use in new insulation jobs and when remodeling. *(Courtesy CertainTeed Corporation)*

If it seems that the cavity may not be filling right, the insulation may have jammed somewhere. Sometimes this can be loosened by lowering a very heavy plumb bob into the cavity or a long stiff wire with the end bent on an angle. These could break up the jam. If the jam cannot be broken, bore a hole below it and insulate the area not filled.

The holes are plugged with a cork, tapered wood, or plastic plugs available from the insulation dealer. After they are in place, glue a piece of plastic vapor barrier over the plug. Finally, replace the siding and make repairs as necessary.

■ Filling Without Removing Wood Siding

An alternative to removing wood siding that some contractors use is to locate the studs with a stud finder and mark each on the siding. Then drill the holes for the nozzle through the siding and sheathing (**5–25**). Insert the nozzle in each hole and fill as just described (**5–26**). Have someone check the hole above to tell when the insulation has gone up the cavity to that hole (**5–27**). Plug the lower hole and move the nozzle to the higher hole. After each hole has been used, glue in a tapered wood plug made for this purpose. After the glue has set,

5–26. Insert the nozzle in the hole and begin filling the cavity. Be certain to wear head, eye, and respiratory protective devices. *(Courtesy CertainTeed Corporation)*

5–25. Bore the proper diameter hole in the center of the cavity between the studs.

(Courtesy CertainTeed Corporation)

5–27. Have someone check the hole above the fill hole so when the insulation reaches there the nozzle can be moved to the higher hole. *(Courtesy CertainTeed Corporation)*

sand the plug flush with the surface of the siding. If there are any small cracks, fill them with wood crack filler and sand the filler when it is dry. Finally, prime each plug and, when dry, paint the entire strip of siding. If the house has been painted some years earlier, this newly painted strip will be noticeable, so consider repainting the entire wall.

■ Opening Bevel Wood Siding

Bevel wood siding may have a plain or rabbeted bevel (5–28). First, cut through any paint that is in the end where the piece being removed butts another piece of siding. With a chisel or pry bar, pry up the bottom edge of the piece of siding (5–29). Do not lift too much or the piece will split. Remove the pry bar and tap the board back in place (5–30). Usually the nail will pop out above the surface of the siding and can be pulled with a hammer (5–31). If this does not occur, cut the nail with a hacksaw blade (5–32). If the siding is hard to slide out, it may be necessary to raise the piece above it as just described. Locate and mark the studs on the vapor

5–29. Slide a pry bar under the edge of the siding near a nail and carefully lift the siding, raising the nail about ⅜ inch. Use an old drywall knife under the bar to protect the siding below.

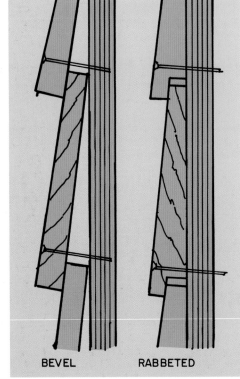

5–28. Bevel wood siding is easier to slide a pry bar under to lift the strip than rabbeted bevel siding.

BEVEL   RABBETED

5–30. After lifting the siding a little, tap it back in place so the nail pops above the surface. Protect the siding so the hammer will not damage it.

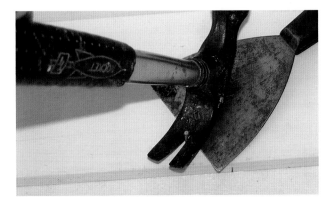

5–31. Pull the nail that has been raised. This technique takes a lot of strain off the piece of siding. Protect the siding from damage.

5–32. If the nail does not pull up a little easily, slide a hacksaw blade under the siding and cut the nail.

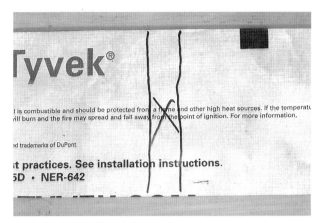

5–33. Locate and mark the studs on the vapor barrier or sheathing.

barrier (**5–33**) and bore the required hole in the center between the studs (**5–34**).

Insert the blowing nozzle and fill the cavity to this level. Glue a cork or tapered wood plug in the hole (**5–35**). These are available at a building supply dealer. Bond a piece of vapor barrier over the hole with mastic. When the row is finished reinstall the siding.

■ Opening Wood-Shingle Siding

Wood shingles used as siding may be applied using a single-course or double-course method (**5–36**). The problems related to removing them are similar; however, double-course shingles have several additional nails.

To remove a single-course shingle, use a chisel to raise the shingle a little above the one below. Use wood wedges to hold the shingles up off those below (**5–37**). Then, using a hacksaw, cut the nails as close to the sheathing as possible (**5–38**). Slide the shingle out. Sometimes it helps if the shingle above the one to be removed is raised slightly with a chisel or wedge.

Another technique is to run a shingle hook under the shingle and work the hook on the end around the nail (**5–39**). Drive the tool out from under the shingle as shown in **5–40**, cutting the nail.

After the shingle has been removed, bore the hole for the nozzle through the exposed shingles and the sheathing (**5–41**). Blow in the insulation, filling the cavity to this point. Some then prefer to glue a tapered wood plug in the hole (**5–42**) and then bond a piece of

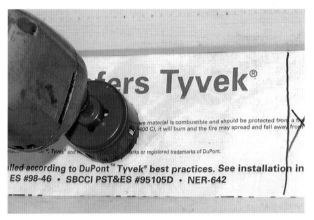

5–34. Bore the nozzle hole in the center of the area between the studs.

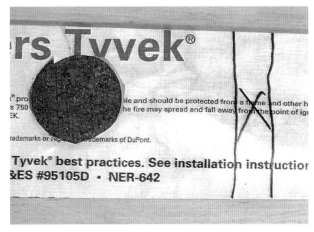

5–35. After the insulation has been blown in the cavity, glue a plug over the hole.

5–36. As you prepare to remove courses of wood-shingle siding, examine it to see if it has been installed single- or double-coursed.

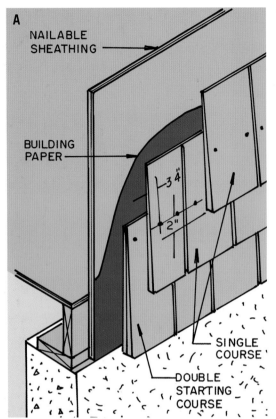

A

NAILABLE SHEATHING

BUILDING PAPER

3 4

2"

SINGLE COURSE

DOUBLE STARTING COURSE

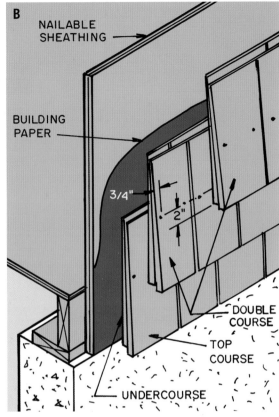

B

NAILABLE SHEATHING

BUILDING PAPER

3/4"

2"

DOUBLE COURSE

TOP COURSE

UNDERCOURSE

5–37. When removing single-course shingles, use a chisel to raise each shingle and slide a thin wood wedge below it.

5–38. After wedging up the shingle, cut the nails with a hacksaw blade. Cut as close to the sheathing as possible.

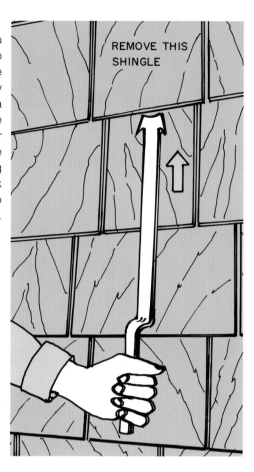

5–39. You can also cut the nails by sliding a shingle hook under the shingle and driving the hook up next to a nail.

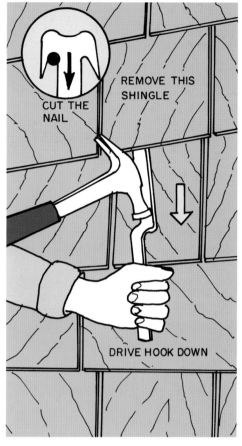

5–40. Hook the cutting edge of the shingle hook around the nail and drive it out with a hammer. It will cut off the nail.

5–41. Bore the hole for the nozzle of the blowing machine through the shingles and sheathing.

5–42. Some people glue a wood plug in the hole.

vapor barrier (**5–43**) over the plug. Now, replace the shingle. Face-nail it through the thick butt end with 6d or 8d galvanized finishing nails.

To remove a double-course shingle, use a chisel to raise the shingles above the one to be removed. Hold it up with a small wood wedge. Next, pry up the shingle to be removed (**5–44**). Slide a hacksaw blade between them and cut the nails holding the shingle to be removed. A shingle hook could be used here instead of a hacksaw. Now, slide the shingle out. Bore the hole for the nozzle through the lower course shingle and the sheathing (refer to **5–39** and **5–40**).

Insert the blowing nozzle and blow in the insulation. When the cavity has been filled to this point, remove the nozzle. Some prefer to glue in the wood plug removed or use special tapered plugs (refer to **5–42**). Lay a piece of builder's felt or vapor barrier over the plug. Bond it with mastic (refer to **5–43**).

Finally, slide the removed shingle back in place. Tap it carefully on the end with a hammer and a block of wood so it is not damaged (**5–45**). Face-nail it through the thick butt end with 6d or 8d galvanized finishing nails.

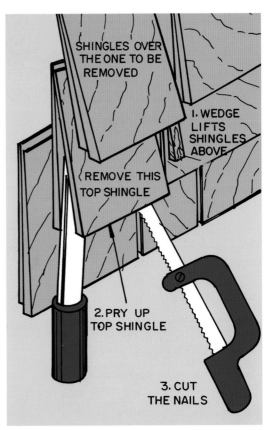

5–44. To remove the top shingle in a double-coursed installation, raise it with a chisel. Cut the nails with a hacksaw blade.

5–43. Seal the plug with a layer of vapor-barrier material.

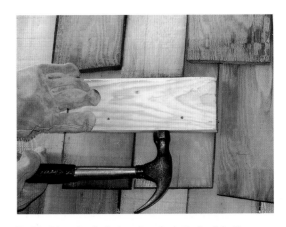

5–45. After the hole has been sealed, slide the removed shingle back in place. Tap it in carefully using a wood block to prevent damage, and then face-nail it securely.

■ Opening Aluminum and Vinyl Siding

A siding tool, often referred to as a zip tool, is used to remove a strip of vinyl or aluminum siding (**5–46**). Siding tools are available at the local building supply dealer.

The siding removal tool is used to unlock the bottom edge where two panels are joined with a lock joint. A typical joint is shown in **5–47**. Insert the tool under the bottom edge and hook it under the lip and slide it along the edge, pulling the lip out of the piece above (**5–48**). Place wedges below the loose piece to keep it from slipping back in place (**5–49**).

Next, slide a pry bar under the nailing flange and pull its nails. Place a piece of wood on the siding below to prevent damage and help in the prying process (**5–50**). Slide the panel down and off the wall.

Now, bore nozzled holes through the vapor barrier and sheathing (**5–51**) and fill the cavity with insulation. Glue the wood plug back in the hole and repair the vapor barrier as shown in **5–52**.

Once the sheathing and vapor barrier are repaired, slide the removed panel in place, and nail the top nailing edge to the sheathing with 3d galvanized siding nails. Place the nails in the center of the nailing slot and drive them in place, but not too tight. The panel needs to be able to expand and contract and slide on the nails. The nails can be pressed in place with a stick. Then place a pry bar on the head and strike the bar with a hammer (**5–53**). Finally, relock the lower lip to the course above with the siding removal tool.

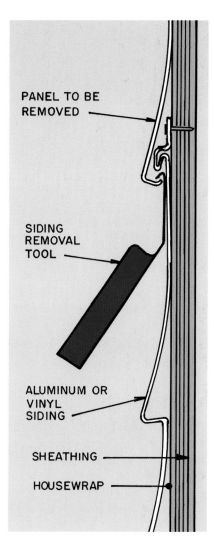

5–47. A typical joint used to secure the lower edge of the course of siding to the course below.

PANEL TO BE REMOVED

SIDING REMOVAL TOOL

ALUMINUM OR VINYL SIDING

SHEATHING

HOUSEWRAP

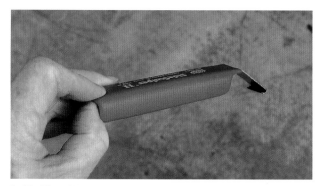

5–46. The siding removal tool is slid under the lip of the panel to be removed and pulls it loose from the lower panel.

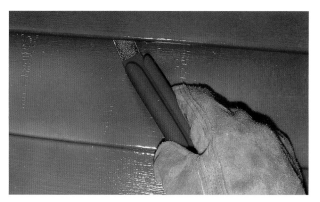

5–48. Slip the siding removal tool into the locked edge and slide it along, separating the two pieces.

5–49. To open the joint, slip the tool under the lip, lift it a little, and slide it along the edge. Wood wedges are inserted to keep the joint from snapping closed.

5–52. After wall cavity has been filled and the hole in the sheathing plugged, glue a piece of vapor barrier over the plug.

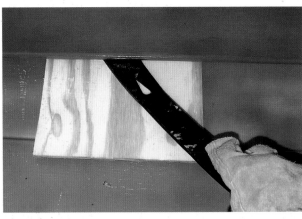

5–50. Once the course is lifted, slide a pry bar below it and pull each nail. Notice that the surface of the course below has been protected by a piece of plywood.

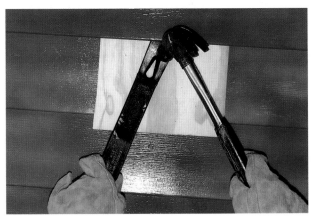

5–53. To reinstall the siding, slide it in place, raise it enough to press a nail through the holes on the top edge into the sheathing. Then place a pry bar on the nail and tap it until the nail is in place. Do not drive tight. The siding needs to be able to expand and contract and must slide on the nail.

5–51. After the panel has been removed, locate the studs and bore the holes for the nozzle.

■ Opening a Brick-Veneer Wall

A brick-veneer house requires that bricks will have to be removed wherever a hole is needed. A skilled brick mason is needed to remove and replace the brick. The new mortar should be close to the same color as the existing weathered mortar.

One way to remove a brick is to drill holes at each corner in the mortar and several in the mortar joint in between. Then, using a mason's chisel, tap out the remaining mortar, and slide out the brick (**5–54**).

If the studs can be accurately located, the removal of one full brick can often provide space for holes in two cavities. Generally, this is difficult to do, so one brick per hole is common. Caution: do not remove more than two bricks. The bricks above are counting on the bricks below for support, so you do not want to remove too many or the bricks above may sag enough to cause some mortar joints to crack.

To replace the brick, put a ⅜-inch-thick layer of mortar on the bottom and sides of the opening. Put a layer of mortar on the top and ends of the brick (**5–55**) and slide it into the opening. Carefully work the brick into the opening. Excess mortar will build up on the edges. Press the mortar with a grooving tool until it is firmly packed. Scrape away all excess mortar (**5–56**). Brush off any mortar still on the face of the bricks with a soft-bristle brush (**5–57**). Spray it with a fine spray several times a day for two days. This will produce a harder mortar.

It is recommended that when possible consider insulating these walls from inside the house. This is discussed later in this chapter.

■ Opening a Stucco Wall

A typical stucco wall detail is shown in **5–58**. To find the studs is difficult because a stud finder cannot be used since the metal lath will block it. Measure over from a corner and produce the first holes; then insert a wire in the holes and feel along until a stud is hit. Pull the wire and use it to measure over to the stud. Mark it on the stucco. To get to the sheathing, it is necessary to cut a hole through the concrete finish, brown and scratch coats. A metal chisel or mason's chisel will produce a hole (**5–59**). Hammer carefully because you do not want to crack the finish around the sides. Then you have to cut through the metal lath. Generally, a hole saw will cut through light metals. Then locate the studs and bore the holes for blowing the insulation. When they have been filled, glue a cork, wood, or plastic plug over them, cover the surface with mastic, and press a piece of builder's felt or plastic vapor barrier into it.

Repair the hole in the stucco by troweling in a layer of stucco patch material (**5–60**). It is available at the local building supply dealer. Fill the hole with several ¼-inch-thick layers. Let each dry before adding another layer. Usually two or three layers are necessary.

5–54. Clean out the mortar as you remove the brick. Bore the nozzle hole through the sheathing.

5–55. After laying mortar on the bottom of the opening (above), lay a thin amount on the top and ends of the brick and slide it into the opening (below).

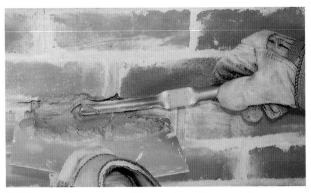

5–56. Form the surface of the mortar with a grooving tool. Try to match the contour used on the other bricks.

5–57. After the mortar has begun to set, carefully brush off any on the face of the brick.

5–58. Typical construction of a Portland cement stucco exterior wall.

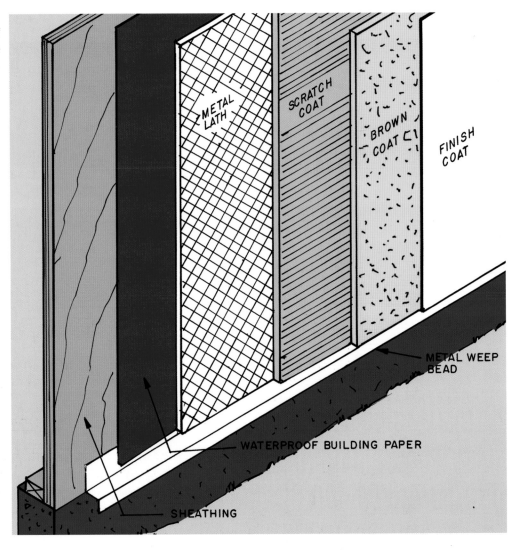

SHEATHING

METAL LATH

SCRATCH COAT

BROWN COAT

FINISH COAT

METAL WEEP BEAD

WATERPROOF BUILDING PAPER

5–59. Use a chisel to cut through the stucco to the metal lath. It can also cut the lath.

5–61. Lay a coat of stucco finish material over the hole after it has been filled. Feather it out on the surface around the hole.

5–60. Use a trowel to fill the hole in the stucco in ¼-inch-thick layers. Let each layer dry before adding the next.

5–62. Many older houses were sided with asbestos shingles, which are now banned. Do not cut or bore holes in them. This could release asbestos fibers, which are harmful.

When the last layer has hardened, trowel a finish coat over the entire area and feather out over the surrounding area (**5–61**). You can get a textured surface by brushing the wet final coat with a fiber brush or swirls by swinging a steel trowel across the patch.

As with brick exteriors, consider insulating the wall by blowing from the inside through holes cut in the drywall. This is discussed later in this chapter.

■ Opening a Wall with Asbestos Siding

Years ago, asbestos shingles were widely used as an exterior siding. They weathered well and provided good service (**5–62**). As it became known that asbestos fibers were a major danger to health, they were banned.

Any work involving these shingles must be done by contractors accredited to work with hazardous materials. **Do not try to remove, cut, or sand them.**

■ Installing Blow-In Insulation from Inside the House

If you are planning to redecorate the inside walls and patch and repair damage to the drywall, blown-in insulation can be installed from the inside by drilling holes through the drywall (**5–63**) and blowing the insulation into the wall through them (**5–64**). This will cause

5–63. After locating the studs with a stud finder, bore the holes in the center of each wall cavity.

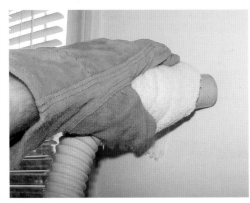

5–64. Fill each stud cavity with the insulation and close the hole with special foam plastic plugs.

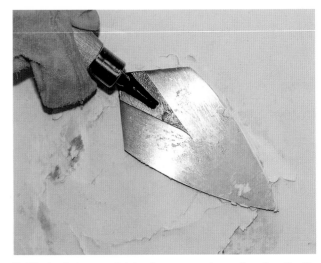

5–65. Apply layers of drywall compound over the plug. It will take several layers. Feather each layer out wider than the one before. When the last coat hardens, sand smooth, prime, and paint.

some disruption of furniture, carpets, curtains, and other interior items, but does preserve the exterior siding. If it does not have to be removed, the exterior siding will not be damaged or need repainting.

Locate the studs with a stud finder. Bore the holes in the center of each cavity about three feet from the floor, about halfway up the wall and 12 to 18 inches from the ceiling. Be aware there may be obstructions in the wall that may keep the insulation from flowing above or below them. To find any obstructions, drop a chalk line down inside the wall from the top hole. If it hits an obstruction, such as 2 × 4 blocking, mark the spot and drill extra holes as needed.

After the cavity is full, patch the holes with specially made foam plastic plugs and cover them with drywall compound. When they are dry, coat and feather the compound as needed to hide the hole (5–65).

■ Insulating an Old House that has a Cathedral Ceiling or a Low Slope or Flat Roof

A situation may occur when the house has a cathedral ceiling, a roof with a very low slope, or a flat roof and the shingles or tar-and-gravel finish roofing need replacing and you would like to increase the insulation in the roof. One way which is sometimes used is to remove the shingles, repair damage to the sheathing, install a layer of rigid foam insulation board over it, and then install a new layer of plywood sheathing. Nail the insulation to the old sheathing and nail the new sheathing through the insulation into the old sheathing. Then install the new shingles on the roof over the cathedral ceiling (5–66) or new tar-and-gravel roofing on the low-slope or flat roof.

An alternative that may prove to be easier, especially if the shingles are in good condition, is to remove the drywall ceiling, install blankets, leaving room for airflow below the sheathing, and install new drywall. Be certain to provide air inflow into this space and an exit at the ridge (5–67).

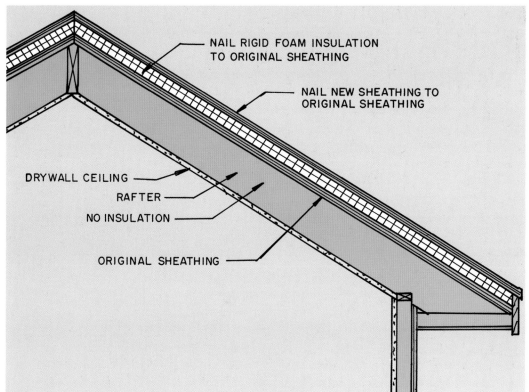

NAIL RIGID FOAM INSULATION TO ORIGINAL SHEATHING

NAIL NEW SHEATHING TO ORIGINAL SHEATHING

DRYWALL CEILING

RAFTER

NO INSULATION

ORIGINAL SHEATHING

5–66. Remove the old shingles or the tar-and-gravel roof, repair the old sheathing, and nail the rigid foam insulation to the old sheathing. Install new sheathing over the insulation and nail it to the old sheathing. Now install the new finish roofing.

5–67. This ceiling has been insulated with pressure-fit blankets. After the plastic vapor barrier is installed over them, the new drywall ceiling can be installed.

■ Insulating Walls That Do Not Have Sheathing

Some very old homes were built without sheathing. The wood siding was nailed directly to the studs. When you remove a piece of siding, the open area is too large to adequately fill the stud cavity with blown-in insulation. To handle this, tack a piece of ¼-inch plywood over the open area and across several studs. Bore a hole in it for the nozzle and fill the cavity. Work along the length of the piece of siding removed. When its end has been reached, remove the plywood and replace the siding. Repeat on down the length of the wall. Then move up the required distance and repeat until the top of the wall is reached (5–68). It is advisable to cover the exposed area with a vapor barrier before replacing the siding. Staple it to the studs.

Another solution it to bore nozzle holes directly through the wood siding, blow in the insulation, glue a

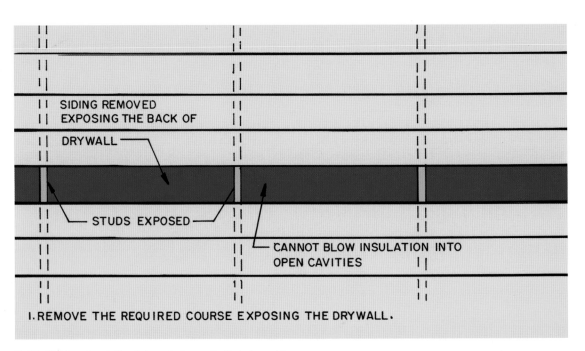

SIDING REMOVED
EXPOSING THE BACK OF
DRYWALL

STUDS EXPOSED

CANNOT BLOW INSULATION INTO
OPEN CAVITIES

I. REMOVE THE REQUIRED COURSE EXPOSING THE DRYWALL.

5–68. To blow insulation into exterior walls that do not have sheathing, remove the required piece of siding, cover the opening with plywood, bore nozzle holes and blow the insulation. Remove the plywood, cover the insulation with a vapor barrier, and replace the siding.

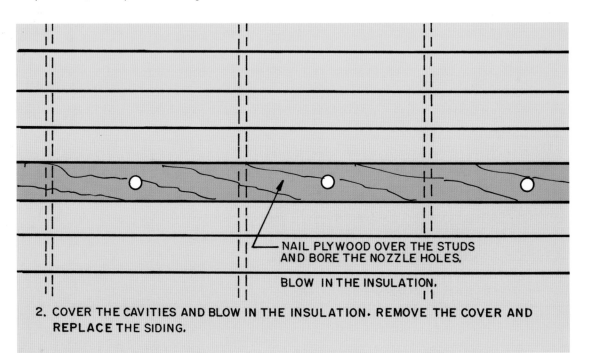

NAIL PLYWOOD OVER THE STUDS
AND BORE THE NOZZLE HOLES.

BLOW IN THE INSULATION.

2. COVER THE CAVITIES AND BLOW IN THE INSULATION. REMOVE THE COVER AND REPLACE THE SIDING.

plug in the hole, and caulk and sand the plug smooth with the siding. This is discussed earlier in this chapter.

Still another possibility is to staple a special fiber mesh made for installing blown fiberglass in open cavities as shown in **5–69**. This is covered in detail in Chapter 4.

■ Insulating an Existing Concrete Floor

If you are planning to install a finished floor covering over an existing on-grade or below-grade concrete floor, it is wise to insulate it before installing the flooring. If the floor is directly on the concrete, it will feel more resilient and the chill factor will be reduced. This will not only save on heating costs, but make the area more pleasant.

Begin by making certain the concrete floor is in a dry condition. If the surface appears damp at times, action must be taken to remove the sources of water. This might be as simple as sloping the land away from the house and putting on gutters. If the surface of the slab appears dry, you can check it for minor moisture penetration by taping a two-foot-square sheet of 6-mil polyethylene sheet over it. After a couple days, remove the sheet and see if moisture has condensed on the sheet (**5–70**). In this case, the slab may need a waterproof coating before the floor installation is started. If the slab cannot be kept dry, do not install a finish floor over it.

When the slab is ready, there are several approaches that can be used. One technique is to dig along the walls butted by the floor and install two-inch-thick polystyrene rigid foam insulation around the foundation (**5–71**). It should extend 12 to 18 inches above grade and at least two feet below grade. In cold northern climates, it would help if it went deeper. The part above ground should be covered with a hard, moisture-resistant material to protect it from damage.

A more thorough approach is to first lay down a polyethylene vapor barrier over the floor. Wrap it up the wall a couple inches and glue it with construction adhesive, overlap the sheets six inches, and bond them with construction adhesive (**5–72**).

5–69. The large opening created when the siding was removed can be covered with a special fiberglass mesh and the insulation blown through holes in the mesh. Leave it in place and replace the siding. *(Courtesy CertainTeed Corporation)*

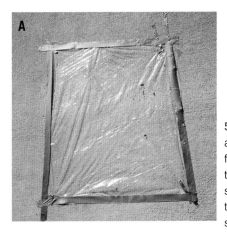

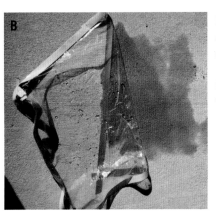

5–70. To check a concrete slab for moisture, tape a piece of sheet plastic to the surface, as shown above left. If moisture collects under it in a day or two, as shown above right, do not install a finish floor over it.

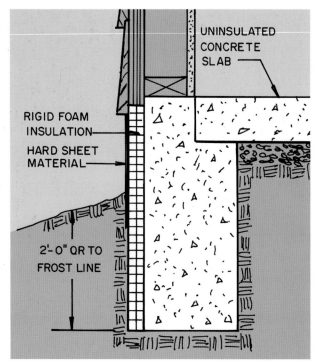

RIGID FOAM INSULATION

HARD SHEET MATERIAL

UNINSULATED CONCRETE SLAB

2'-0" OR TO FROST LINE

5–71. Uninsulated concrete slab floors can get some relief from frozen soil by installing rigid foam insulation on the exterior of the foundation wall.

Now, nail 1 × 3-inch pressure-treated wood sleepers around the edge of the room (5–73). Secure them to the concrete floor with 2½-inch masonry nails. Wear eye protection because they occasionally shatter and are dangerous. A better technique is to use power-actuated concrete fasteners. Then install 1 × 3-inch sleepers parallel with the long dimension of the room. Space them 16 or 24 inches on center. Next, place rigid foam insulation between them (5–74). If you use 1 × 3 sleepers, you will only get to use ¾-inch insulation. Some people prefer to rise 2 × 4–inch sleepers because they use 1½-inch-thick insulations.

If strip wood flooring is to be used, it can be nailed to the sleepers (5–75). If carpet, vinyl floor covering, or ceramic tile are to be used, the sleepers are covered with a plywood subfloor (5–76). If the sleepers have been spaced 24 inches on center, use ¾-inch plywood for the subfloor.

If carpet is to be installed, another technique used involves installing 1 × 2-inch pressure-treated sleepers along the wall. The tackless carpet strips that hold the carpet tight are nailed to these (5–77). Then bond rigid

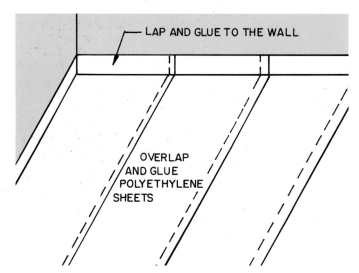

LAP AND GLUE TO THE WALL

OVERLAP AND GLUE POLYETHYLENE SHEETS

5–72. Cover the slab with six-mil polyethylene plastic sheeting. Overlap the sheets six inches and glue them with adhesive.

NAIL 1" x 3" WOOD SLEEPERS TO THE FLOOR ALONG THE WALL

5–73. Nail 1 × 3-inch pressure-treated wood sleepers around the perimeter of the room. Some prefer to use 2 × 4-inch sleepers.

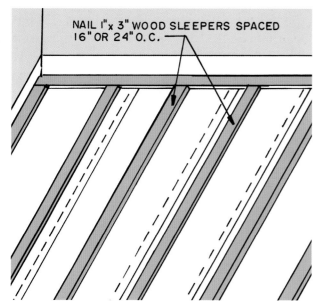

5–74. Space 1 × 3-inch sleepers parallel with the long wall spaced 16 or 24 inches on center. Fill the spaces between with rigid foam insulation.

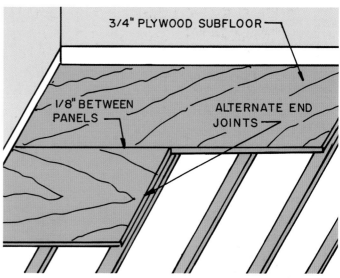

5–76. The sleepers are covered with plywood if ceramic tile, vinyl floor covering, carpet, or wood parquet blocks are to be installed.

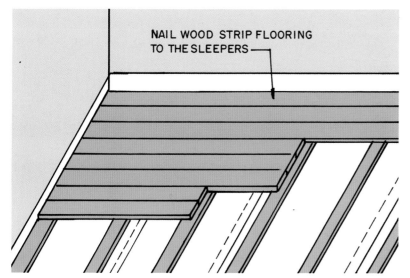

5–75. Nail the wood strip flooring to the sleepers.

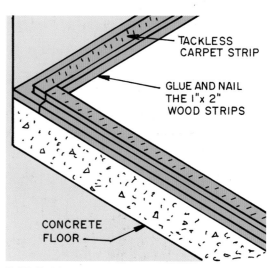

5–77. Tackless carpet strips are nailed to the sleepers along the walls.

insulation panels to the concrete area, leaving a ³⁄₁₆-inch space between them (**5–78**). The carpet is installed over this in the normal manner. If ceramic or vinyl tile or wood flooring is to be installed, plywood panels can be installed over the insulation and secured to the floor with concrete fasteners (**5–79**).

An easier way to install a wood subfloor over a concrete floor is with a patented product made up of engineered wood panels two feet square that have a high-density polyethylene moisture barrier with molded-in cleats that raise the wood panel ¼ inch off the concrete floor (**5–80**). This air space permits air to circulate, which helps dry up condensation that may form on the concrete and allows it to breathe. This also acts as a thermal break, preventing the transmission of cold from the concrete to the wood subfloor.

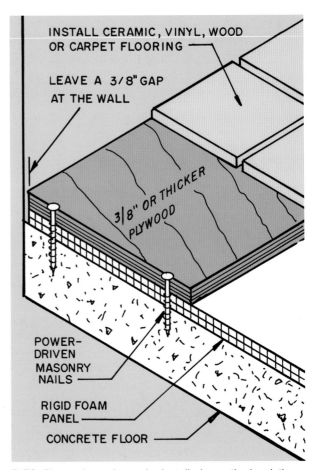

INSTALL CERAMIC, VINYL, WOOD OR CARPET FLOORING

LEAVE A 3/8" GAP AT THE WALL

3/8" OR THICKER PLYWOOD

POWER-DRIVEN MASONRY NAILS

RIGID FOAM PANEL

CONCRETE FLOOR

5–79. Plywood panels can be installed over the insulation, allowing ceramic tile, vinyl floor covering, carpet, and wood flooring to be installed.

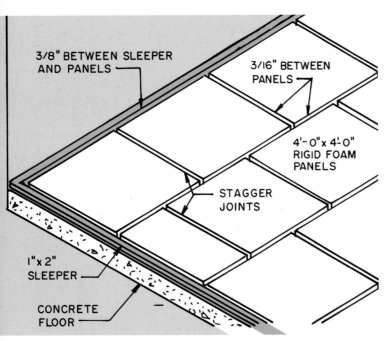

3/8" BETWEEN SLEEPER AND PANELS

3/16" BETWEEN PANELS

4'-0" x 4'-0" RIGID FOAM PANELS

STAGGER JOINTS

1"x 2" SLEEPER

CONCRETE FLOOR

5–78. Fill the area with rigid foam insulation panels. Bond to the concrete slab with an approved adhesive.

5–80. The wood subfloor is made of two-foot-square engineered wood panels that have a patented polyethylene, molded moisture barrier bonded to the bottom.
(Courtesy Dricore Division, Longac Wood Industries)

The engineered wood panels are laid on the concrete floor and are pressed together with nails or glue to create a floating floor (**5–81**). In some cases, minimal anchoring to the concrete might be required. Follow the manufacturer's instructions. When completed, the room will have a strong wood subfloor ready to receive the finish flooring (**5–82**).

■ Sound Control

Older houses generally had no special actions taken to control the movement of sound between rooms and from exterior sources. As a house is remodeled, it is a good time to consider insulating to control sound transmission, as well as heat loss and gain. Sound control is covered in Chapter 4.

5–81. The panels are laid edge-to-edge on the concrete floor.

(Courtesy Dricore Division, Longac Wood Industries)

5–82. The finished installation provides a strong wood subfloor ready to receive the finish flooring.

(Courtesy Dricore Division, Longac Wood Industries)

6

INSULATING BASEMENTS, CRAWL SPACES, AND ATTIC ROOMS

Three areas that require some special attention but which are often neglected are basements, crawl spaces, and living areas built in attic space. A review of the information in this book on sealing a space, proper placement of insulation, and consideration of moisture are important as the special needs of these areas are considered.

■ Constructing Attic Rooms

If you are considering converting attic space into a heated and cooled living area, insulation is one of the many things to be considered. Other factors include a permanent stair, natural light and ventilation with dormers or operable skylights, and adequate natural ventilation of the attic space surrounding the room enclosure.

The framing used to enclose the living space can take on various designs. Those in **6–1** are typical.

Begin by considering insulating the floor, which is the ceiling of the room below. It will most likely have insulation already if the unfinished attic is above a heated and cooled area. If it has some insulation and is above a heated and cooled room, additional insulation will not be needed. If it has no insulation, some prefer to omit it and let the energy in the room below flow into this second-level room. If the attic room is over an unheated area, such as a garage, the floor (garage ceiling) should be insulated to the standard recommended for that area. The vapor barrier should be next to the subfloor (**6–2**).

Sometimes the attic already has a subfloor installed so it could be used for storage. Look between the panels to see if there is insulation. If there is none and insula-

tion is needed, have a contractor blow insulation below the subfloor. Blown fiberglass or dry, blown cellulose are commonly used.

Since it is difficult to blow insulation more than four to six feet, it may be necessary to remove some of the flooring every six feet. Wires and bridging below the floor also hinder blowing the insulation. Usually the insulation is installed by inserting the hose four to six feet under the floor and pulling it out slowly as the insulation fills the space. If there are obstructions, the hose will hit them. You will then have to remove flooring in that area if a full layer of insulation is to be laid.

If the attic space does not have a subfloor and requires insulation, first seal all sources of air leaks in the ceiling below. (Review Chapter 2 for information on sealing leaks.) Then install the insulation. Perhaps the easiest thing to do is lay in blankets with the vapor barrier side down next to the drywall ceiling.

Begin by insulating the ceiling (**6–3**). Install as discussed in Chapter 4. The vapor barrier should face the room and be next to the drywall ceiling material. The ends of the ceiling insulation should butt firmly against that to be placed in the rafters forming the sloped part of the ceiling.

Next, insulate the sloped ceiling formed by the rafters (**6–3**). If the thickness of the insulation used tends to block the airflow above the insulation, install baffles (**6–4**). They are stapled to the roof sheathing. This will ensure a channel for the air to flow from the soffit up and out of the ridge vent or gable end vents. Then install the blankets starting at the ceiling down to the top of the kneewall (refer to **6–3**). As with other blanket installation, blankets with a kraft vapor barrier can be installed by stapling them to the face of the rafters or stapling the flange to the sides. If pressure-fit unfaced batts are used, press them in place and cover them with 6-mil polyethylene

sheeting. Be certain the blanket seals tightly against the top of the kneewall and butts the ceiling insulation so there is no gap.

Then install blankets in the kneewall. These are installed as described in Chapter 4 for full exterior walls (refer to **6–3**). Be certain the insulation seals with the plate on top of the kneewall studs and the floor. The vapor barrier faces the room.

Normally a door is built in the kneewall to provide access to the insulated ceiling behind it (**6–5**). This gives access to electrical to plumbing systems, and provides storage in that area. The door can be a ¾-inch-thick sheet of plywood. Prepare seals around the door opening to stop air leaks and glue or nail two inches or more of rigid foam insulation to the back of the door (**6–6**).

An access opening is made in the ceiling to provide access to the attic above (**6–7**). Weather-strip the edges so the plywood panel has no air leaks. Glue or nail rigid foam insulation to the back of the panel.

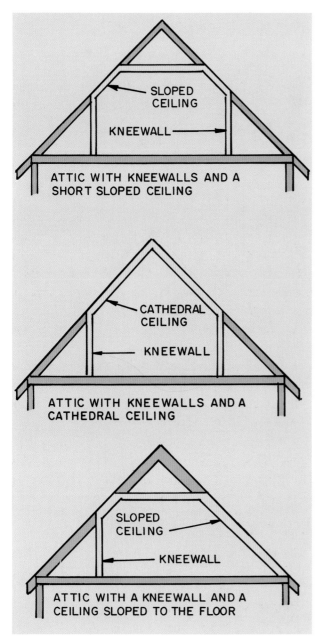

6–1. These are commonly used methods for building and insulating attic rooms.

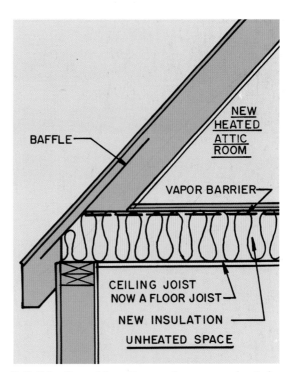

6–2. If the floor of the attic room is over an unheated area, such as a garage, it should be insulated according to local codes. Do not block the airflow from the soffit vent.

6–3. The steps to insulate an attic room include first insulating the horizontal ceiling, then the sloped ceiling, and finally the kneewall.

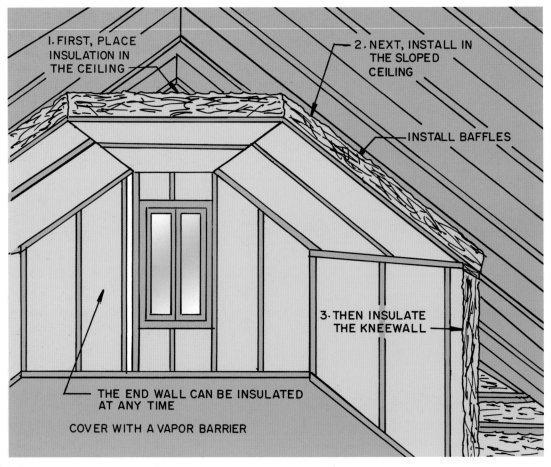

1. FIRST, PLACE INSULATION IN THE CEILING

2. NEXT, INSTALL IN THE SLOPED CEILING

INSTALL BAFFLES

3. THEN INSULATE THE KNEEWALL

THE END WALL CAN BE INSULATED AT ANY TIME

COVER WITH A VAPOR BARRIER

6–4. Baffles are often needed to keep the insulation from touching the roof sheathing, blocking airflow.

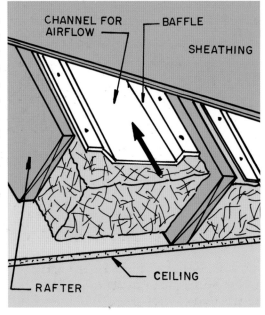

CHANNEL FOR AIRFLOW

BAFFLE

SHEATHING

CEILING

RAFTER

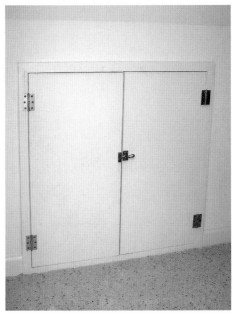

6–5. Doors are usually built in the kneewall to provide access to the attic area behind it.

6–6. Insulate the kneewall access door with several inches of rigid foam insulation. Weather-strip the door around the edges.

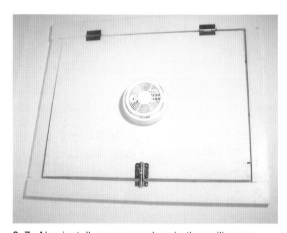

6–7. Also install an access door in the ceiling so wiring, plumbing, and insulation can be reached if necessary.

■ Insulating Crawl Spaces

Many houses are built with the first floor over a crawl space. This has the advantage of being able to run electrical and plumbing lines below the floor and makes them accessible for repair. Heating and air-conditioning units and ducts are also located there.

The first thing to do is be certain the crawl space is dry. The foundation should have been waterproofed on the exterior and the earth sloped away (6–8). Any cracks in the masonry should be cleaned out and filled and the waterproof coating applied over the repair.

Even if the crawl space is dry, considerable moisture from the exposed earth floor will flow into the air. The earth floor should be covered with 6-mil polyethylene sheets that are overlapped 12 inches and glued or taped. They are laid six inches up the foundation and taped or glued to it (6–9). Any tears that occur over the years from crawling on it should be repaired.

It is recommended that after the foundation has been installed and before the wood framed floor is built, the

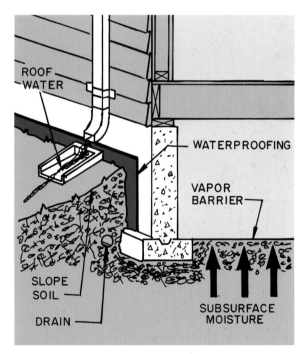

6–8. The crawl space must be very dry. Waterproof the foundation, direct surface water away, and cover the earth floor with a vapor barrier.

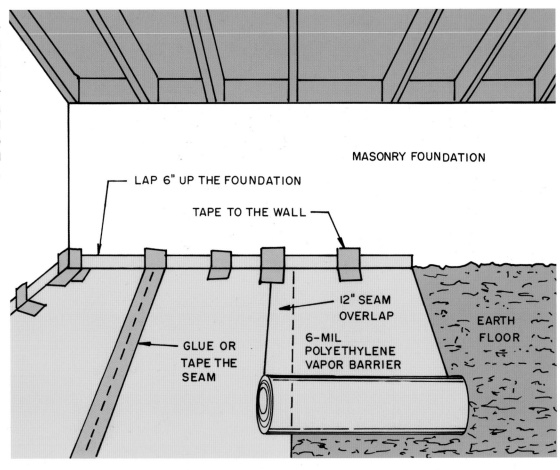

6–9. The earth floor in a crawl space should be covered with a 6-mil polyethylene vapor barrier. All seams should be sealed and it should lap up the foundation and be taped to it.

MASONRY FOUNDATION

LAP 6" UP THE FOUNDATION

TAPE TO THE WALL

12" SEAM OVERLAP

EARTH FLOOR

GLUE OR TAPE THE SEAM

6-MIL POLYETHYLENE VAPOR BARRIER

earth floor of the crawl space be covered with 6-mil polyethylene. This immediately blocks the buildup of moisture under the floor as the house is built. Since it will probably get damaged during construction, it can be replaced or covered with a second layer of polyethylene after the house is weathertight.

If you choose to not cover the crawl space floor with polyethylene during construction, insulate the overhead wood-framed floor as discussed earlier in this chapter before covering the earth floor so the polyethylene is not damaged. Then lay a sheet of polyethylene along a foundation wall and insulate that foundation (**6–10**). Continue across the floor with additional rows of polyethylene, as shown in **6–11**. The vapor barrier should face the crawl space.

When using fiberglass blankets and batts, there are two ways the rim joist is usually insulated (**6–12**). When the floor joists run perpendicular to the rim joist, short pieces of insulation are cut to fit between the joists. When the joists run parallel with the rim joist, the insulation can run full length parallel with the floor joists.

The exterior foundation walls can also be insulated by bonding expanded polystyrene insulation panels to the masonry with a mastic (**6–13**). The exposed foam boards do present a smoke and fire hazard, so must be covered with ½-inch gypsum wallboard or other code-approved fire-resistant material if the area has a gas- or oil-fired furnace. Another option is to use a fire-rated foam board. This panel has a foil facing on both sides and has a 15-minute fire rating. Check the local building code. Some people recommend bonding 6-mil polyethylene sheeting to the foundation with an adhesive mastic and mechanically fastening the rigid insulation over it with power-driven masonry nails.

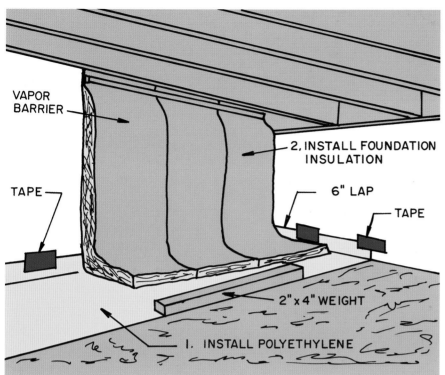

VAPOR
BARRIER

2. INSTALL FOUNDATION
INSULATION

6" LAP

TAPE

TAPE

2" x 4" WEIGHT

1. INSTALL POLYETHYLENE

6–10. Lay a row of polyethylene along a foundation wall and install the insulation. Lap the polyethylene up the wall about six inches.

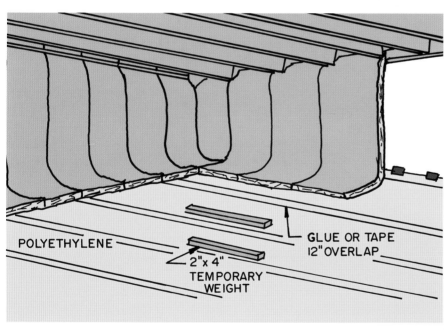

POLYETHYLENE

2" x 4"
TEMPORARY
WEIGHT

GLUE OR TAPE
12" OVERLAP

6–11. Continue across the earth floor with layers of polyethylene as you install sections of insulation on the wall.

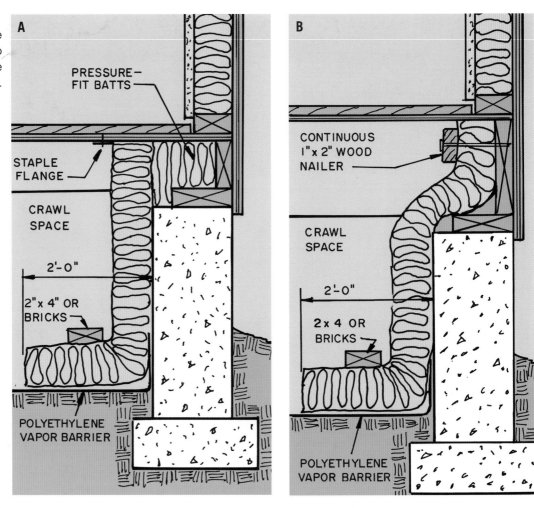

6–12. There are two ways to insulate the rim joist.

A

PRESSURE- FIT BATTS

STAPLE FLANGE

CRAWL SPACE

2'-0"

2"x 4" OR BRICKS

POLYETHYLENE VAPOR BARRIER

B

CONTINUOUS 1"x 2" WOOD NAILER

CRAWL SPACE

2'-0"

2 x 4 OR BRICKS

POLYETHYLENE VAPOR BARRIER

Some people run the insulation down to the footing or at least to the frost line. Be certain to caulk or foam around all pipes and other things that penetrate the foundation.

Foundations can also be insulated with sprayed foam insulation. The foam is laid on in thin layers, which expand in thickness as the foam cures. A typical application is shown in **6–33**, on page 155. This material has a high R-value per inch. It also seals any air leaks and forms a vapor barrier (**6–14**).

The energy code specifies that if the crawl-space foundation is insulated to R-10 it is not necessary to insulate the floor of the living area above. Check the local code.

After the house is occupied, service technicians will have to enter the crawl-space foundation to care for mechanical equipment, and the homeowner is going to store things in the space. This leads to frequent damage to the polyethylene sheet on the floor. It can be protected by covering these areas with old carpet, thin sheets of plywood or OSB, or some other durable material.

One last consideration is what to do with the vents built into the foundation (**6–15**). These may be required by codes; however, their usefulness is in doubt. The idea behind the vents is to close them in the winter during the heating season to keep the crawl space warm, and then open them in the summer to allow moisture to escape. However, many people believe it is best to seal the crawl

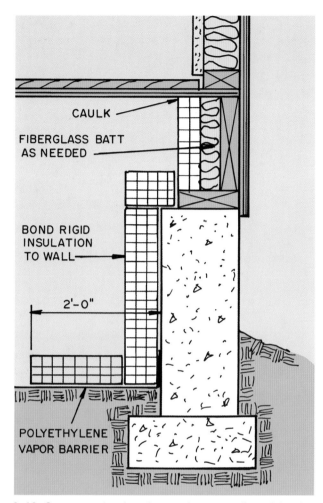

6–13. One way to insulate the crawl-space walls and the rim joist is by using rigid foam insulation.

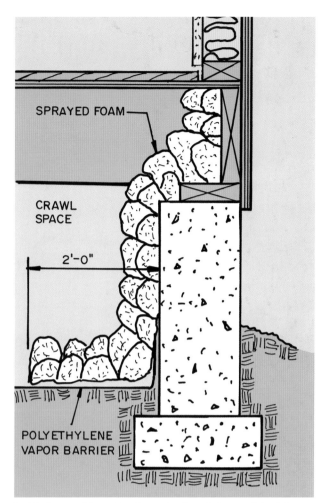

6–14. Sprayed foam insulates the foundation and rim joist and seals all air leaks.

space so it is watertight and fully insulated as just described and keep the vents closed all the time. In this case, cover the vents in the crawl space with two-inch pieces of rigid insulation, and foam or caulk the edges to get an airtight seal (6–16). The justification for this is that in many climates the outside air in the summer when the vents are supposed to be open has a higher humidity than the air in the insulated, watertight crawl space and actually introduces moisture into the area.

Typical code requirements for ventilating crawl spaces require openings having a net-free area of at least one square foot for each 150 square feet of foundation area if the ground is not covered with a vapor barrier. If a vapor barrier is placed over the ground, the vent opening requirements can be reduced to 0.1 square foot for every 150 square feet of floor area.

As part of the planning for a well-insulated, moisture-proof crawl space, a supply of conditioned air is recommended. A heating and air-conditioning contractor can design and install a system to change the air in the crawl space. Typically, a small fan (6–17) is located in the crawl space and it draws conditioned air from the living area above. This could be from a floor register located in a large open room (6–18), or a register from the air-conditioning system located in the crawl space. Local codes will usually specify the

6–15. Foundation vents have sliding doors that shut them closed when needed. They also have screens to keep out insects.

6–16. Foundation vents can be permanently closed and insulated by installing pieces of rigid foam over them and sealing around the edges with foam.

6–17. This inline ventilation fan draws conditioned air from the living area and discharges it into the crawl space.
(Courtesy Soler and Palau, Inc.)

acceptable system. In many houses, there are enough holes in the subfloor that conditioned air leaks into the crawl space without the need for a fan.

■ Insulating Basements

Before insulating a basement, make certain it is water-tight and dry. Any water or high levels of moisture will cause mold to form and ruin the insulation and any wood framing that has been installed. A wet basement will also cause damage to the wood floor, the ceiling, and even exterior and interior walls. Sealing a wet base-ment is a major undertaking and requires careful con-sideration before it is started. Usually professional help is required.

INSTALLING RIGID FOAM INSULATION

Rigid foam insulation is installed on basement walls in several ways. A frequently used method is to install wood furring strips vertically. Apply a waterproof paint or bond polyethylene sheeting to the wall with mastic before installing the furring. Furring strips generally used are 1 × 2 or 1 × 3 wood pieces, although 2 × 4 members are also used (**6–19**).

It should be noted that one-inch furring provides for the installation of a ¾-inch-thick insulation panel, which gives an R-rating of around 4 to 6. While this cuts the cold from the masonry wall somewhat, in cold climates 2 × 4-inch furring strips placed with the four-inch side against the wall will allow 1½-inch-thick rigid panels, which will given an R-rating of about 8 to 12. Under certain conditions it might be better to build a 2 × 4-stud wall and use 3½-inch blankets as shown later in this chapter.

Notice that a furring strip is located at the top of the wall butting the overhead joists. At the floor, the furring strip is kept ½ inch off the concrete floor. The vertical strips are spaced to accept the rigid panels and sheets of drywall. They are secured to the wall with 1¾-inch concrete nails. Some place a dab of mastic in several locations on the strips. If the basement has windows or an exterior door, the furring strip is installed around them (**6–20**).

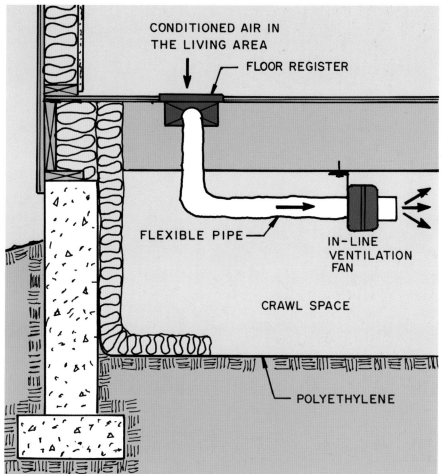

CONDITIONED AIR IN
THE LIVING AREA

FLOOR REGISTER

FLEXIBLE PIPE

IN-LINE
VENTILATION
FAN

CRAWL SPACE

POLYETHYLENE

6–18. The air in the crawl space can be ventilated by an inflow of conditioned air from the living area.

The rigid insulation must be covered with ½-inch drywall or some other fire-resistant material to meet fire codes. This is required because the plastic foam presents a fire and smoke hazard. Since drywall panels are 4 × 8 feet, the furring must be spaced so the edge of each sheet of drywall extends to the center of each furring strip (6–21). Notice that the 1 × 2 inch furring strip is only 1½ inches wide, so the drywall has only a ¾-inch nailing surface. This is enough to install it properly; however, the 1 × 3 strip is actually 2½ inches wide, which gives you a 1¼-wide nailing surface. This gives a little room for error in installing the furring strips. A 2 × 4 inch furring strip installed with the wide side on the wall will give a 3½-inch-wide nailing surface.

The rigid panels are cut to fit firmly against the furring. They are bonded to the masonry wall with manufacturer-recommended mastic or construction adhesive. It must be moisture-resistant. Place the adhesive on the back of the panel in the pattern recommended by the manufacturer. One frequently used pattern is shown in 6–22.

The rim joist must be insulated. One way is shown in 6–19. Look at other suggestions in the section on insulating crawl spaces in this chapter.

Another installation method used is to install the rigid insulation horizontally. The horizontal furring is applied to suit the width of the insulation panel. The vertical furring strips are installed so the edge of the

6–19. Basement walls to be insulated with rigid foam insulation have wood furring strips nailed to the foundation and the insulation is placed between them. The gypsum drywall is nailed to the furring. Notice that the rim joist must be insulated.

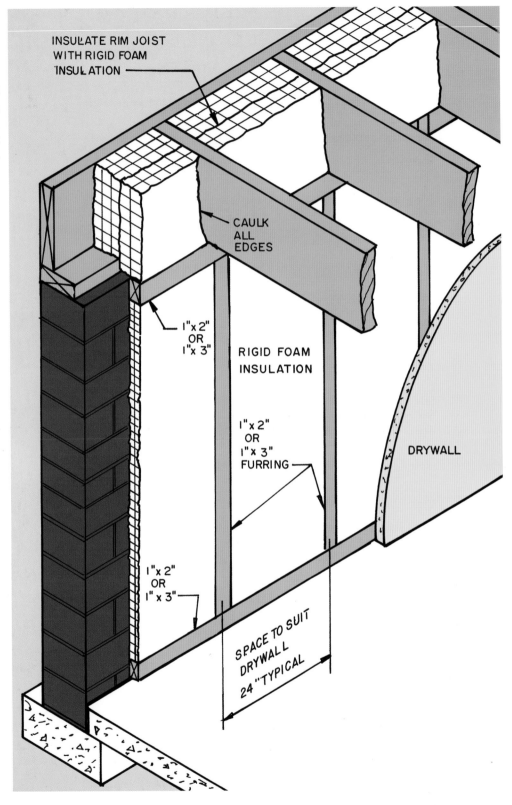

INSULATE RIM JOIST WITH RIGID FOAM INSULATION

CAULK ALL EDGES

1"x 2" OR 1"x 3"

RIGID FOAM INSULATION

1"x 2" OR 1"x 3" FURRING

DRYWALL

1"x 2" OR 1"x 3"

SPACE TO SUIT DRYWALL 24 "TYPICAL

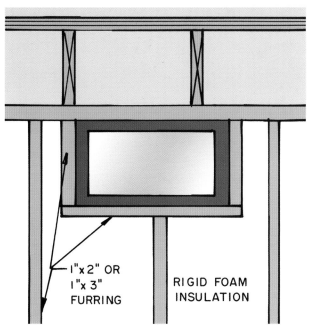

6–20. Install furring strips around windows and doors in the foundation so gypsum drywall can be secured around them.

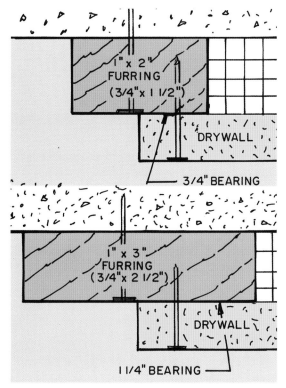

6–21. Space the furring strips so the gypsum drywall has at least a ¾-inch bearing surface.

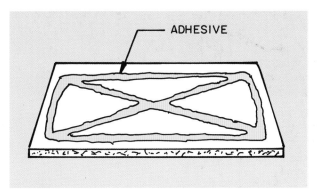

6–22. Manufacturer-recommended mastic or adhesive is applied to the back of the rigid foam panel in a pattern recommended by the manufacturer. This is one example.

drywall panel falls on the center of the vertical panel. This means they are placed 24 inches center to center (6–23). The drywall is nailed to the horizontal and vertical furring.

Since rigid foam insulation is moisture-resistant, a vapor barrier is not usually installed over it.

Another approach to insulating the foundation with rigid foam panels is to bond the panels to the foundation with an approved adhesive. This provides moisture control as well as insulation. Then place 1×2 or 1×3-inch wood furring strips over the insulation and secure them to the masonry wall with power-actuated concrete nails. They must be long enough to go through the furring and insulation and into the masonry. The drywall is then secured to the furring strips (6–24).

INSULATING WITH FIBERGLASS BLANKETS

It is important that the masonry will be waterproofed and dry. If it gets moist or moist interior air gets to it, condensation will form and mold will develop inside the wall.

Basement walls can be insulated with 1×2-inch furring spaced to hold special fiberglass blankets designed for this purpose. They are unfaced blankets ¾ and 1¾ inches thick. They are pressure-fit between the furring as shown in 6–25. They are covered with a 6-mil polyethylene vapor barrier and drywall. R-values range from 3 to 6.

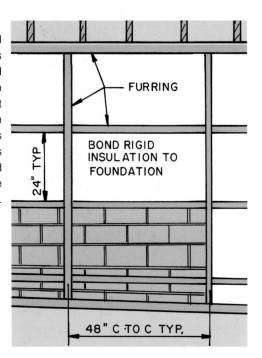

6–23. These rigid foam panels are installed horizontally. Plan the furring layout so the gypsum wallboard has nailing surfaces on the edges and center of the panel.

FURRING

BOND RIGID INSULATION TO FOUNDATION

24" TYP.

48" C TO C TYP.

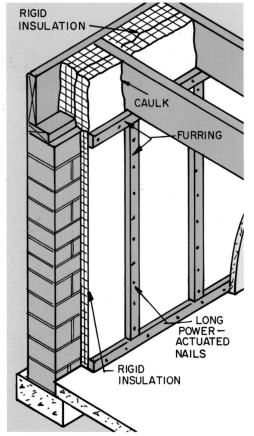

6–24. Some people prefer to bond the rigid foam insulation to the masonry and install the furring on top.

RIGID INSULATION

CAULK

FURRING

LONG POWER–ACTUATED NAILS

RIGID INSULATION

6–25. These unfaced fiberglass blankets are pressure-fit between wood furring nailed to the foundation. They are covered with 6-mil polyethylene and gypsum wallboard. *(Courtesy CertainTeed Corporation)*

If the basement is to be used for storage and finished walls are not required, fiberglass masonry wall insulation is available in widths of 48 and 72 inches that have an R-value of 11. They are stapled to the wood plate on top of the masonry wall (6–26). The blankets have either a white reinforced polypropylene or reinforced foil facing. They do not need a fire-resistant covering.

As with other types of insulation, some people apply a waterproofing paint on the masonry wall or bond a sheet of polyethylene on it with mastic.

BUILDING A STUD WALL

To get R-values similar to these in stud-framed exterior walls, install a standard stud wall over the foundation. This typically uses 2 × 4-inch studs, but 2 × 6 studs will give space for thicker insulation. When the wall runs perpendicular to the overhead joist, the top plate is

6–26. These fiberglass blankets are designed to insulate foundation walls in areas where they will not need to be covered with a finish wall material. *(Courtesy CertainTeed Corporation)*

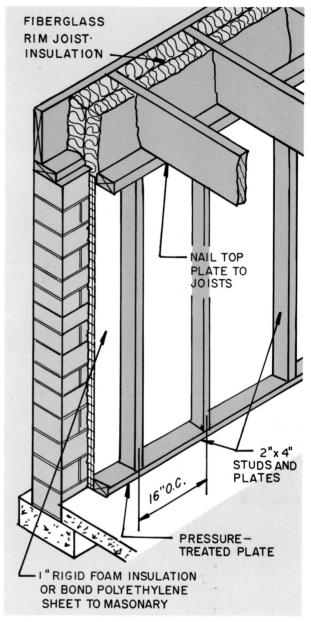

FIBERGLASS RIM JOIST INSULATION

NAIL TOP PLATE TO JOISTS

2"x 4" STUDS AND PLATES

16"O.C.

PRESSURE-TREATED PLATE

1" RIGID FOAM INSULATION OR BOND POLYETHYLENE SHEET TO MASONARY

6–27. The stud wall is set next to the foundation over rigid insulation or polyethylene bonded to the wall. This wall is running perpendicular to the joists, so the top plate is nailed to the joists.

nailed to them (**6–27**). If it runs parallel to the joists, blocking must be installed to which the top plate is nailed (**6–28**).

The insulation is installed in the same way as frame exterior walls. The vapor barrier will face the basement because it will be the warmer side (**6–29**). Either faced or unfaced insulation is covered with a 6–mil polyethylene vapor barrier. The vapor barrier faces the basement. The wall is then covered with ½-inch gypsum wallboard. Review the information on insulating exterior walls.

Before you install the insulation blankets, the wiring and electric boxes for switches and outlets must be installed. Install outlet boxes with the bottom 12 inches above the floor. Bore holes for the wire at least 12 inches above the box and at least 1¼ inches in from the back edge of the stud (**6–30**). Run the wires through the

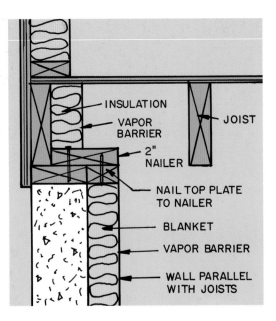

6–28. When the framed wall runs parallel with the joists, blocking is installed to provide a nailer for the top plate.

INSULATION

VAPOR BARRIER

JOIST

2" NAILER

NAIL TOP PLATE TO NAILER

BLANKET

VAPOR BARRIER

WALL PARALLEL WITH JOISTS

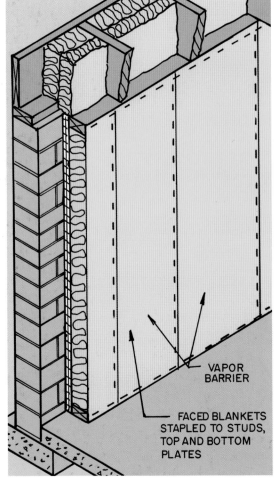

6–29. Either faced or unfaced blankets can be used. The vapor barrier must face the basement.

VAPOR BARRIER

FACED BLANKETS STAPLED TO STUDS, TOP AND BOTTOM PLATES

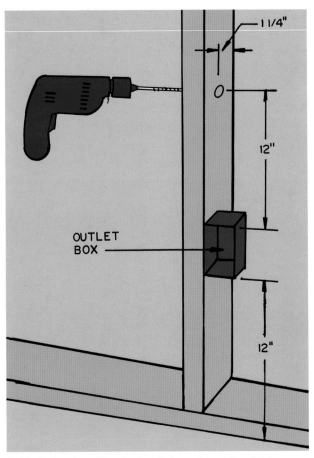

1 1/4"

12"

12"

OUTLET BOX

6–30. Before installing the insulation, place all outlet boxes and run all wires.

holes in the studs and into the boxes (**6–31**). Be certain to follow electric codes or have a licensed electrician do the job.

Next, install the insulation so it fits behind and around the box. Then, after the drywall has been installed, caulk the crack between the box and the edges of the drywall (**6–32**). See Chapter 2 for more information on sealing openings to prevent air leaks around electric outlet boxes.

When you install drywall over the insulated wall, cut it ¾ inch short of the floor so moisture from the concrete floor does not wick up into the edge of the drywall. You could put a plastic vapor barrier on the floor under the bottom plate and drywall. Consider using a pressure-treated bottom plate.

INSULATING WITH SPRAYED FOAM

Masonry walls are also effectively insulated with sprayed foam. The foam sticks to masonry and makes sealing and insulating basement and crawl-space walls very effective. It can be sprayed directly on the wall, as shown in **6–33**. If the wall is to be finished with drywall, a wood stud wall can be built next to the foundation and the foam sprayed between the studs (**6–34**). This work must be performed by certified contractors. See additional information in this chapter.

6–33. This concrete block basement wall is being insulated by spraying foam insulation directly on it.
(Courtesy North Carolina Foam Industries)

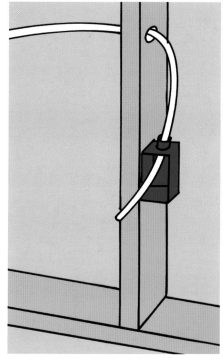

6–31. Run wires in the holes drilled in the studs and pull through each outlet box.

6–34. This basement wall will have a drywall finish material. A wood frame wall has been built next to it and the cavity is being filled with foam insulation.
(Courtesy North Carolina Foam Industries)

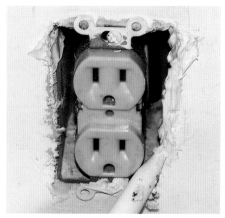

6–32. After the drywall has been installed, caulk the crack between the outlet box and the drywall.

7

HOME VENTILATION

Over the past few years, emphasis has been placed on building "tight" houses. This refers to construction in which air leaks are sealed. (Review Chapter 2 for information on air leaks.) Older houses typically allowed natural air leakage which served as the ventilation system for the house. Poorly fitted doors and windows and gaps in wall construction are typical examples. These areas tended to allow fresh air to infiltrate the home, but the air was not controlled. They also allowed air pollutants, moisture, and odors to flow to the outside, but this too was uncontrolled. Older houses therefore had excessive heat loss in the winter and heat gain in the summer. This increased energy costs. They also had cold drafts that made living a bit uncomfortable.

To get the most comfortable and healthy living environment, tight houses need a controlled ventilation system which allows the occupant to decide when ventilation is needed to purify the air and how much is needed. This ventilation system should also control ventilation in special areas such as the bath and kitchen, which have more severe problems than most other areas of the house.

Ventilation systems not only provide better-quality indoor air, but can reduce damage to the house. If the windows have condensation, mold, and mildew forms, odors remain for hours and the paint begins to peel, this indicates the level of humidity is high and ventilation is needed.

Indoor air pollution is a major health risk for the occupants. Air pollution is in higher concentrations indoors than outdoors. Typical problems include formaldehyde in the glue in old laminated and pressed wood products. Some products have eliminated this problem. Other pollu-

tants include various cleaning products, new cabinets, aerosol spray, solvents, carpet, wood stoves, radon, wood-burning fireplaces, some types of insulation, kerosene heaters, and unvented or malfunctioning heater units. Carbon monoxide is a frequent killer.

Symptoms of polluted air include nausea, vomiting, skin rashes, headaches, respiratory inflammation, fatigue, and dizziness. Long-term exposure can lead to a variety of health problems.

■ Codes for Ventilating the Living Area

As you plan a new house or get into a remodeling project, it is important to consider how ventilation to the living area will be provided. The first thing to do is consult the local building code. Local codes are usually based on the International Residential Code for One- and Two-Family Dwellings. The older codes—BOCA National Codes, SBCCI Standard Codes and ICBO Uniform Codes—have been merged with the International Residential Code. This code when followed ensures that the quality of the indoor air meets minimum requirements by supplying an adequate quantity of fresh outdoor air.

The industry standards established by the American Society of Heating, Refigeration and Air-Conditioning Engineers (ASHRAE) provide the primary reference for residential ventilation. They are recorded in the standard, ASHRAE-62, Ventilation for Acceptable Indoor Air Quality. This requires a minimum inflow of fresh outdoor air to be 15 cubic feet per minute per person in the room and a minimum overall air change of 0.35 air changes per hour in living areas. This standard also provides procedures to obtain acceptable indoor air quality by using the Ventilation Rate Procedure (VRP) and Indoor Air Quality Procedure (IAQP), which relates to controlling contaminants within the air space. The VRP specifies the rate at which outdoor air should be delivered to the interior space. The requirements for outdoor air requirements specified in ASHRAE-62 are in **Table 7–1**.

Codes allow habitable rooms in residences to have natural ventilation provided by glazed areas equal to 4 to 8 percent of the floor area. Where this is not available, mechanical ventilation is required. Generally, the code requires a system capable of supplying 15 cubic feet per minute per occupant typically expected to use the room. In addition to a mechanical ventilation system designed for one room, a whole house ventilation can supply the same fresh air requirements.

■ Overview of Ventilation Systems

The ventilation system needs an **exhaust system** to vent pollution, odors, and moisture and a **fresh air system** to bring in new air. Rooms that have odors and high moisture, such as the kitchen and bath, require special exhaust systems and can receive fresh air from an inflow or whole-house fresh-air system. Other rooms such as bedrooms, living and dining rooms, and recreation areas will be on the whole-house ventilation system.

Whatever ventilation system is used, the air inlets and exhaust outlets are placed within the house to produce natural airflow patterns from the inlets to the exhaust outlets.

Natural ventilation in old houses is through leaks in the doors, windows, and walls. In new tight houses, natural ventilation is provided by opening windows and doors and the use of passive ventilators. Natural ventilation depends a great deal on the differences in pressure in the house and the outside caused by wind and differences in temperature between the indoors and outdoors. The pressure difference causes inflow and outflow of the air in the house.

Mechanical ventilation uses various powered fan units to induce airflow from inside the house to the exterior and airflow of outside air into the house.

■ Passive Ventilation

Passive ventilation is provided by various devices such as vents through the wall. They provide a natural flow of outside air into the house, as well as a means of moving stale inside air to the outside. They are very small openings that permit only a small, easily controlled airflow and therefore do not create a draft. They provide greater

TABLE 7–1.

OUTDOOR AIR REQUIREMENTS FOR VENTILATION OF RESIDENTIAL BUILDINGS (ASHRAE-62)

Application	Outdoor Air Requirements
Living Areas	0.35 ACH* but not less than 15 cfm* (7.5 L/s**) per person
Kitchens	100 cfm*** (50 L/s) intermittent or 25 cfm (12 L/s) continuous or openable windows
Baths, Toilets	50 cfm (25 L/s) intermittent or 20 cfm (10 L/s) continuous, or openable windows for each bath and toilet
Garage Separate from Dwelling	100 cfm (50 L/s) per car

ASHRAE 62 (c) American Society of Heating, Refrigerating and Air-Conditioning Engineers, Inc., www.ashrae.org.

*ACH refers to air changes per hour   **L/s refers to liters per second

***cfm refers to cubic feet per minute

security to those in the house as compared to having open windows, and will not let rain enter the house.

These passive through-wall air inlets are generally not used if the house has a forced-air heating/cooling system. What occurs is that the forced airflow into a room builds up air pressure and will cause air to vent to the outside rather than flow into the room. Other air inflow systems are available for use in houses with forced-air heating/cooling systems.

Passive ventilating devices may be manually adjusted to control the airflow; be self-regulating by reacting to changes in temperature, air pressure or humidity; or be fixed, permitting no closing of the venting unit.

A typical passive through-the-wall venting air inlet with no means of regulating airflow is shown in **7–1**. This unit provides continuous airflow. It would seldom be used to provide a source of fresh air to a living area.

Passive through-wall fresh air outlets that have con-

trols to self-regulate the airflow may have a self-regulating damper or be controlled by a humidity sensor that controls a damper. A unit with a self-regulating damper that is mounted through the wall with a round adjustable sleeve is shown in **7–2**. It has accessories that facilitate installation on bevel siding. A rectangular version mounts through a 1¾-inch-wide slot in the wall (**7–3**). The exterior has a hooded grille and insect screen. The flow of air controlled by a self-regulating grille that deflects the air upwards. A fresh-air inlet unit controlled by a humidity sensor is shown in **7–4**. It automatically adjusts the inflow of fresh air according to the interior air humidity level in each room in which one is installed.

Generally, these units are installed near the ceiling, which allows the fresh air to move across the room and avoids any draft on the occupants.

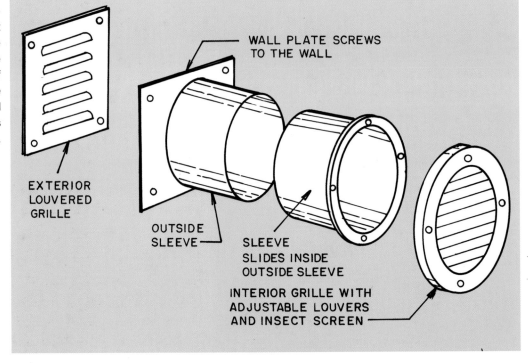

7–1. A typical through-wall air inlet does not allow control of the airflow. It is adjustable to go through walls of varying thickness. Be certain to caulk around it where it penetrates the wall.

EXTERIOR LOUVERED GRILLE

WALL PLATE SCREWS TO THE WALL

OUTSIDE SLEEVE

SLEEVE SLIDES INSIDE OUTSIDE SLEEVE

INTERIOR GRILLE WITH ADJUSTABLE LOUVERS AND INSECT SCREEN

7–2. This round, self-regulating fresh air inlet has a plastic damper that automatically adjusts the free opening to provide a draft-free regulated amount of incoming air independent of wind pressure.
(Courtesy American ALDES Ventilation Corporation)

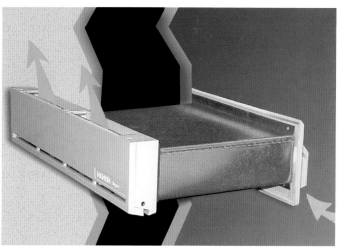

7–4. This humidity controlled fresh air inlet automatically adjusts the incoming airflow according to the interior humidity levels. The makeup air is modulated according to the need of the room in which the unit is installed.
(Courtesy American ALDES Ventilation Corporation)

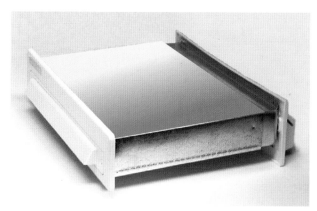

7–3. This rectangular self-regulating fresh-air inlet has an airflow regulating damper on the interior side. The interior grille also deflects the airflow upwards, producing draft free fresh air. *(Courtesy American ALDES Ventilation Corporation)*

■ Mechanical Ventilation

Mechanical ventilation can be as simple and inexpensive as the use of any of the various types of fans available. Another type uses fan units and ducts to vent specific appliances, such as a range, or a room such as a bathroom. A complete whole-house system is a complex arrangement of heat- or energy-recovery units and ducts to the exterior and rooms.

FANS

Natural ventilation can be enhanced by the use of ceiling fans, window fans, and small, portable fans. They move more air, providing a more comfortable situation. If **ceiling fans** are used (**7–5** and **7–6**), install one in each room. They should hang 10 or 12 inches below the ceiling. A typical room will require a fan with a 36- to 44-inch-diameter blade. They are controlled by a variable-speed switch, so the amount of airflow can be controlled. Some people prefer to have it blow down in the summer and up toward the ceiling in the winter. In the winter, they are not used for cooling but to move the heated air that rises to the ceiling down the walls to the floor. Typically, the fan will be run on the slowest speed

7–5. Ceiling fans are very useful in distributing the air in a room so the overall temperature is uniform. They are used in the summer and winter. In the winter, some people like to set them to blow up toward the ceiling. In summer, they can be set to blow down into the room.

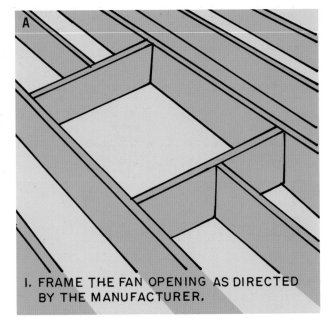

I. FRAME THE FAN OPENING AS DIRECTED BY THE MANUFACTURER.

7–6. Ceiling fans should be controlled by a variable-speed switch mounted in the typical electric outlet box.

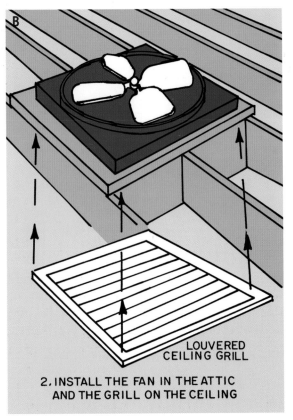

LOUVERED CEILING GRILL

2. INSTALL THE FAN IN THE ATTIC AND THE GRILL ON THE CEILING

because you do not want a draft. In older houses, the ceiling light can be replaced with a fan. Some fans have a light on the bottom, so the room still has a light. In new homes, the same installation can be made.

Whole-house fans are large exhaust fans centrally located in the living area (**7–7**). They are mounted in the ceiling and vent into the attic. They pull fresh outside air into the house through open windows (**7–8**). In addition to changing the air in the house, they provide excellent attic

7–7. A large whole-house ventilation fan is mounted in the ceiling in a central location. This is an older type and is noisy.

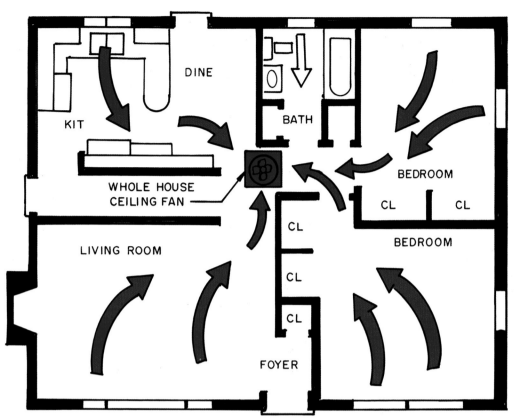

7–8. Large ceiling-mounted whole-house fans pull air from every room in which a window has been opened. They require more louver area in the attic than is needed for natural-air attic ventilation.

ventilation. The flow of air can be regulated by varying the speed of the fan with a variable-speed switch (refer to **7–6**). The cooling can be varied where needed by adjusting the size of the window opening. For example, at night the bedroom windows can be opened and those in the living room closed or at least almost closed. Fans of various capacities are available. Typically, they range in sizes providing 30 to 60 air changes per hour. This varies with the house and climate. A heating and air-conditioning consultant can determine what is best for a house. If you have no air-conditioning, a larger-capacity fan will be recommended. In cooler northern climates, a smaller fan can be used. To size a fan, find the cubic feet of space you want to cool. To do this, multiply the square feet of the areas to be cooled by the height of the ceiling and divide by 60 minutes. This will give the number of cubic feet per minute the fan must cool.

Since a large volume of air is vented into the attic, the amount of attic ventilation must be greatly increased. Depending upon the volume of air moved, the venting should be two or three times that for normal attic ventilation. One square foot of attic ventilation will handle about 750 cubic feet per minute.

Since the fan pulls unfiltered outside air into the house, it will bring in dust, insects, and pollen. Some types of filters should be placed in the window opening. Some people install furnace air-return filters, but these do not do a perfect job.

The fan opening in the ceiling is a big air leak at times when the house is on air-conditioning or heating. While the fan has louvers that open when it is on and close when it is off, considerable air leakage occurs. Plan to have some type of tight sealing cover to go over the fan opening.

Fans will large motors and blades are noisy. Mount the fan to the framed ceiling opening with rubber gaskets to reduce the vibrations from entering the ceiling joists. The fan is quieter if run on slow speeds.

A quiet, energy-efficient whole-house fan is shown in **7–9**. It has two fans which run at variable speeds and a motorized dual-door assembly which seals it, so there are no air leaks. It is installed in an opening framed in the ceiling (**7–10**) and the unit is placed in it and is mounted on gaskets to dampen noise vibrations (**7–11**). All that is visible is a louvered grille on the ceiling (**7–12**).

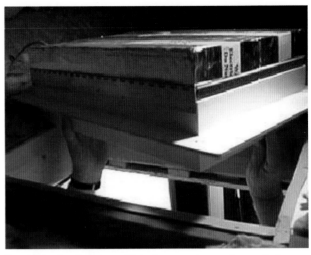

7–11. The fan is lowered into the opening and mounted on manufacturer-supplied gaskets, which dampen vibration.

7–9. This highly efficient whole-house fan is mounted in the ceiling. It has two small-diameter fans and runs very quiet. It also has motorized doors which open when it starts and close when it stops sealing all air leaks.
(Courtesy Tamarack Technologies, Inc.)

7–12. The fan is covered by a louvered grille, which blends in with the finished ceiling. *(Courtesy Tamarack Technologies, Inc.)*

Another small motorized ventilator is shown in **7–13**. It is designed for use in ventilating sunrooms, solariums, greenhouses, and other similar spaces. It has a low profile when not running and has a motorized lift on the cover which opens when it runs. It is adapted for use on solid roof installations over spaces such as a loft or balcony room.

The fan in **7–14** is a wall-mounted in-line exhaust fan that is connected to a vent grille in the ceiling (**7–15**). The fan unit is installed inside the exterior wall and all that shows on the exterior of the house is a small

7–10. The whole-house fan is mounted in an opening framed in the ceiling. *(Courtesy Tamarack Technologies, Inc.)*

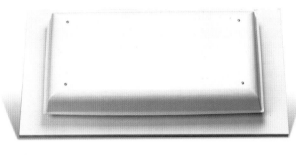

7-13. This small motorized ventilator is used on sunrooms, greenhouses, and other glass-enclosed spaces (*Courtesy Tamarack Technologies, Inc.*)

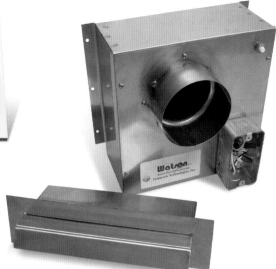

7-14. This in-line exhaust fan is mounted in the wall and vents through a grille in the ceiling.

(Courtesy Tamarack Technologies, Inc.)

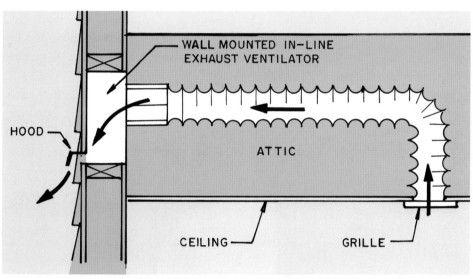

7-15. The wall-mounted in-line exhaust ventilator is connected to a grille in the room to be vented.

(Courtesy Tamarack Technologies Inc.)

hood. It is used for exhaust vents such as commonly used in bathrooms. Airflow from a hall or other rooms is needed to vent the room. Since the fan is in the exterior wall, the sound level in the room is low.

The ceiling ventilation fans described in the sections on bathroom and kitchen ventilation that follow are other examples of exhaust-only systems.

The through-the-wall direct exhaust unit shown in **7-16** moves 100 cubic feet per minute. It is mounted in the exterior wall and used to ventilate a room. When turned on, a cover motor pushes the cover open, forming

7-16. This through-the-wall power ventilator will vent any type of space. The cover opens and closes automatically as the fan starts and stops.

(Courtesy Tamarack Technologies, Inc.)

7–17. This unit provides filtered fresh air to the house interior. It moves the air through ducts to four rooms. Since it is in the attic, very little fan noise reaches the room. The venting hood is small and not noticeable. *(Courtesy Tamarack Technologies, Inc.)*

a hood. When the fan is turned off, the cover motor pulls the cover closed, tightly sealing the exterior opening. The room should have an inflow of air from other rooms in the house. A fresh-air supply system is an effective and inexpensive way to meet the needs for an inflow of fresh air.

■ Fresh-Air Supply Systems

Houses need a steady supply of fresh outside air if they are built airtight. This is especially needed if a number of exhaust-only fans are in use. The unit in **7–17** directs fresh air through ducts to four locations. It has a large intake duct on the exterior wall. The internal fan pulls the air through replaceable filters. The low-velocity air exits from grilles mounted six inches below the room ceiling, where it blends with the air in the room. It can be run continuously or wired to other fans, such as a bathroom fan, and operates when they run. This provides a positive pressure, which helps with the exhaust process (**7–18**).

■ Bathroom Ventilation

Plumbing codes specify that a bathroom must have a window that can be opened or some form of mechanical ventilation. Actually, even if you have a window, it is a good idea to put in an exhaust fan, because the window is seldom opened. The fan running for around 30 minutes during a shower will carry the air with high moisture content out of the room and return the moisture content to normal. If you do not remove moisture, windows will sweat and mildew will form on interior sur-

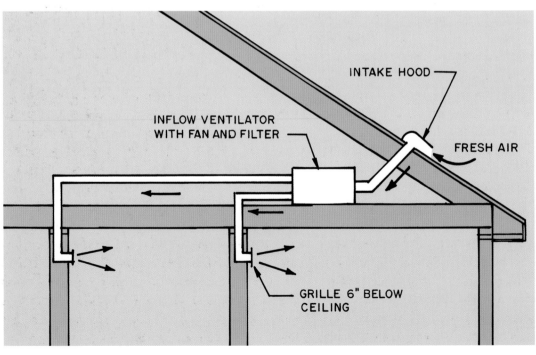

INTAKE HOOD

INFLOW VENTILATOR
WITH FAN AND FILTER

FRESH AIR

GRILLE 6" BELOW
CEILING

7–18. A fresh air-supply system moves outside air through a filter and to rooms through ducts.

faces, causing a smell and the paint and wallpaper to deteriorate. Hopefully, the exterior wall has a vapor barrier to keep the moisture from entering it and damaging the insulation, studs, sheathing, and exterior siding.

Check the local building code for ventilation requirements. Typically, they require a window to provide 1.5 square feet of open area or a ventilation fan that provides eight air changes per hour.

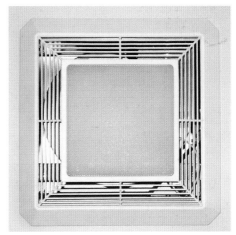

7–19. This bathroom ceiling vent has a light and ventilating louvers around it.

SELECTING THE FAN SIZE

Codes typically require that a bathroom fan should provide eight air changes per hour. To select a fan that will move this much air, first calculate the cubic feet in the bathroom. For example, if the bathroom measures eight by ten feet and has an eight-foot ceiling, multiply these to get the capacity This bathroom has $8 \times 10 \times 8 = 640$ cubic feet. Since 8 changes per hour are required, multiply 640×8 to get 5,120 cubic feet per hour to be moved. Fan capacities are given in cubic feet per minute, so divide 5,120 by 60 minutes and you get 85.3 cubic feet per minute. The fan selected should move at least 85.3 cubic feet of air per minute.

A frequently used ventilation system uses a single fan in the ceiling of the bathroom. There are a variety of units available. Some contain a light and fan (**7–19**), while others will have a fan, light, and electric heater (**7–20**). The heater provides a rapid source of localized heat to warm a person after they step out of the shower. Some people prefer to have the light and fan be activated whenever the wall switch is turned on. Others do not want the fan fanning every time they step into the bathroom, so each has its own switch.

There are bathroom fans that have automatic humidity and motion sensors and a night light. The humidity sensor starts the fan when it senses excess moisture in the air and turns off when the moisture level returns to normal. The most commonly used fan control is a timer switch. You can set the time to allow the ventilating fan to run a predetermined number of minutes after you leave the room. Usually a 30-minute run will remove most of the excess moisture.

To operate efficiently, the fan needs a steady volume of air that is not available if the bathroom door fits tightly

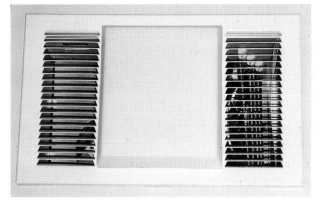

7–20. This bathroom ceiling vent has a light, ventilating louvers, and electric heat.

to the floor. Leave ½ to ¾ inch of space at the floor.

Some fans run quieter than others. Noisy fans can be heard all over the house and this can be annoying. Select a fan with a low sone rating. A **sone** is a unit of loudness. Select a fan with a sone rating of 2 or less.

A single ventilating fan has a duct that runs from the side of the fan to an outside wall and vents into the soffit (**7–21**). Since the soffit has a continuous vent used to move air into the attic, if the bathroom vent discharges air here this moist air will likely be moved into the attic where it can cause damage. The best solution is to run all vents through the roof (**7–22**). The ducts should be smooth inside and avoid turns because this slows down the air and reduces the amount of flow.

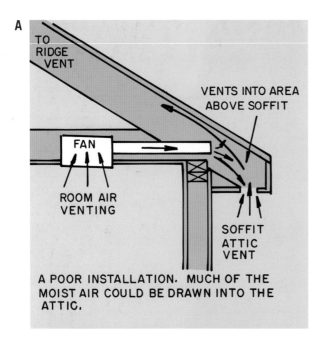

A

TO RIDGE VENT

VENTS INTO AREA ABOVE SOFFIT

FAN

ROOM AIR VENTING

SOFFIT ATTIC VENT

A POOR INSTALLATION. MUCH OF THE MOIST AIR COULD BE DRAWN INTO THE ATTIC.

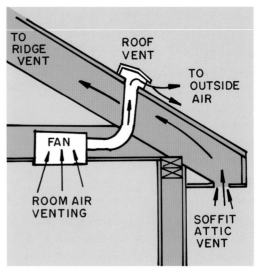

TO RIDGE VENT

ROOF VENT

TO OUTSIDE AIR

FAN

ROOM AIR VENTING

SOFFIT ATTIC VENT

7–22. The most effective way to vent a bathroom ceiling fan is through the roof. This is more expensive but is a good installation.

(Courtesy Tamarack Technologies, Inc.)

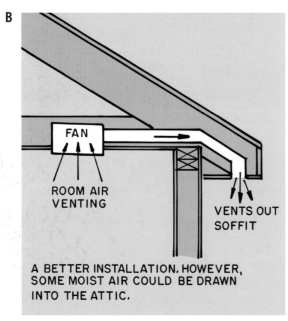

B

FAN

ROOM AIR VENTING

VENTS OUT SOFFIT

A BETTER INSTALLATION. HOWEVER, SOME MOIST AIR COULD BE DRAWN INTO THE ATTIC.

7–21. When bathroom ceiling fans are vented into the soffit, often a large amount of the moist air flows into the attic.

Roof vents are available in kits which contain everything needed to install the vent, including directions (7–23). The flexible pipe is held to a round pipe in the bottom of the vent cover. Most kits supply a plastic strip to hold the flexible pipe to the vent pipe. This is adequate and will possibly create a leak. The use of automotive hose clamps provides a better connection (7–24). Always seal the connection with duct tape, as shown in 7–25.

Since most houses have several bathrooms, it is a good practice to ventilate them with a central exhaust ventilator (7–26). These units are quiet and are mounted in the attic, so the fan noise is not noticed in the bathroom (7–27). The central unit can serve several bathrooms, and all that appears in the ceiling is the vent grille (7–28). The unit should be vented through the roof. The manufacturer provides recommended installation instructions and fan-capacity data. The fan can be operated manually, automatically by a programmable time-of-day timer, dehumidistat, or run continuously. The airflow from each room can be regulated by manually adjusting the vanes in the ceiling grille or with preset air-

7–23. This is a typical roof vent kit.

7–25. The flexible, expansive duct is clamped to the pipe in the bottom of the vent cover. The end of the duct is sealed to the pipe with duct tape.

7–24. It is recommended that the duct be connected to the pipe below the roof vent with an auto-hose clamp. Then wrap it with duct tape.

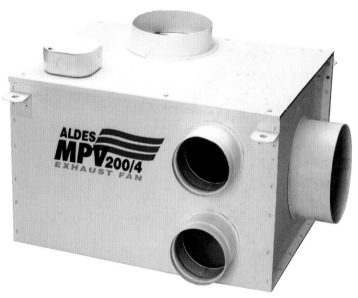

7–26. A central exhaust ventilator is mounted in the attic and is very quiet. It can ventilate several bathrooms. *(Courtesy Matthews Graphic Design-American ALDES Ventilation Corporation.)*

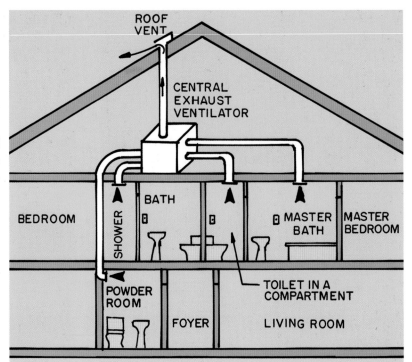

7–27. Flexible ducts run from the central exhaust ventilator to the various bathrooms. It is vented through the roof.

ROOF VENT

CENTRAL EXHAUST VENTILATOR

BEDROOM

SHOWER

BATH

MASTER BATH

MASTER BEDROOM

POWDER ROOM

TOILET IN A COMPARTMENT

FOYER

LIVING ROOM

BATH 1   MASTER BATH   BATH 4

BATH 2   BATH 3

7–28. Flexible ducts run from the exhaust ventilator to ceiling grilles in each bathroom and the exhaust vent runs from the top of the unit out of the roof.

flow regulators. This central exhaust ventilator can also be used to change the air in other rooms and provide different cubic foot airflow capacities in each room.

■ Kitchen Ventilation

Adequate ventilation of the heat and fumes generated by cooking activities is very important. Cooking activities generate moisture, odors, fumes, and grease in the air that cling to the cabinets, walls, ceiling, curtains, flooring, and other exposed items. Range hoods are commonly used to dispense these pollutants (7–29). There are available a wide variety of hoods, and the choice partially has to do with how you want the hood to influence the appearance of the kitchen. The hood in 7–30 is shallow and fits up against the cabinet. When in use, it slides out as far as necessary to cover the range. In 7–31, the hood is a standard depth but is covered to match the cabinets, so it is not noticed. Island counters with a cooktop or range are popular and also require a hood (7–32) or a downdraft unit. The hood forms an attractive architectural feature along with the cabinets.

7–29. A hood is an effective way to remove fumes produced as foods are cooked on a range or surface unit.

7–30. This hood shows only a narrow edge. It is pushed under the cabinet and is pulled out to cover the range when needed.

7–31. The hood has been blended in with the cabinets by banding it with wood that matches the cabinets.

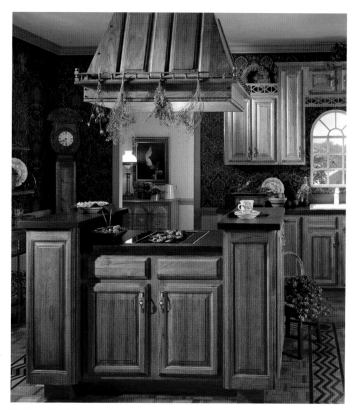

7–32. This island cabinet contains a cooktop. An attractive hood vents the fumes and is a dominant element in the design of the kitchen. *(Courtesy Wellborn Cabinet, Inc.)*

HOOD FAN CAPACITIES

To achieve satisfactory removal of the fumes from cooking, the hood fan must have adequate capacity to move the amount of air needed to completely exhaust them. Air movement is rated in cubic feet per minute (cfm). The recommended capacity of a range hood for use with residential ranges and cooktops varies, depending upon the association making the recommendations and the hood manufacturer. Typically, a hood over a range in a residence should move 40 to 60 cfm per lineal foot of hood. The hood should extend three inches beyond the ends of the range or cooktop. Since ranges are generally 30 inches long, a 36-inch hood would be recommended. A 30-inch hood would be usable on most cooktops. The fan capacity for this installation would be 3.0 ft. 3 40 = 120 cfm up to 30 ft. 3 60 = 180 cfm. In general, a fan capacity of 150 cfm is widely used as a standard. Hoods over island counters require a larger ventilating capacity. Typically, 180 to 200 cfm is recommended. Ranges and cooktops with downdraft ventilating systems have the same fan capacity recommendations as hoods (7–33). Downdraft units pull the air down and do not need a hood.

When you are buying a hood, the rating should be clearly marked on the label. If a larger professional-type range is installed, it will generate considerably more heat than the typical residential range. It will need a larger and more powerful hood to pull off the heat and cooking odors and vapors (7–34).

The selection of the capacity of the roof cap or wall hood is important to the efficient performance of the hood fan. The net-free area of the passage where the air is most restricted should be at least 1.5 square inch per 10 cfm of fan capacity. This provides the minimum required vent area to handle the airflow from the hood.

RANGE HOODS

Range hoods are effective in removing the fumes generated by cooking. There are a wide range of units available, so a study of the capabilities is important. Some have a single-speed fan motor, while others have controls that vary the fan speed, which is helpful because the need for exhaust will vary greatly depending upon the type and intensity of cooking.

Range hoods remove the pollutants and exhaust them to the outdoors. They also provide a light for the range (7–35). They have aluminum mesh filters that trap grease and are removed and cleaned with normal detergents (7–36).

Another type filters the air from cooking and recycles it back into the room (7–37). This uses filters that must be removed and cleaned. One type holds a microwave and also filters the air, returning it to the room (7–38).

While hoods serve as an air-purifying feature, they also can be used to produce a dynamic design feature in the kitchen, as shown by the cabinet and hood installation in 7–32 and 7–39.

7–33. Downdraft cooking units have ventilating grills on the surface and pull the fumes down into the vent duct.

7–34. Large professional ranges generate a lot of heat and, since larger cooking activities occur, require a larger and more powerful hood.

7–35. The hood provides excellent lighting of the range or surface unit.

7–38. This unit serves as a hood over the range and holds a microwave. The fumes run through a mesh filter and are vented above the microwave. *(Courtesy Sharp Electronics)*

7–36. Hoods use some form of mesh filter to trap grease. They are cleaned with a detergent that will cut grease.

7–37. Some hoods are not vented to the outside. They run the fumes through a filter on top of the hood and circulate the filtered air back into the room.

7–39. This hood is color-coordinated with the decorative cabinets that hold a cooking surface unit, making the installation a beautiful assembly of cabinets and hood. *(Courtesy Merillat Industries)*

RANGE AND COOKTOP HOOD INSTALLATION

Range hoods should discharge directly to the outside using a single wall duct that is smooth on the inside. All joints should be taped so the duct is airtight. Ducts must never discharge into a crawl space or attic.

The ducts should be stainless or galvanized steel or copper. Some codes permit downdraft systems to use polyvinyl chloride ducts and have detailed installation requirements. All hood installations must have a back-draft damper to block the flow of air from outside into the house and block any flow from inside the house to the outside when the fan is not in operation.

The installation of a hood over a range or cooktop requires at least 24 inches between the cooking surface and the hood (**7–40**). In some cases, they are placed a few inches closer. If a hood is not used, there

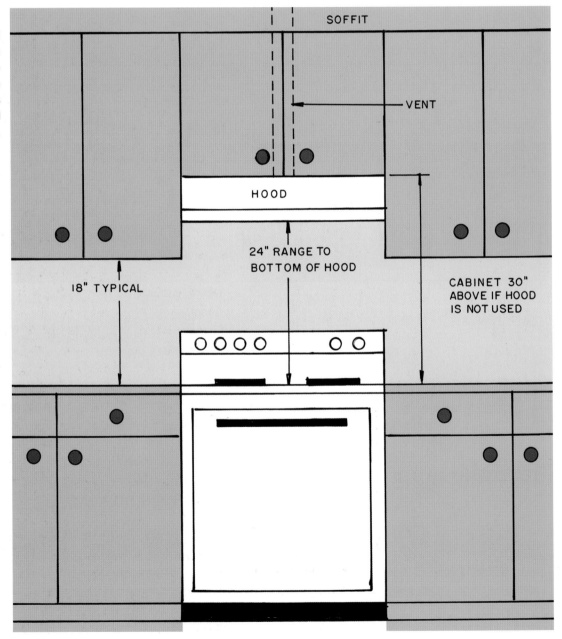

7–40. This hood should be 24 inches above the range. If no hood is used, the bottom of the cabinets over the range should be 30 inches.

should be at least 30 inches between the surface of the range and the bottom of the cabinet. Often a hood is used that will also carry a microwave. The recommended height will vary depending upon the recommendation of the hood manufacturer. If in doubt, leave 18 to 24 inches (**7–41**).

If the range is on an exterior wall, the easiest way to vent the hood is directly through the wall (**7–42**). This has the advantage of a short duct with no elbows. Any

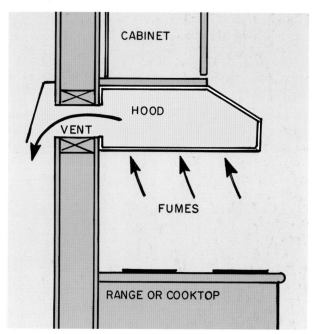

7–42. When the range is on an exterior wall, vent it directly through the wall.

changes in direction of the duct reduces the flow of air. A long duct also reduces airflow.

Possibly the most frequently used path for the ducts is through the soffit over the cabinets or between the ceiling joists (**7–43**). This system requires at least one elbow, but this is a minor obstruction to airflow (**7–44**). What is important is to be certain the length of the duct does not exceed 30 feet. If the length is longer, consider installing an in-line duct ventilation fan to boost the volume of airflow (**7–45**). If the duct is in the attic, it in many climates will be subjected to freezing temperatures. It should have a slope toward the outside wall, so any moisture that condenses drains away rather than possibly draining back into the fan in the hood. Also insulate the duct so the moisture is less likely to freeze. Selection of a good wall vent is important. It should have a backdraft louver which closes the pipe when the fan is not running. All duct joints should be sealed with aluminum-faced duct tape and caulk the places where the duct passes through the ceiling or wall.

Another way to vent a hood is through the roof (**7–46**). This provides a straight run (**7–47**). The cap should be one recommended by the hood manufacturer.

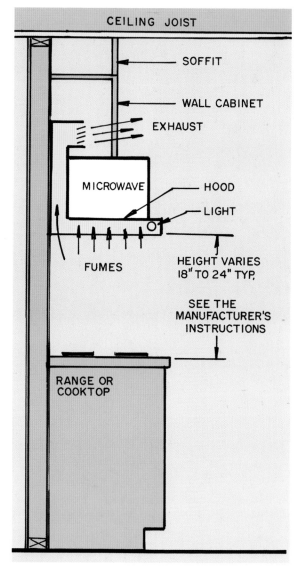

7–41. This ductless hood also carries the microwave.

7–43. This vent runs between the ceiling joists to an exterior wall. Notice that the fan is in the attic, which reduces noise in the kitchen.

(Courtesy Matthews Graphic Design-American ALDES Ventilation Corporation)

The roof cap should be installed following the directions that come with it, so a leak is not created.

Downdraft cooking units require a different plan for ventilation of the cooking fumes. While the hood just discussed pulls the fumes up from the cooking surface, the downdraft system draws in the fumes and pulls them down into the ventilating ducts. One type has a venting gill on the surface of the cooking unit, as shown in **7–33**, on page 170. The fumes are moved down and out ducts through the wall or below the floor (**7–48**). Another type of surface unit has a small raised panel across the back. It rises or tilts forward when the fan is turned on. When the fan is not running, it is lowered (**7–49**).

■ Clothes Dryer Exhaust

A clothes dryer generates a lot of moisture and lint. The dryer should have a filter that catches the lint (**7–50**). The exhaust duct should be sized and installed as directed by the dryer manufacturer. They must vent to the outside and should have a screen over the opening in the outside wall as well as a backdraft damper. The ducts should be smooth inside and have smooth connecting joints so airflow is not interrupted. They must be airtight. Ducts should not be longer than 25 feet and must be reduced in lengths of 45°or 90° in the duct. Again, observe the manufacturer's recommendations.

Dryers can be vented through the outside wall above or below the floor as done for kitchen hood vents.

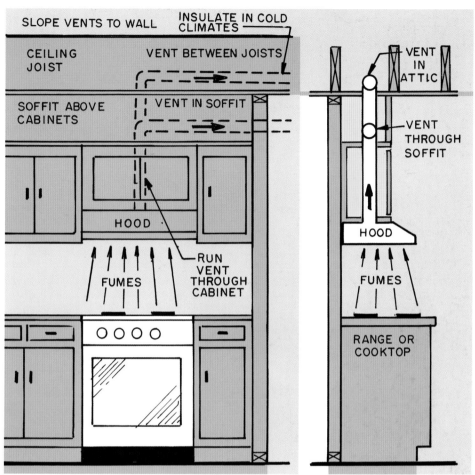

7–44. Range hoods can be vented through the soffit over the cabinets or between the ceiling joists.

SLOPE VENTS TO WALL

INSULATE IN COLD CLIMATES

CEILING JOIST

VENT BETWEEN JOISTS

SOFFIT ABOVE CABINETS

VENT IN SOFFIT

VENT IN ATTIC

VENT THROUGH SOFFIT

HOOD

RUN VENT THROUGH CABINET

FUMES

HOOD

FUMES

RANGE OR COOKTOP

7–45. This in-line centrifugal duct exhaust fan provides extra airflow volume on long vent lines. *(Courtesy Soler and Pala, Inc.)*

Another good system runs the duct out the roof (**7–51**). Since this duct may exceed the 25-foot limit, a duct booster fan has been installed on it in the attic. The booster also allows any lint that has gotten past the filter to pass on out the roof.

■ Whole-House Ventilation Systems

As today's houses become more airtight and older houses have air leaks sealed (see Chapter 2), the need for a whole-house ventilation system to refresh the interior has become apparent. There are a number of systems in use which are designed to change the air approximately three times per hour. The design of such a system requires the help of a qualified heating and air-conditioning technician. Following is a discussion of some of the systems in use.

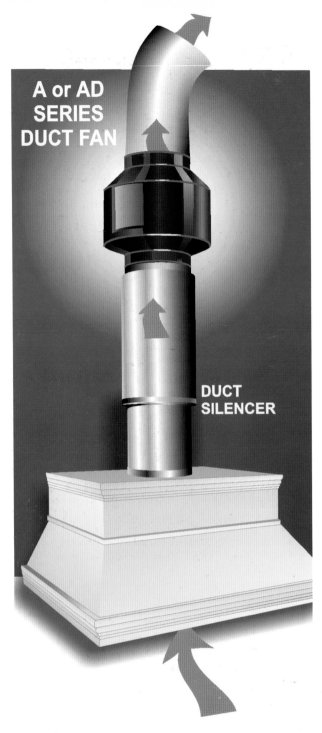

A or AD SERIES DUCT FAN

DUCT SILENCER

7–46. This hood is vented through the roof. The duct fan is in the attic and has a duct silencer, which greatly reduces noise in the kitchen. The speed of the fan can be varied to suit the amount of airflow needed for the cooking underway.

(Courtesy Matthews Graphic Design-American ALDES Ventilation Corporation)

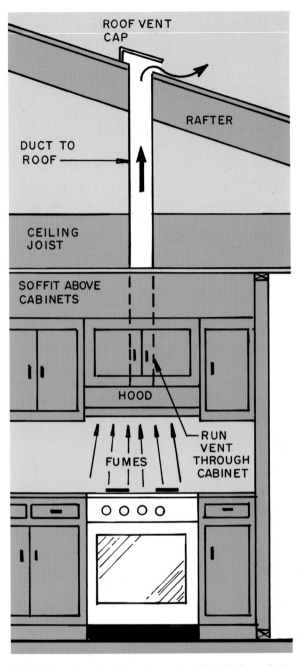

ROOF VENT CAP

RAFTER

DUCT TO ROOF

CEILING JOIST

SOFFIT ABOVE CABINETS

HOOD

FUMES

RUN VENT THROUGH CABINET

7–47. The range hood can be vented directly through the roof. Since there are no turns in the duct, this is the most efficient installation.

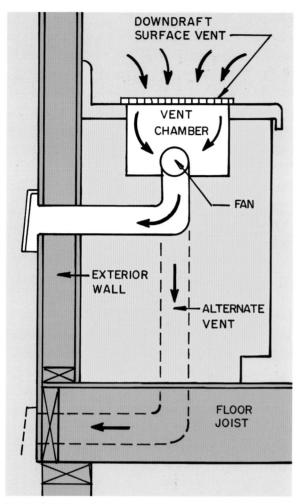

DOWNDRAFT
SURFACE VENT

VENT
CHAMBER

FAN

EXTERIOR
WALL

ALTERNATE
VENT

FLOOR
JOIST

7–48. This downdraft cooking unit pulls the cooking fumes into a vent on the surface and discharges them to the outside air.

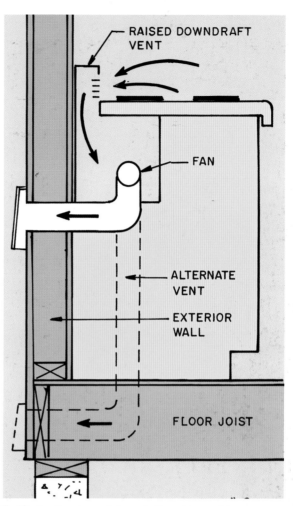

RAISED DOWNDRAFT
VENT

FAN

ALTERNATE
VENT

EXTERIOR
WALL

FLOOR JOIST

7–49. Another type of downdraft cooking unit has a small raised panel on the surface that pulls the cooking fumes out of the house.

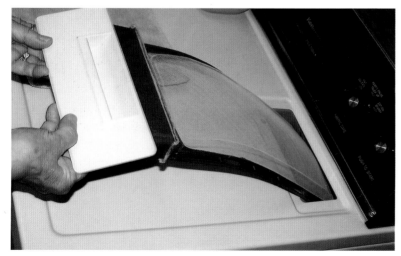

7–50. A dryer must have a filter to collect any fiber particles so they do not get into the vent and possibly clog the vent in the wall.

7–51. This dryer has a dryer booster fan installed in the attic. It has a pressure-sensitive switch which turns on the fan automatically when the air pressure in the duct increases due to the dryer fan running. It also switches off automatically. *(Courtesy Mattews Graphic Design-American ALDES Ventilation Corporation)*

EXHAUST VENTILATION ONLY

A typical exhaust-only system requires inlet sources so the air being removed is replaced with fresh outside air (**7–52**). The inlet grilles should have louvers so the amount of airflow can be regulated. The location of the inlet grilles should be so the air is evenly distributed throughout the house. In the winter, they could create cold drafts in areas where people sit, relax, and visit. Care should be taken to provide a way to seal appliances such as wood-burning stoves and fireplaces because a considerable backdraft could occur. Also seal the basement or crawl space so air containing moisture and possibly radon is not pulled into the house. This system is not recommended for houses that are tightly sealed against air leaks unless an inlet air supply is installed.

INFLOWING SUPPLY AIR ONLY

This system uses fans to bring in fresh outside air, which increases the air pressure inside the house. The pressure forces stale inside air out through ventilating grilles or leaks in the windows, doors, walls, and ceilings (**7–53**). Since it brings in untreated air, it can bring in dust unless filtered and increases the moisture in the interior air, which may cause condensation to form on walls, ceilings, and windows.

An inflow-only supply system is generally not used because of the problems that can occur at various times of the year. In addition to moisture and dust, the incoming air in the winter is cold and will increase heating costs. A pre-heater could be added to increase comfort as the inflowing air mixes with the existing air in the house.

BALANCED AIR-SUPPLY SYSTEMS

A balanced air-supply system will have a heat-recovery or energy-recovery ventilator that brings in fresh outside air and exhausts stale interior air (**7–54**). The ventilator is connected to the various rooms through a system of ducts to evenly distribute the air.

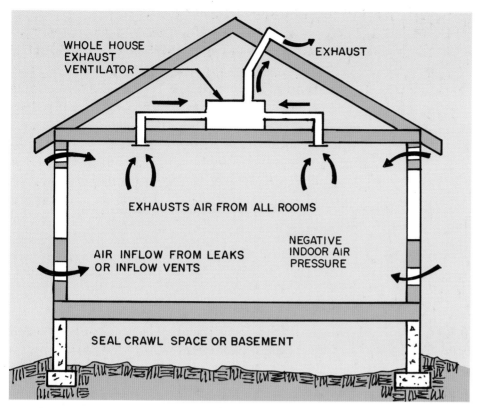

WHOLE HOUSE EXHAUST VENTILATOR

EXHAUST

EXHAUSTS AIR FROM ALL ROOMS

AIR INFLOW FROM LEAKS OR INFLOW VENTS

NEGATIVE INDOOR AIR PRESSURE

SEAL CRAWL SPACE OR BASEMENT

7–52. This illustrates a whole-house exhaust-only ventilating system. It produces negative inside air pressure, causing air to enter through inflow vents and leaks in the construction.

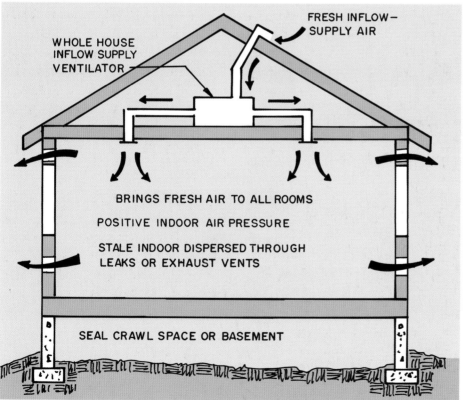

FRESH INFLOW— SUPPLY AIR

WHOLE HOUSE INFLOW SUPPLY VENTILATOR

BRINGS FRESH AIR TO ALL ROOMS

POSITIVE INDOOR AIR PRESSURE

STALE INDOOR DISPERSED THROUGH LEAKS OR EXHAUST VENTS

SEAL CRAWL SPACE OR BASEMENT

7–53. This illustrates a whole-house supply air-only system. It produces a positive air pressure in the house which forces interior air to vent through outflow vents and leaks in the construction.

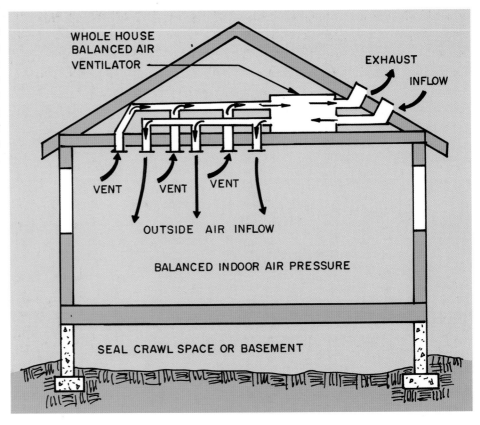

7–54. This illustrates a balanced whole-house ventilation system which perates exhaust and inflow air-supply systems. It evenly distributes the air because it maintains average indoor air pressures equal to those outside.

WHOLE HOUSE
BALANCED AIR
VENTILATOR

EXHAUST

INFLOW

VENT VENT VENT

OUTSIDE AIR INFLOW

BALANCED INDOOR AIR PRESSURE

SEAL CRAWL SPACE OR BASEMENT

HEAT-RECOVERY VENTILATORS

Heat-recovery ventilators (HRV) improve air quality and provide balanced ventilation (**7–55**). The HRV has a heat-recover core in the center and fans on each end to bring in fresh air and exhaust stale interior air (**7–56**). The HRV brings in fresh outdoor air which is drawn through filters and the heat-exchange core, where it is heated by the stale outgoing air (**7–57**). This saves considerable energy. The HRV distributed this preheated air through the ductwork of a forced-air system or through a series of ducts installed especially for the HRV.

The HRV usually has one fan for bringing in the outdoor supply air and one for moving the exhaust air. The ventilator is kept running continuously and is controlled by manual on-off switches, high-low speed switches, or a variable-speed control and humidity controlled by a dehumidistat, which sets it on high speed when the humidity in the living area rises about a set level. Some HRVs have a heater that will help heat the incoming air

7–55. Heat-recovery and energy-recovery ventilators improve the quality of interior air and save energy by utilizing the heat and coolness of the interior air being exhausted.
(Courtesy Fanteck, www.fantech.net)

as needed. In freezing weather, the incoming air may be cold enough to freeze the heat-exchange core, so an electric preheat coil is used to raise the temperature of the incoming air so it is above the freezing point. This is a very effective and desirable ventilation system and it is recommended for use in states in the northern third of the United States and all of Canada.

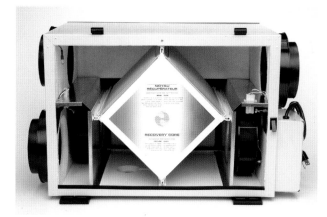

7–56. Fans move the venting and incoming fresh air through the core in the center of the ventilator. *(Courtesy Fanteck, www.fantech.net)*

ENERGY-RECOVERY VENTILATORS

Energy-recovery ventilators (ERV) bring in fresh outdoor air that is filtered, cooled, and dehumidified by the stale outgoing air. The unit appears much like the heat-recovery unit in **7–56**. The air passes through an energy-recovery core. The airflow is the same as shown in **7–57**. The ventilator then distributes the cooled dehumidified air through the ductwork of a forced-air system or through ducts installed especially for this ventilation system.

If the outdoor air temperature reaches a predetermined level below freezing, an automatic defrost cycle occurs and the unit turns on the exhaust fan, thus blowing warm inside air through the core, increasing the effectiveness of the defrost.

The installation of ERV units is very important in the southern states where air-conditioning is a major consideration and useful in states in the middle of the United States where heating and air-conditioning demands are about equal.

7–57. The stale interior air is pulled from the interior by the heat-recovery ventilator and vented to the outside. A second fan pulls in fresh outside air and passes it to the inside of the house. As they pass in the heat recovery core the cool outside air is warmed by the existing stale inside air.

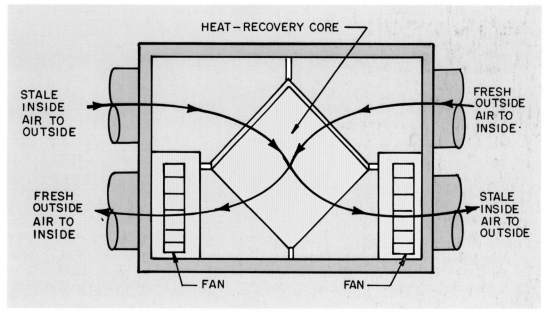

WHOLE-HOUSE AIR-FILTRATION SYSTEM

A whole-house air-filtration system collects airborne particles and allergens, including things such as smoke, dust particles, animal dander, dust mites, bacteria, and attached viruses (**7–58**). Typically, a unit will clean the air in the entire house once every hour. The filtration unit is connected to the existing ductwork of a forced-air furnace or air handler (**7–59**).

7–58. The air-filtration unit can be mounted on the air handler or furnace. The removable filter removes airborne particles and allergens. *(Courtesy Fanteck, www.fantech.net)*

■ Venting Attics

Attic ventilation is needed for summer and winter weather conditions. In the summer, attic temperatures can reach 150°F or higher. The ceiling insulation absorbs heat and holds it into the evening hours, causing increased air-conditioning costs. The hot air must be vented by natural means or with power ventilating fans. In the winter, moisture in the air can turn to frost on the rafters and sheathing. When the air starts to warm in the spring, this melts and drips on to the insulation, which then loses its effectiveness and often has to be replaced. The ceiling material can also get soaked and wet through to the room sides. It will have to be replaced over time. If the attic ceiling insulation has a vapor barrier, this will protect the ceiling material from damage.

If the attic is not vented, it will hold any heat that passes through the ceiling, so in the winter the snow on the shingles might melt and drain toward the fascia. As the melted snow passes over the roof overhang, it can freeze. This causes an ice dam, forcing the melted snow to back up under the shingles and, if it penetrates the shingles and underlayment, will eventually damage the sheathing and even leak onto the ceiling (**7–60**). The

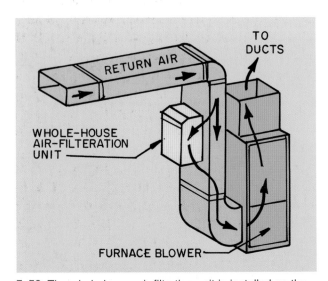

7–59. The whole-house air-filtration unit is installed on the return air duct before it reaches the furnace. The filtered air is heated or cooled and returned to the house by the furnace blower through the system of ducts.

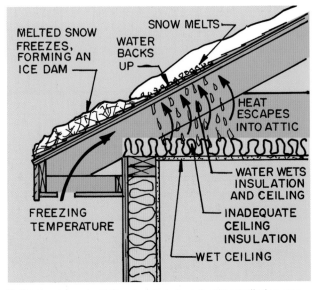

7–60. Inadequate ceiling insulation and attic ventilation can allow an ice dam to form, which can then back up water which might leak through the shingles.

vented attic air should be the same temperature as the outside air, so the snow will not melt.

A key to a dry attic also involves sealing all air leaks that may run from the basement, crawl space, or the living areas of the house through walls, ceilings, and other vertical openings. Moisture from these areas will flow into the attic, greatly increasing the moisture available to cause damage. Review Chapter 2 for detailed information on controlling air leaks. It is also important that the ceiling have a vapor barrier and adequate insulations.

ATTIC VENTING SYSTEMS

Possibly the most widely used effective attic venting systems involve installing continuous soffit vents (**7–61**) and the use of baffles at the outer wall to keep the ceiling insulation from blocking the airflow from the soffit (**7–62**). Baffles plus the use of ridge vents (**7–63**) form a system that provides continuous airflow from the soffit out through the ridge vent (**7–64**).

Another attic venting system widely used has vents in the gable ends (**7–65**). These are not very effective. When the wind blows perpendicular to the ridge, it moves along the top of the ceiling joists and vents out the soffit vents on the other side, leaving a large volume of unvented air near the ridge (**7–66**). When the

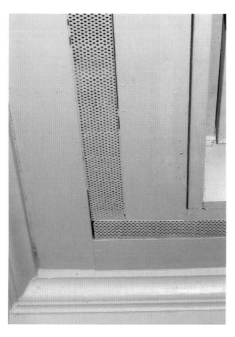

7–61. Continuous soffit vents provide a wide, uniform flow of air into the attic.

wind flows parallel with the ridge, it drops to the top of the ceiling joists after entering the attic, flows along them, and rises and vents out of the gable end vent on the other side (**7–67**). This leaves a very large volume of unvented air along the ridge.

Some people like to use electric roof fans (**7–68**), often called power ventilators. They are placed high on the roof near the ridge. The controls include a thermostat which turns on the fan when the attic air reaches the set temperature. It also has a humidistat that turns on the fan when the moisture in the attic air reaches a predetermined level and off when the set level is reached.

It is important to select the right size ventilator and the required number to change the air in the attic as required by code.

On some architectural styles, a cupola is a prominent architectural feature (**7–69**). It will also provide attic ventilation at the ridge.

■ Air Purification

So far, this chapter has given details showing various ways effective ventilation systems remove stale, smelly air from inside the house and replace it with filtered outside air. This greatly improves the living conditions. The new inflowing air is run through various types of filters, which remove some of the impurities. However, a lot of things could be missed. Some of these are dust, pollen, airborne dust mites, and indoor odors. If the house does not have a fresh-air inflow air system, the need for interior air purifiers is even more important.

Other things are forming inside the house, such as bacteria that live primarily on kitchen and bath counters and refrigerators, and migrate to the rest of the house through the heating system. Mold spores form in damp places such as carpets, drapes, inside walls (including wet insulation), in crawl spaces and basements, and in wet areas of bathrooms and kitchens. These and other irritating substances cause allergies to act up, give a person headaches, and inflame asthma. In addition, they cause a wide variety of odors such as the typical musty smell in wet bathrooms and under the house.

To clean up a polluted house, first work to find and remove the mold and other contaminating substances.

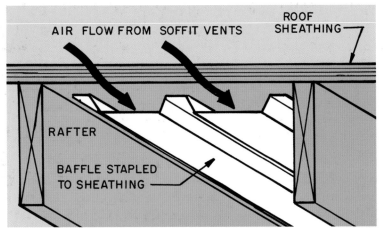

AIR FLOW FROM SOFFIT VENTS

ROOF SHEATHING

RAFTER

BAFFLE STAPLED TO SHEATHING

7–62. Baffles are installed on the roof sheathing at the exterior wall to keep the insulation from blocking the airflow from the soffit vent.

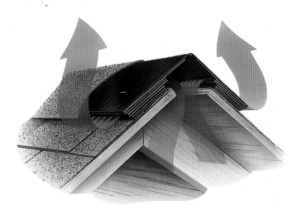

7–63. Ridge vents are the best way to provide the venting of the air in the attic. *(Courtesy Cor-A-Vent)*

7–64. The proper venting of an attic requires an uninterrupted flow of air from the soffit vent out the ridge vent.

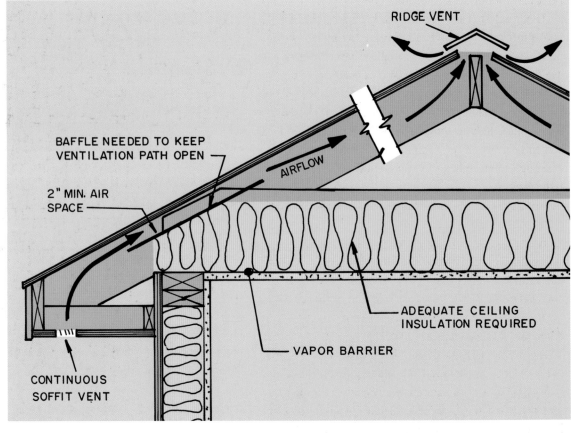

RIDGE VENT

BAFFLE NEEDED TO KEEP VENTILATION PATH OPEN

AIRFLOW

2" MIN. AIR SPACE

ADEQUATE CEILING INSULATION REQUIRED

VAPOR BARRIER

CONTINUOUS SOFFIT VENT

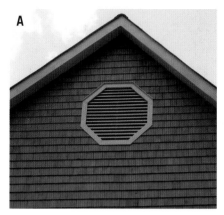

7–65. Gable-end vents are widely used; however, they are not as effective as ridge vents. Some people mount exhaust fans behind them that are activated by a therm static control.

Then purify the air. Even with the major causes removed, indoor air still needs to be purified.

The final step to produce really pure, healthful air and eliminate the harmful things is to install an air-purification system. Several small portable systems are available. One system (7–70) combines a high-intensity ultraviolet light with a specially developed metal hydrophilic coating on an engineered matrix, producing a Radiant Catalytic Ionization (RCI) screen. This RCI screen reduces airborne contaminants and odors while creating super oxide ions and hydro-peroxides. This reduce odors, volatile organic compounds, and attacks micro-organisms (7–71). This unit helps remove smoke odors, dust, fungi, stale air, allergens, mold, pollen salmonella, E-coli, pollen, and general house dust.

Another air purifier uses filters through which the air is moved with a fan (7–72). The filter removes dust and pollen, while a separate carbon filter removes odors from the air. Depending upon the design and type of filter, they will last typically from four months to a year.

As you choose an air purifier, consider the number of air changes per hour (ACH), and the clean-air delivery rate (CADR) the unit is certified to deliver for the room size specified for it. Recommended clean-air delivery rates for various room sizes are shown in **Table 7–2**, on page 187. Air purifiers are tested and certified by the Association of Home Appliance Manufacturers. Their seal of certification will appear on the unit, indicating it meets the clean-air delivery rate for the specified room size.

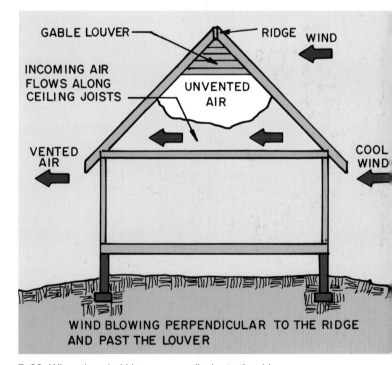

7–66. When the wind blows perpendicular to the ridge, an airflow is generated along the floor and it vents out the soffit vents on the other side, leaving a large area where attic air remains unchanged.

7-67. When the airflow is parallel with the ridge, the cooler exterior air sinks to the top of the ceiling joists and moves along until it is pulled out of the gable end vent on the other side, leaving a large volume of unvented air.

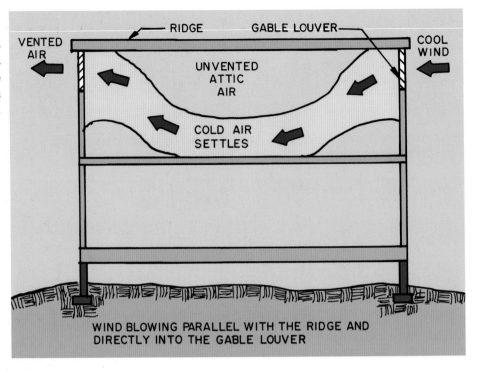

7–68. Electric roof fans can be activated with a thermostat control when the weather is hot and a humidistat when moisture in the air rises above a pre-set setting.

7–69. Cupolas are part of the architectural style of some houses. They provide some attic ventilation at the ridge in parts of the attic.

7–70. This air purifier uses radiant catalytic ionization and ultraviolet light to reduce odors, airborne germs, mold, mildew, bacteria, dust, and other impurities from the air.

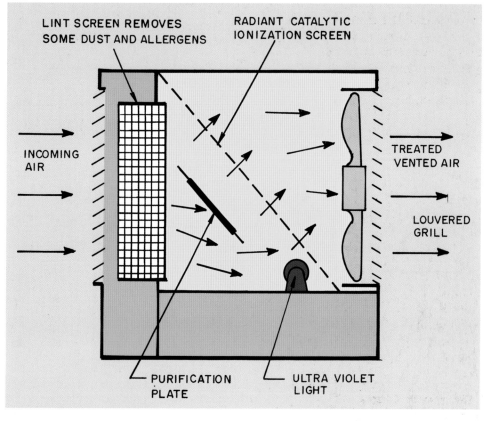

7–71. A typical diagram of an air purifier using ultraviolet light and an ionization screen to pull dust, mold, allergens, odors, and other pollutants from the air.

LINT SCREEN REMOVES SOME DUST AND ALLERGENS

RADIANT CATALYTIC IONIZATION SCREEN

INCOMING AIR

TREATED VENTED AIR

LOUVERED GRILL

PURIFICATION PLATE

ULTRA VIOLET LIGHT

7–72. This air purifier uses a series of filters to pull a high percentage of dust, pollen, allergens, and odors from the air.

TABLE 7–2.

ROOM CLEAN-AIR DELIVERY RATES

Room Size (Ft.)	Minimum CADR*
8 × 10 or less	50
10 × 12	80
12 × 12	100
12 × 16	120
14 × 14	130
14 × 16	145
16 × 18	186
16 × 20	200
18 × 18	210
18 × 20	230
20 × 20	250
20 × 24	300

METRIC EQUIVALENTS CHART

INCHES TO MILLEMETERS AND CENTIMETERS

MM—Millemeters   CM—Centimeters

Inches	MM	CM	Inches	CM	Inches	CM
⅛	3	0.3	9	22.9	30	76.2
¼	6	0.6	10	25.4	31	78.7
⅜	10	1.0	11	27.9	32	81.3
½	13	1.3	12	30.5	33	83.8
⅝	16	1.6	13	33.0	34	86.4
¾	19	1.9	14	35.6	35	88.9
⅞	22	2.2	15	38.1	36	91.4
1	25	2.5	16	40.6	37	94.0
1¼	32	3.2	17	43.2	38	96.5
1½	38	3.8	18	45.7	39	99.1
1¾	44	4.4	19	48.3	48	101.6
2	51	5.1	20	50.8	41	104.1
2½	64	6.4	21	53.3	42	106.7
3	76	7.6	22	55.9	43	109.2
3½	89	8.9	23	58.4	44	111.8
4	102	10.2	24	61.0	45	114.3
4½	114	11.4	25	63.5	46	116.8
5	127	12.7	25	66.0	47	119.4
6	152	15.2	27	68.6	48	121.9
7	178	17.8	28	71.1	49	124.5
8	203	20.3	29	73.7	50	127.0

INDEX

Abestos siding, opening a wall with, 131, 132

Access hatches, to attics, 28, 29

Acoustical ceiling tile, stapling to wood furring nails, 102, 105

Acrylic latex caulk, sealing small openings with, 21, 22

Airborne sound, 99, 100

Air infiltration
description of, 7
preventing, 20

Air leaks
analyzing, 14, 15, 16
in ceilings, sealing, 23, 24
factoring in, when improving energy efficiency, 7, 8
in floors, 32, 33
locations of, 20, 21
materials for sealing, 21, 22
sealing in inside places, 43

Air purification, 183, 185–187

Aluminum foil
installing, 67
perm ratings of, 64

Aluminum siding, opening, 127, 128

American Society of Heating, Refigeration and Air-Conditioning Engineers, 156

Association of Home Appliance Manufacturers, 185

Attics
constructing, 140, 141–142, 143
folding stairs for, sealing leaks in, 29
insulating with foam insulation, 88, 89, 90
and moisture problems, 19
preventing airflow in, 43, 44
venting, 182, 183–186

Baffles
in attic venting system, 183, 184
stapling to roof sheathing, 75, 77
using on cathedral ceilings, 88, 89

Balanced air-supply system, 178, 179

Balloon framing, 118, 119

Barrier boxes
air-vapor, around electric outlet, 80
air-vapor, installing, 35, 36

Basements
and air leaks, 32
insulating, 148, 149–155

Bathroom ventilation, 164, 165–168, 169

Baths, outdoor air requirements for, 157

Batts
faced, installing, 68, 69
pressure-fitting, 70, 71
typical R-value of, 46
use as insulation materials, 47–48

Beadboard. *See* Expanded polystyrene

Bevel wood siding, opening, 122

Blankets
butting, 72

faced, installing, 68–69

fiberglass, insulating basement walls with, 151, 152, 153

pressure-fit, insulating ceilings with, 133

sound-attenuation, over suspended ceilings, 102, 104

sound-attenuation, on partitions, 102

use as insulation materials, 47–48

Blower-door test, 14, 15

Blow-in insulation
fibrous, installing, 84, 85, 86
installing from inside the house, 131, 132

BOCA National Codes, 156

Brick-veneer wall, opening a, 128, 129

British thermal units, 45, 45

Building felt, perm ratings of, 64

Carbon monoxide warning unit, 9

Carpet strips, nailing to sleepers, 137

Cathedral ceilings
insulating, 75, 76, 77, 92, 93
in old houses, insulating, 132, 133
using foam insulation on, 88, 89

Ceilings
access door in, 141, 143
with attics above, insulating, 92, 93
cathedral, insulating, 92, 93
cathedral, using foam insulation on, 88, 89
cavities, insulating, 72, 73
controlling sound in, 102, 104. 105
fans for, 27, 159, 160
insulating, 74–78, 79

Cellulose
dry, blown, installing, 90, 91–92, 93
dry, blown, and vapor barriers, 94, 95
as insulation, composition of, 49
typical R-value of, 46
wet, spray, insulating, 93, 94

Chases, finding and sealing, 43, 44

Chimneys
and combustible insulation, 78
sealing openings around, 31
with vent-pipe air leaks, 29, 30–31

Clothes dryer exhaust, 174, 177, 178

Clothing for insulation, 63

Combustion type furnaces, 9

Comfort mask, 62

Concrete
block basements, insulating, 155
floors, insulating, 82, 83, 135, 136–138, 139

Conduction, 4

Convection, 4

Cooktop hood installation, 172, 173, 174

Cotton insulation
installing, 89, 90
use as insulation material, 48

Crawl spaces
and air leaks, 32
insulating, 143, 144–147, 148

Cupola, as attic venting system, 183, 186

Dew point, 17

Diffusion, 17

Digital manometer, 14, 15

Direct sound, 99

Disappearing stairs, insulating, 113, 114, 115

Doors
insulating, 79, 80, 81
seal for, 42

Downdraft cooking unit, 170, 174, 177

Drywall clips, 109, 110

Electric cable air leaks, 23

Electric roof fans, 183, 186

Electric systems, and insulation placement, 79, 80

Electric wires
frayed, 64
working into insulation, 80, 81

Energy Star label, 6, 7

Energy-recovery ventilators, 181

E-value, 52

Exhaust-only ventilating system, 178, 179

Exhaust ventilator, for bathrooms, 166, 167, 168

Expanded polystyrene
bead board, perm ratings of, 64
composition of, 49, 50
typical R-value of, 46

Exterior doors, sealing, 41, 42

Exterior walls
ability to resist airborne sound, 102, 105
air-sealing, 34–37, 38
cavities, filling, 120, 121
controlling sound in, 102, 105
insulating, 115, 116–118, 119
made of Portland cement stucco, 130
sheathing, 67, 68, 69
and water vapor, 16, 17, 18

Extruded polystyrene
board, perm ratings of, 64
typical R-value of, 46

Eye protection, 61

Faced blankets and batts, installing, 68, 69

Face-stapling, 69, 70

Fans
bathroom, 165, 166–167, 168
enhancing natural ventilation with, 159, 160–164

Fiberglass
blankets, cutting, 68, 69
blankets, installation of, 65
blankets, insulating basement walls with, 151, 152, 153
blowing machine, 120
typical R-value of, 46
use as insulation material, 47, 48

Fibrous insulation
blow-in, installing, 84, 85

loose, how it is made, 49
Fireplace, and combustible insulation, 78
Flat roofs
  insulating, 78
  old house with, insulating, 132, 133
Floors
  air leaks in, 32, 33
  cavities in, insulating, 72, 73
  concrete, 82, 83
Foam gaskets, 22
Foam insulation
  filling gaps in window frame with, 37
  properties and insulating values of, 52
  sealing air leaks with, 7
Foundation vents, 146, 148
Fresh-air supply sytems, 164
Furnace vent-pipe air leaks, 29, 30–31, 32
Furring strips, installing reflective insulation
  with, 95, 97
Gable end vents, 183, 185
Garage, outdoor air requirements for, 157
Granular insulation, composition of, 49
Granulated cork sheets, composition of, 50
Hacksaw blade, cutting shingle nails with, 123,
  124
Hearing protection, 63
Heat, how it is transferred, 4, 5
Heat ducts
  in ceiling, 28
  flexible, 13
Heat flow, principles of, 4
Heat-recovery ventilators, 180, 181
Heat register, and air leaks, 8
High-density fiberglass, typical R-value of, 46
High Efficiency Particulate Arresting respi-
  rator, 62
Hole saw, 119
Home Energy Rating Systems, 5
Home ventilation
  air purification, 183, 185–187
  attic ventilation, 182, 183–185, 186
  bathroom ventilation, 164, 165–167, 168
  clothes dryer exhaust, 174, 175
  codes for, 156, 157
  kitchen ventilation, 168, 169
  mechanical ventilation, 159, 160–163,
    164
  passive ventilation, 157, 158, 159
  whole-house ventilation system, 175,
    176–181, 182
House wrap
  sealing air leaks with, 7, 8
  using on door or window rough openings, 35,
    36, 37
Humidity-controlled fresh-air inlet, 159
ICBO Uniform Codes, 156
Impact Isolation Class, 106, 107
Indoor Air Quality Procedure, 157
In-line
  centrifugal duct exhaust fan, 173, 175

exhaust fan, enhancing natural ventilation
  with, 163
  ventilation fan, 148
Inset-stapling, 69, 70
Insulation
  adding to existing house, 108–138
  adding, factors when considering, 11
  for attics, 140, 141–142, 143
  for basements, 148, 149–155
  batts,butting, 72, 73
  batts, installing, 68, 69, 70
  batts, as insulation material, 47, 48
  blankets, importance of, 9
  blankets, installing, 68, 69, 70
  blankets, as insulation material, 47, 48
  blankets, wraparound, 12
  blow-in, installing, 84, 85, 86, 131, 132
  and building code fire regulations, 55, 56
  ceiling, increasing, 67, 111, 112, 113
  cellulose, 89, 90–93, 94
  choosing a, 45
  cotton, 89
  for crawl spaces, 143, 144–148, 149
  determining how much is needed, 7, 59
  for floors, 81, 82–83
  hazards of, 56
  loose-fill, 49
  radiant barriers, 52, 53, 54, 97, 98, 99
  reflective, 95, 96–96. 97
  rigid, 49, 50, 51
  R-values of, 46
  safety techniques when installing, 23, 59,
    61–63, 64
  sound-deadening materials, 47
  sprayed-foam, 51, 52, 86, 87–89, 90
  unfaced, installing, 70, 71, 72
  vapor barriers, description of, 54, 55
  vapor barriers, locating, 64, 65–67
  for windows and doors, 79, 80, 81
Interior radiation-control coatings, 98, 99
International Energy Conservation Code, 16
International Residental Code for One- and
  Two-Family Dwellings, 156
Island cabinet, 169, 170
Kitchen
  outdoor air requirements for, 157
  ventilating, 168, 169
Kneewall, building doors in, 141, 142, 143
Kraft paper insulation facing
  installation of, 65
  perm ratings of, 64
Latex primer, perm ratings of, 64
Light fixtures, and combustible insulation, 78
Living areas, outdoor air requirements for, 157
Loose fill insulation
  typical R-value of, 46
  use as insulation material, 49
Low slope roofs
  insulating, 78
  old house with, insulating, 132, 133

Mason's chisel,opening a stucco wall with,
  129, 131
Masonry walls,installing reflective insulation
  on, 96, 97
Mechanical ventilation
  description of, 157
  means of, 159, 160–163, 164
Metal-resilient channels, 106, 107
Mineral wool
  installing, 86, 87–88, 89
  use as insulation material, 48
Mold and mildrew, 19
National Home Energy Rating Guidelines,
  adoptation of, 5, 6
National Institute for Occupational Safety and
  Health, 61
Naural ventilation, 157
Noise-Reduction Coefficient
  definition of, 47
  for selected materials, 100, 101
Old houses
  insulating, with cathedral ceiling, low slope,
    or flat roof, 132, 133
  insulating, to control sound, 139
Outlet boxes
  controlling ceiling fans with, 160
  caulking cracks in, 155
  insulating, 86
  pulling wires through, 155
Paper dust mask,61
Partitions, reducing sound transmission in, 102
Passive ventilation, 157, 158, 159
Perlite, typical R-value of, 46
PicoCurie, 16
Plumbing
  air leak, 23
  placing insulation in, 79, 86
Pocket window, installing a, 40
Polluted house, cleaning up a, 183, 184–187
Polyethylene
  foam insulation, on water pipes, 12, 13
  sheet, perm ratings of, 64
  vapor barriers, installation of, 65, 66
Polyisocyanurate
  rigid foam sheets, composition of, 50
  typical R-value of, 46
Polyurethane
  caulk, sealing small openings with, 21, 22
  low-expansion foams, sealing air leaks with,
    21, 22
  rigid insulation, composition of, 50
  typical R-value of, 46
Pressure-fit blankets, insulating ceilings with,
  133
Radiant barriers, installing, 97, 98, 99
Radiant Catalytic Ionization screen, 185
Radiant insulations
  composition of, 52, 53
  types of, 53, 54
Radiated heat, how it is transferred, 5, 6

Radiation-control coatings, 98, 99
Radon, 16
Range hoods
  capacities of, 169, 170
  decription of, 168, 169
  for kitchens, 170, 171–177, 178
Recessed lights
  and air leaks, 24
  and combustible insulation, 78, 79
Reflective insulation
  composition of, 53
  installing, 95, 96, 97
  sealing air leaks with, 7
Replacement windows
  assembled, installing, 40
  for double-hung windows, 38, 39, 40
Residential buildings, ventilation of, 157
Respiratory protection, 61
Rigid insulation
  board, typical R-value of, 46
  composition of, 49, 50, 51
  foam, installing in basements, 148, 149–150,
    151
  sealing air leaks with, 7
Rim joists
  in basement wall, insulating, 148, 149
  insulating when using blankets and batts,
    144, 146
  sealing, 89, 90
Rock wool, typical R-value of, 46
Roofs
  truss-frame, insulating, 89
  vents, 166
Room Clean-Air Delivery Rates, 185, 187
Rotary brush, removing excess cellulose with,
    94
R-values of insulation, 45, 46, 59, 60
Sash replacement kit, 38, 39, 40
SBCCI Standard Codes, 156
Sealing materials, 21, 22
Self-regulating fresh air inlet, 158, 159
Siding
  aluminum, opening, 127, 128
  bevel, opening, 122, 123
  removing, 117, 118, 119
  R-values of, 59
  vinyl, opening, 127, 128
  wood-shingle, opening, 123, 124–126
Sill sealer, 22, 32
Single-course shingle, removing, 123, 124
Smoke alarms, 27
Smoke generator, 15
Smoke pencil, 15

Smoke pipe installation, 32
Soffic vents, as attic venting system, 183
Sone, 165
Sound control in older houses, 139
Sound-deadening materials, 47
Sound Intensity, 100, 101
Sound rating indicators, 100, 101–105
Sound-Transmission Class
  definition of, 47
  ratings system for living areas, 100, 101
Sprayed-foam insulation
  basement foundations, using on, 146, 147
  composition of, 51, 52
  installation technique, 86, 87–89, 90
  masonry walls, insulating with, 155
Stack effect, definition of, 10, 11, 17
Standard fiberglas, typical R-value of, 46
Storm door, replacing old door with, 42, 43
Storm windows
  installing, 38, 39
  reducing air infiltration with, 12
Story Jig, 91
Stucco wall, opening a, 129, 130, 131
Stud framing, bracing, 67, 68, 69
Supply-air-only ventilation system, 178, 179
Surface-mounted lights, and air leaks, 25,
    26
Suspended ceilings
  reducing sound transmission in, 102
  sealing air leaks in, 23, 24
Thermal
  boundary. *See* Thermal envelope
  bridging, definition of, 67, 68
  conductance, definition of, 47
  conductivity, definition of, 47
  envelope, definition of, 20
  envelope, and placement of insulation, 57,
    58, 59
  properties, specifying, 45–46, 47
  radiation, definition of, 4
  resistance, description of, 46
  transmittance, definition of, 47
Through-the-wall air inlet, 158
Through-the-wall direct exhaust unit, 163
Toilets, outdoor air requirements for, 157
Truss-frame roofs
  insulating, 89
  stapling radiant barriers to, 9
Unfaced insulation, installing, 70, 71, 72
Urea formaldehyde, typical R-value of, 46
Urethane, typical R-value of, 46
Vapor barriers
  installing in basement, 153, 154

  locating in attic, 140, 141
  locating in geographic areas, 64, 65
  materials for, perm ratings of, 64
  polyethylene, laying down over floor, 135,
    136
  recent developments in, 19
Vapor retardant paint, perm ratings of, 64
Ventilation for Acceptable Indoor Air Quality,
    156
Ventilation Rate Procedure, 157
Ventilation, home
  attics, 182, 183–185, 186
  bathroom, 164, 165–167, 168
  codes for, 156, 157
  kitchen, 168, 169–173, 174
  mechanical, 159, 160–163, 164
  passive, 157, 158, 159
  as preliminary energy consideration, 8, 9
  whole-house, 175, 176–182
Vermiculate, typical R-value of, 46
Vinyl siding, opening, 127, 128
Wall primer, as vapor barrier, 67
Walls
  with abestos siding, opening, 131, 132
  basement, with drywall finish material, 155
  basement, insulating, 148, 150
  brick-veneer, opening, 128, 129
  cavities, insulating, 72, 73
  masonry, installing reflective insulation on,
    96, 97
  stucco, opening, 129, 130, 131
  stud, building a, 152, 153–154, 155
Water heaters, insulating, 12
Water vapor
  and exterior walls, 16, 17, 18
  importance of controlling, 8
Weatherstripping
  accordion-type, 42
  double, 42
  tubular-type, on exterior doors, 41, 42
Wet, sprayed cellulose, insulating with, 93,
    94
Whole-house
  air-filtration system, 182
  fans, description of, 160, 162–163, 164
  ventilation system, 175, 176–179, 180
Windows
  framing around, 118
  insulating, 79
  slides for, reducing air leakage in, 37, 38
Wood and cane fiberboard, composition of,
    50
Wood sleepers, 136, 137, 138

STERLING BOOKS BY WILLIAM SPENCE

- *Basic Woodworking* (co-author Duane Griffiths)
- *Building Your Dream House*
- *Carpentry and Building Construction: A Do-It-Yourself Guide*
- *Constructing Bathrooms*
- *Constructing Kitchens*
- *Constructing Staircases, Balustrades, and Landings*
- *Doors and Entryways*
- *Encyclopedia of Construction Methods & Materials*
- *Encyclopedia of Home Maintenance and Repair*
- *Finish Carpentry: A Complete Interior & Exterior Guide*
- *Home Carpentry and Woodworking*
- *Installing and Finishing Drywall*
- *Installing and Finishing Flooring*
- *Insulating, Sealing & Ventilating a House*
- *Interior Trim: Making, Installing, & Finishing*
- *Residential Framing: A Homebuilder's Construction Guide*
- *Roofing Materials and Installation*
- *Windows and Skylights*
- *Woodworking Basics: The Essential Benchtop Reference* (with L. Duane Griffiths)

ABOUT THE AUTHOR

William P. Spence is a do-it-yourself expert who has authored more than three dozen books for Sterling Publishing Co., Inc. and for other publishers. He also has written articles extensively for magazines and journals. Spence has been a professor of technical arts and applied sciences at Virginia Commonwealth University, Richmond, and Western Michigan University, Kalamazoo, as well as Chairman of the Department of Industrial Education and Art, and Dean, College of Technology, at Pittsburg State University, Pittsburg, Kansas. He has also worked in industry as General Manager and Design Draftsman for manufacturers in Virginia, has worked as a cabinetmaker, and became involved in real estate sales and land development with Sandhill Properties, Inc. of Whispering Pines, North Carolina. He earned a doctorate in education and a masters in education at the University of Missouri as well as a bachelor of science and bachelor of science in education at Southeast Missouri State University. He also served in the U.S. Navy. He makes his home in Pinehurst, North Carolina where he is currently writing technical books full time.